THE ICARUS FACTOR

THE ICARUS FACTOR

THE RISE AND FALL OF EDGAR BRONFMAN JR.

ROD McQUEEN

DOUBLEDAY CANADA

Library and Archives Canada Cataloguing in Publication

McQueen, Rod, 1944–
The Icarus factor : the rise and fall of Edgar Bronfman Jr. / Rod McQueen.

Includes bibliographical references and index.
ISBN 0-385-65995-4

1. Bronfman, Edgar Jr., 1955– 2. Executives—Canada—Biography.
3. Consolidation and merger of corporations. 4. Seagram Company.
5. Vivendi Universal Corporation. I. Title.

HD9390.C22B754 2004   338.8'092   C2004-903129-5

Jacket image: © Dan Borris/CORBIS OUTLINE/MAGMA
Jacket design: Kelly Hill
Printed and bound in the USA

Published in Canada by
Doubleday Canada, a division of
Random House of Canada Limited

Visit Random House of Canada Limited's website: www.randomhouse.ca

BVG   10   9   8   7   6   5   4   3   2   1

For Sandy
who has always believed in me

CONTENTS

That which you inherit from your fathers,
you must earn in order to possess.
—GOETHE, *Faust*

INTRODUCTION

THE TWO CHIEF EXECUTIVE OFFICERS were perched on stools at the Internet Café in Paris. Edgar Bronfman Jr. looked formal, even European, in his Armani suit. In a classic case of role reversal, Vivendi chairman and CEO Jean-Marie Messier had taken off his suit jacket as if he were trying to emulate an American businessman ready to roll up his sleeves.

As the third-generation CEO of the family-controlled Seagram Co., Edgar Jr. had his heritage very much in mind that morning. Before the two men announced the $34-billion merger of their two companies, Edgar Jr. took Messier aside and told him, "You know what they say in the U.S. about entrepreneurial families? The first generation creates, the second makes the fortune, and the third destroys it. I represent that third generation. But with this, I'm assuring the future of the generations to follow."

Even the date was auspicious. June 20, 2000, was the seventy-first birthday of Edgar Bronfman Sr. "I can think of no better present to give my father, his children, his grandchildren, and his great-grandchildren than this world-beating company we are creating today," said Edgar Jr. at the news conference. "I'm proud of what we've accomplished. It completes Seagram's translation from a traditional company into a leading force in the global media and entertainment industry."

Edgar Jr. had indeed done well. In 1994, when he succeeded his father as CEO, the family's Seagram shares were worth $4 billion. In June 2000, based on the negotiated price per share of $77.35, the family's holdings had doubled in value to $8.2 billion. Mind you, the broad measure of the stock market—the Dow Jones Industrial Average—had almost tripled during the same six-year period. Still, praise for Edgar Jr., who in the past was widely criticized as a naive dilettante, had never been so fulsome. "Bronfman, one of Hollywood's favorite punching bags, may finally get some respect," said Betsy Streisand in *U.S. News & World Report*. "If they ever erect a family business hall of fame, the Bronfmans should be a shoo-in on the first ballot," wrote Gordon Pitts in *The Globe and Mail*. "Few could match their accomplishments: They guided their liquor giant Seagram Co. Ltd. into the third generation; rebuilt its business model; and sold when the time seemed right, amply rewarding family and non-family shareholders."

Editorial writers at *The Gazette* in Montreal, the city where Seagram's head office had been located for more than seventy-five years, were not so sure. "It's the end of an era in Canadian business. The deal is a confirmation of Samuel Bronfman's concern . . . that the financial colossus he built might not survive the third generation," said *The Gazette*. The editorial paid tribute to the legacy of Mr. Sam, as he was called, congratulated the second generation for their philanthropy, but damned Edgar Jr. with faint praise. "The high price for the company is seen by some as a vindication of chairman Edgar Bronfman Jr.'s strategy to transform it into an entertainment giant in the six years he has run the company."

The Gazette was wise to withhold applause. Within two years, Vivendi Universal became crippled by $19 billion in debt, the share price plummeted, and the high-flying Messier was ousted. What was supposed to be the capstone of Edgar Jr.'s career would instead become his epitaph. "There's something in life called The Great Equalizer. I don't know what it is, I don't know where it is, I don't know how it is," says David Culver, former CEO of Alcan Aluminum Ltd. and a long-time Seagram director. "I only know one thing about The Great Equalizer. If you're flat on your back on the floor, He's paying no attention. But if you're on the cover of *Time* magazine, He's waiting there. I think it happened to Edgar Jr. The history is there. How many billion dollars has the family lost? That's The Great Equalizer at work."

Because the Bronfman family swapped all of their Seagram holdings for shares of Vivendi, the losses were devastating. From that peak of $8.2 billion, during the next two years the value of those family holdings, including proceeds from shares they sold along the way, fell by almost three-quarters to $2.2 billion. Mr. Sam had predicted this dynastic tragedy in a 1966 interview with *Fortune.* "Members of a family don't want to work as hard as employees—and you can't fire them. I tell my sons and son-in-law that they have to think about what the little children will do. The thing is that it depends on how those little minds develop. You've heard about shirtsleeves to shirtsleeves in three generations. I'm worried about the third generation. Empires have come and gone," said Mr. Sam.

The sale of Seagram and the financial ruin that followed is too much for the old-timers, who blame Edgar Sr. for letting his son run amok. "Even to this day Senior thinks Junior is a genius. I think his admiration of his own son exceeded his good judgment," says Mel Griffin, who joined Seagram in 1945, rose to become a senior officer and director, and then retired in

1988. "I don't know whether he recognizes that his son has wrecked the company." As for what Mr. Sam might think, "He'd be rolling in his grave, I'm sure. He was pretty single-minded about Seagram and the liquor business. There's hardly anything left of the Seagram Co. I knew," says Griffin.

Mr. Sam, who died in 1971, has no equal in Canada as an entrepreneurial founder and family business leader. Through sheer determination, gut instinct, and a few corners cut as far as the law was concerned, Mr. Sam made Seagram a household word in more than 150 countries. George Weston, who started a biscuit company that became a food conglomerate, and Roy Thomson, in media and oil, also launched vast Canadian-based global family empires that prospered into the third generation, but both of those families relied on professional management. Seagram was different. The Bronfman family not only maintained control of the company but also held the top job into the third generation. Everything went well until Edgar Jr. sold his heritage with such disastrous results.

As a business writer for twenty-five years, I lived and worked in Canada, England, and the United States but had only followed the family from a distance and had never written about them at any length. In the summer of 2002, Edgar Jr.'s plunge from the heavens captured my attention. Were external forces the cause or had he done himself in? In January 2003, five months after I'd begun researching this biography, I was able to secure an appointment with my New York-based subject to ask if he would agree to interviews. Among those I met that week was Michael Wolff, media columnist with *New York* magazine. We had a drink at Bemelmans, the bar at the Carlyle Hotel, while he poured venom into my ear. "He's one of the great lightweights who's ever played with this much money. The story includes farce and incredible paternal and family indulgence. Everybody I know who moves in those circles makes fun of him. Edgar is a star-fucker of significant proportions." Well, I thought, at least strongly held opinions won't be hard to find.

At Lexa Partners, Edgar Jr.'s venture capital firm in Lever House on Park Avenue, even the view was instructive. Kitty-corner across the street was the magnificent Seagram Building, designed by architect Mies van der Rohe in the 1950s. There Edgar Jr. had been on the fifth floor, here he was on the fourth, a discreet nod to his newly lower status. Of all the possible locations after the debacle, Edgar Jr. had rented space where he could not help but see the very windows where he used to work. He was either a bear for punishment or saw himself as a deposed king in exile awaiting a summons from his former subjects to make a triumphal return to the throne.

Edgar Jr. arrived for our meeting wearing a turtleneck sweater and a taupe-coloured suit. Taller than average at six foot two, slender, and strikingly handsome, his manner was gracious, his demeanour reserved. Unlike some famous scions or celebrity chief executives, he did not consume all the oxygen in the room. His reddish-brown hair was short, sculpted, and swept back in a fashionable length that neither stood up nor lay down. He sported one of those carefully groomed three-day-growth beards of the sort favoured by Alec Baldwin and others of his Hollywood ilk. Until 1990, after he separated from his first wife, Edgar Jr. was clean-shaven. Perhaps he concluded that growing a beard would give him *gravitas*.

When we shook hands, his skin felt silken, as if he enjoyed daily massages with luxurious lotions. The nails were carefully manicured, giving off just the slightest sheen. His only jewellery was a thin gold wedding band that he removed from time to time then flipped among the fingers of both hands as if seeking solace in marriage and family, hearth and home.

Of other movements there were few. His contained manner and gentle voice bespoke a privileged upbringing during which someone had always done his bidding long before he was aware of his own needs, let alone had given any command. He sat erect, his hands folded on the table, alert and listening. As time passed, he relaxed a bit, draping an arm on the back of the chair beside him, his jacket by now unbuttoned.

If Edgar Jr. suffered from one of the seven deadly sins, it was not sloth, the affliction of some third-generation wastrels who loll about rather than add lustre to the family firm. He has worked too hard to be called lazy, but his sin might just be vanity. During our meeting he often looked over my shoulder as if checking his reflection in the wall of glass behind me. He seemed to like what he saw. If style is the man himself, Edgar Jr. is a mostly manufactured model. Call it studied tousle. I thought of Dolly Parton's self-deprecating description: "It costs a lot of money to look this cheap." In that same vein, Edgar Jr.'s motto might be: "It takes a lot of effort to look this laid-back."

I told him that business stories were best told and under-stood when presented through the prism of a person. I said I wanted his voice in the book for accuracy and balance. I pro-posed twelve to fifteen hours of interviews in three or four clumps spread out over the next year, hoping, of course, there would be more. I requested access to corporate archives and his help opening doors of former Seagram and Vivendi colleagues. I told him I wanted to interview family members even though I was well aware that in the case of his wife, for example, her comments would be predictably complimentary. He raised his right hand, made a *comme ci, comme ça* motion, and said, "Some days." His face softened into a lopsided smile, the first I'd seen.

My pitch lasted about five minutes. "If I was going to make the case that you just did, I would have said precisely the same things," he began, then stepped back. "Nothing would make me happier than if you were to say you weren't doing this book, but I know that's not going to happen." He said he'd consider my proposal, adding, "I won't take too long."

Two weeks later, word arrived that he'd agreed. Two interviews were set for March.

When next we met, Edgar Jr. presented his only condition for continued access. "To the extent that there are going to be people, as with any subject—and probably, given this industry, more than usual—who will have their own agendas and their own points of view and their own issues, I'd like the opportunity, if I can, to respond to those things. You can then choose to edit and disseminate it in the way that you feel appropriate, but I'd like at least the opportunity." I readily agreed. He then pushed his point one puzzling step further. "If someone says, 'He's a pedophile,' I'd like to be able to say, 'I'm not.'"

That peculiar remark sent him into a lengthy monologue about *Capturing the Friedmans,* a harrowing documentary he had just seen about a father and son arrested for sodomizing young male students to whom they gave computer training in their home in Great Neck, New York. The family supplied much of the videotape used in the documentary, scenes that showed them trying to make sense of events and being destroyed in the process. "You can't get it out of your mind," he said.

The wide-ranging interview with him that followed was strangely tinged by the dark tone of that documentary, where truth and delusion mingle. He was frank and revealing, although he indicated there were some matters that he was not prepared to talk about just yet.

The second interview, scheduled for later in the week, was cancelled on the morning it was to take place because of a "family emergency." Edgar Jr.'s secretary e-mailed me a few days later with three more dates in April. But life with Edgar Jr. never follows a straight line, as I was beginning to learn. The middle interview of the three was cancelled the week before it was scheduled to happen.

I arrived fifteen minutes early for the first session in that shortened series only to have Edgar Jr. announce that he was leaving for London in fifteen minutes. "Believe me," he said, "I don't want to go to London and back in thirty-six hours." All my interviews that week were cancelled. He apologized, saying, "I don't want to piss off the guy who's writing a book about me." Indeed, I was beginning to get a little miffed. He had now cancelled four successive interviews on short notice. I suggested that I accompany him to the airport, saying that we could at least cover some topics while riding together in the car. His nose wrinkled. "I like to be like this, across the table, in the office, where I can focus." He said he was returning Wednesday evening and planned to spend Friday with his children before taking everyone to his country place for the weekend. I asked about Thursday.

As we waited for his secretary to bring his diary, I removed from my briefcase a photocopied page from the yearbook I had viewed that morning at the prep school he attended. All Collegiate graduates in the class of '73 had been given a full page to do with as they chose. Each had supplied a photograph of himself, some more than one. Most pages included a quote from sources as diverse as Friedrich Nietzsche and the Rolling Stones. Edgar Jr. was the only one among the forty-one grads who had not identified himself by name. The picture that took up the full page looked like a young Edgar Jr. with collar-length hair, and it was in the right place alphabetically, but I wanted to be sure, so I showed him the photocopy and asked, "Is this you?"

Edgar Jr. stared wordlessly at the page. In such circumstances most people will blurt some remark like, "Look at the hair" or "How young I was." Instead, he silently stared in apparent disbelief or narcissistic rapture, it was hard to tell which. Finally, he said slowly, "I regret to say it is."

Lonnie Conte arrived with the diary and stood beside him. Edgar Jr. continued to stare at his own photo, then finally mustered another comment: "Take a look at your boss."

She said nothing. I put the page away. He was surprised to find that his Thursday was open. He agreed to meet me at 11:30 A.M. "I'll give you a whack of time," he said, "three or four hours. We'll take a break after two hours."

On Thursday, I again arrived early. Through the glass boardroom wall I could see Edgar Jr. in a meeting that was just breaking up, so I had yet to take a seat as he bade his guest goodbye in the reception area. He was wearing a royal blue V-neck sweater and dark pants. Without the protective armour of a business suit, his slender frame was almost boyish—but the body language was bizarre. Edgar Jr. was actually cringing at the sight of me. He was slightly stooped, both elbows were tucked at his sides, his forearms raised with the palms showing as if he were fending me off, even though I was standing six feet away. He shook hands reluctantly, muttered a greeting, then scuttled down the hall.

The reason for his skittish behaviour was soon revealed. He would be giving me no more interviews. His reasons were remarkably similar to what he'd previously said. The only sentence that sounded slightly different was, "I don't want to facilitate my voice in the book."

I wondered if this was just a ploy to get me to abandon the project, so I told him I would be proceeding despite his decision to back out. "I have a book contract," I said, "and I thought we had a deal." I wondered if he'd been spooked by some of the content of our earlier interview. Perhaps there were aspects of his early years that he wished he hadn't revealed, such as the troubled state of his mother after his parents separated. Maybe there were darkened rooms into which he did not wish to go. "Let's park all talk of family to the side," I said. "This is a business biography. From here on, we'll just talk about the deals."

My suggestion made no difference. He said that he would not prevent friends and colleagues from speaking to me, but he would not encourage the participation of family members.

His sudden decision was baffling. I couldn't imagine a man so fearful about the retelling of his own life that he worried what he might say to me in a moment of weakness. Or maybe his altered view meant that Edgar Jr. no longer trusted his own judgment after his decision to sell Seagram. His self-esteem, never strong, must have been at a particularly low ebb. As if those weren't reasons enough, the Bronfman family had a complicated history when it came to books about them. Edgar Jr. fit right into the maybe-yes-maybe-no family mould.

The family's first attempt to commission an official corporate history ended tragically in 1970 when the writer, Terence Robertson, claimed that he had uncovered material the family did not want made public, then committed suicide. John Scott, former editor of *Time* Canada, toiled for several years on a Seagram corporate history that came to grief in the 1980s for reasons he won't talk about even yet. Next the family hired journalist Erna Paris, then paid her to stop work before she had even begun. Finally, the family commissioned Michael Marrus, a history professor at the University of Toronto, who in 1991 produced the authorized *Mr. Sam: The Life and Times of Samuel Bronfman*. Edgar Bronfman Sr. has been the family's only author, and has three books to his credit: *Good Spirits, The Making of a Jew,* and *The Third Act.* The first two are autobiographical, the third deals with retirement. His younger brother Charles decided that he too would publish a memoir. He retained Sir Martin Gilbert, biographer of Winston Churchill, who produced a 90,000-word manuscript tentatively entitled *Conversations with Charles.* At last report Charles had decided that the book would not be published.

This is the first book to look closely at Edgar Bronfman Jr. In 1978, when Peter C. Newman's *Bronfman Dynasty* was published, Edgar Jr. was only twenty-three and still four years away from joining Seagram. This book is neither better nor worse for Edgar Jr.'s change of heart, but it is certainly different, and falls squarely into that category of biography known as unauthorized. Moreover, Edgar Jr. intervened in my interview process and told some of the people I contacted not to speak to me. Most, however, did agree to talk. This book is the product of 150 interviews with high school friends, associates from his movie and Broadway days, as well as former colleagues at Seagram and Vivendi.

Those interviews fell mainly into two camps. The first comprised friends who loved him and colleagues who were happy to do his bidding. The second group included his detractors: securities analysts, journalists, and industry critics who treated him as a whipping boy. But that second group also encompassed people who worked closely with Edgar Jr. and couldn't always understand where he was going or were mystified about what he wanted them to do.

To be sure, there's more to a man than who's for him or against him. This is a story about duty and destiny, passion and performance, family and failure. Above all, it is a cautionary tale about the complex relationship between a father and a son.

Edgar Sr. and Edgar Jr. are modern-day versions of Daedalus and Icarus. Daedalus built wings so he and his son could escape Crete. In the Greek myth, Icarus didn't heed his father's warning. He flew too close to the sun, thereby melting the wax with which his wings were fastened, and fell to his death.

Edgar Sr. gave his son everything—everything except the one thing he needed most: guidance. He encouraged Edgar Jr. to fly ever higher, but unlike Daedalus, he issued no warning about the dangers ahead. For his part, Edgar Jr. tried so hard to please his father that he went well beyond what the wings of his talent would allow. The consequences were just as catastrophic as in those bygone times.

ONE

BITTEN BY THE BUG

LATE IN THE AFTERNOON of May 16, 1955, Ann Loeb Bronfman was in labour at Manhattan's Lenox Hill Hospital. Her husband, Edgar Miles Bronfman, phoned the Park Avenue apartment of her parents to tell the staff he wanted dinner served at 7:30 P.M. A nurse, who overheard his instructions, reminded him that labour could last for hours. He advised her that the baby would arrive between 6:00 P.M. and 6:30 P.M. After that, he planned to have a 7 P.M. cocktail, followed by his meal, then return to the hospital. At precisely 6:17 P.M., Ann and their new son, Edgar Miles Bronfman Jr., meekly complied.

Edgar Jr.'s life was controlled by his father right from the night of conception, when Edgar Sr. predicted the exact date of birth. Edgar Sr. had previously forecast the family's eventual size and the birth order: two boys, a girl, a boy, and then a girl. He got the number right, missing out only on the sex of the last child.

Edgar Sr. and Ann were living at the time on Aberdeen Avenue in Montreal's wealthy enclave of Westmount. They planned to move to New York, the location of the U.S. headquarters of Seagram, the family spirits and wine business, but Edgar Sr. was waiting until the month following Edgar Jr.'s birth, when he would turn twenty-six and be safely beyond the U.S. military draft. Ann was an American, and Edgar Sr. intended to become an American citizen, so the couple travelled to New York for the birth of their first two boys.

Edgar Sr.'s behaviour, including such pretentious capacity for prophecy, was part real, part façade. He'd grown up in the shadow of such a famous and fearsome father that he'd had to adopt a hard-shelled persona just to survive. By the 1950s, when Edgar Sr. went to work for the family firm, Mr. Sam was the richest man in Canada, with a net worth of C$400 million. His prosperity was all the more amazing given his humble origins and the notorious nature of the enterprise.

Sam was born in 1889 while his family was en route from Bessarabia, bound for a better life in the Canadian West. His hardscrabble career began as a hotel owner before he ventured into spirits, the ideal family business given that the name Bronfman means "whisky man" in Yiddish. The Canadian government banned interprovincial shipments of liquor in 1918, but Sam found a loophole that allowed the sale of his hooch for medicinal purposes. Business got even better after the Volstead Act of 1919. The "noble experiment," as supporters in the U.S. called it, or Prohibition, as it was better known by drinkers denied their daily tot, was a bonanza for the gangsters who handled distribution. The Canadian government turned a blind eye to burgeoning whisky exports in return for tax revenue.

No Bronfman was ever found guilty of any wrongdoing, but a brother-in-law was murdered in 1922 and Sam's brother had a few close calls. Harry Bronfman, one of the four brothers in the business, was charged with witness tampering and attempting to bribe a customs officer, but was acquitted.

In 1924, Mr. Sam moved to Montreal, created Distillers Corp., and built a distillery in the Montreal suburb of Ville LaSalle. By 1928 he had made enough money from burgeoning U.S. sales to erect a Montreal head office. The five-storey limestone building on Peel Street looked like a baronial Scottish castle, with a gargoyle, turrets, parapets, and a portcullis guarding the entrance. Mr. Sam could also afford to buy Joseph E. Seagram & Sons Ltd. of Waterloo, Ontario, a distiller with brands such as Seagram 83 and V.O. that had been popular in the U.S. for decades. With the acquisition, the company name changed to Distillers Corp.-Seagrams Ltd. (The modern-day name, Seagram Co., came about in 1975.)

Throughout that freewheeling era, Sam claimed to be oblivious about the final destination of his products. "We loaded a carload of goods, got our cash, and shipped it," he said. "We shipped a lot of goods. Of course, we knew where it went, but we had no legal proof. And I never went on the other side of the border to count the empty Seagrams bottles." According to Michael Marrus, who wrote the family-financed biography of Sam, "Sam and his brothers kept basically within the framework of Canadian law, nestled comfortably in the loopholes of provincial and federal regulations as they supplied American bootleggers from coast to coast."

Because legitimate U.S. producers had been inactive, when Prohibition ended in 1933, Seagram had the largest supply of aged whisky. Sam's brands were soon top sellers in the U.S. market. To help meet growing demand, former bootleggers became distributors and Mr. Sam bought distilleries in Lawrenceburg, Indiana, and Relay, Maryland. He also set up a U.S. headquarters in New York's Chrysler Building. By 1955, the year of Edgar Jr.'s birth, one-third of all beverage alcohol sold in the U.S. was a Seagram brand.

Mr. Sam was short, balding, and driven. He desperately sought legitimacy and tried to get beyond his bootlegging background, but never during his lifetime was he regarded as anything but an arriviste who'd built his fortune using questionable means. In 1935, Seagram agreed to a negotiated settlement that included paying $1.5 million in U.S. taxes and duties on Prohibition-era shipments. (All figures are in U.S. dollars unless otherwise specified.)

In the 1950s, after their schooling was complete, Edgar Sr. and his brother Charles both joined the family business. Beyond the easy entree, their hard-nosed father offered them few favours as they learned the business from the distillery floor up. Sam was ruthless and given to violent displays of foul-mouthed temper. His management technique was to divide and conquer; he would pit one son against the other in order to maintain his control over them and make them strive for his acknowledgment. In the twenty-room family home with a staff of ten at 15 Belvedere Road in Montreal, Sam was distant at best, a threatening presence at worst. As the eldest, Edgar Sr. tried to tough it out by constantly fighting with his father. Charles, who was two years younger, would do anything to avoid confrontation. He learned to be supple or seek safe haven by hiding behind Edgar Sr. Sisters Phyllis and Minda fled to college as soon as they could, then married as a means of escaping their irascible father. Only their mother, Saidye, could handle Sam. At family gatherings she would sing to him the Eddie Cantor song, "You've got the cutest little baby face."

As Edgar Sr. and Charles moved up through the company ranks, they divvied up the duties. Edgar Sr. wanted to live in New York because U.S. operations accounted for 90 percent of sales. As the second son, Charles was content to remain at home in Canada and accept a lesser role.

Edgar Sr. married Ann Loeb, an American with a patrician heritage. In 1931, when Sam was bootlegging, Ann's father, John Langeloth Loeb, and grandfather Carl M. Loeb founded an investment banking firm later known as Loeb, Rhoades & Co. Her mother, Frances, was a Lehman, but she was also related to the Altschuls and the Lewissohns, two other powerful German-Jewish families on Wall Street.

Ann attended Choate Rosemary Hall, a Connecticut boarding school, where she was elected a vice-president in her freshman year, played on the varsity tennis team, and was editor of *Question Mark,* the literary magazine. After graduating in 1950, she studied literature at Bennington College in Vermont, and was married on January 7, 1953, during her third year. Edgar Sr. had spent two boisterous years at Williams College in Williamstown, Massachusetts, before eventually graduating from Montreal's McGill University in 1951.

Some members of Ann's family were willing to overlook the scandalous Bronfman past for the sake of Ann's future. After all, Joseph Kennedy had a similar checkered history dealing in whisky, and he'd gone on to serve as U.S. ambassador to Britain. Moreover, the Bronfmans were rich, even by Wall Street standards. At the wedding, John Loeb said, "Now I know what it feels like to be a poor relation." Other family members were less enthralled. Said Mrs. Arthur Lehman, "But those Bronfmans have just come down out of the trees."

Nine months later, when Sam and Saidye's first grandchild arrived, Samuel Bronfman II was named after the family patriarch, contrary to Jewish custom. A child is normally named after a relative who has recently died, but Edgar Sr. sought to please his father and flout tradition. It was Ann who suggested that their second son be named after his father. Edgar Sr. was delighted with the idea, but he worried that two Edgars around the house might cause confusion. So Edgar Jr. was called Gary until he was five, at which time he announced he wanted to be called Edgar so that he had a five-letter name just like Sammy and his younger sister Holly.

The family moved to the U.S. from Montreal in December 1955, when Edgar Jr. was seven months old. Edgar Sr. bought a 23-acre parcel of land, part of the estate that had been in the Loeb family for three generations, in suburban Westchester County twenty-five miles from Manhattan. He built a brick mansion designed by Mott Schmidt in the American Georgian style that was popular with wealthy families such as the Astors, Rockefellers, and Vanderbilts. As a child, Edgar Jr. enjoyed an opulent life in a home resplendent with eight bedrooms, a living room, dining room, library, and children's playroom. The manicured grounds included a clay tennis court and swimming pool, far different environs than most of the lads he later knew as he was growing up. One year, Edgar Jr.'s class spent a sunny day in spring roaming the grounds, swimming in the outdoor pool, and playing tennis. "It was like going to a camp for a day, but it was somebody's house, it was quite amazing," remembers Henry Schulson, now director of a children's museum in Chattanooga, Tennessee.

In Edgar Jr.'s earliest memory he was four years old, walking up the driveway towards the house with Sam, Holly, and their nanny. Ann was expecting, so the conversation was about whether the new arrival would be a boy or a girl. Sam and Edgar Jr. predicted a baby boy; Holly said a girl. What is interesting is not the topic but that Edgar Jr.'s first recollection does not involve a parent. "They both were very impactful in different ways as 'rifle shots,' but neither were ever very present in our lives," he says. Edgar Jr. and his siblings spent most of their time being looked after by their nanny and the rest of the household staff, which included a cook, a laundress, a maid, and a groundskeeper who lived on the property.

Although Edgar Jr. was the second-born of five, he was very much a middle child. He was bracketed between Sam, who was eighteen months older, and Holly, who was fifteen months younger. Matthew came along in 1959, four years after Edgar Jr., and Adam followed four years later, in 1963. As the first-born, Sam was treated more strictly than the rest and battled against all rules. Holly was the little princess who could do no wrong. Edgar Jr., who got along better with his parents than did Sam, was the resident diplomat who wanted to please. "I would settle fights. I would explain my siblings' positions to my parents when there were issues between them. I was generally the facilitator or the peacemaker," Edgar Jr. recalls.

As with most middle children, he was expected to help out with the younger ones, so he learned responsibility early and came to be seen by them as their protector. When Edgar Jr. was five, Holly asked him: "What happens if Dad dies?"

"Well, Mom will take care of us," he said.

"What if Mom dies?"

"Well, Nanny will take care of us."

"What if Nanny dies?"

"Holly, don't worry, I will always take care of you."

That leadership role has lasted. During the 1990s, Holly ran a yoga and meditation centre in New York. When she married her third husband in 2000, Holly asked for some changes in her family trust. The lawyers were reluctant. For help in the impasse she turned not to her father but to Edgar Jr.

In Edgar Jr.'s cosseted world, familial love took the form of indulgence, not affection. On New Year's Day when Edgar Jr. was four and Sam was six, the family was visiting their grandparents in Montreal. Edgar Jr. and Sam announced that they'd like to go bowling. Mr. Sam phoned Michael McCormick, a loyal Seagram retainer, and told him, "We want to go bowling." "Who's we?" asked McCormick. "Me and my little jewels," replied Mr. Sam. The manager of a local bowling alley obligingly opened his establishment on the holiday so the lads could knock down pins in splendid isolation. Between frames, they served themselves ice cream and dispensed soft drinks at the soda fountain.

Meals at home were not family events when everyone shared news of the day, so Edgar Jr. did not grow up hearing at dinner about the family business or discussing great public events. The children ate together at 6 P.M., then disappeared to do their homework or get ready for bed. Edgar Sr. and Ann would eat later, often in the library, while watching television. There were rooms into which Edgar Jr. and his siblings were not allowed to go for fear they might trigger alarms protecting the artworks. Sometimes, when the children were finished their homework, the entire family would gather. Woe betide the child who sat in Father's favourite chair. "Get out of my tree," he'd bellow. So often did he utter the phrase that his children ended up calling him Tree, a nickname that a mellowed Edgar Sr. used in later years when signing letters to them.

By the time he was ten, Edgar Jr. had learned some piano and would play "What the World Needs Now is Love," over and over again. Even to his friends, the plaintive "love, sweet love" of that Burt Bacharach/Hal David hit seemed to represent what was missing most in Edgar Jr.'s young life. "The father was a very standoffish person. He wasn't warm with anybody, and he certainly didn't seem warm with Edgar's friends. Leonard Bernstein was very warm with Alex's friends," says Leslie Reif, now a teacher in San Francisco, referring to another famous father in their group. "I didn't get the same feeling with the

Bronfmans. Maybe it was a larger staff. It was just not the same type of environment."

Answers to the questions that troubled Edgar Jr. were more likely to come from his mother than his father. "More than anything, he just wasn't around," says Edgar Jr. "He worked a lot, he travelled a fair amount. I remember she used one piece of imagery which is in some senses extremely obvious, but it was impactful because I was eight or nine years old. We were talking about African-Americans. She always told me all people were just the same. No matter who you cut, they bleed just like you do. Inside we're all alike, and . . . the outside is just a difference of appearance. She always believed that, and she was powerful in describing her feelings."

When he was eight, Edgar Jr. ran away from home. His adventure was short-lived; he was back in an hour. His mother sat him down and told him that running away from a problem was like writing down the problem on a piece of paper and leaving the paper behind, sitting on a table. "You can run away for ten years, you can run away for twenty years, one day when you come back that problem's still going to be there," she told him. "You can really never run away from your problems, you have to deal with them."

Ann knew whereof she spoke. "I don't think either her father or her husband were particularly gentle with her," says Edgar Jr. "I think she felt that they both had high expectations of her. Certainly she felt her father was not at all forgiving. Expectations were either met or unmet, there were no gradations. I think that she probably felt that she disappointed him more often than not."

Edgar Jr. did not take sides or sit in judgment. His world was still small and he needed everyone in it. "My dad was an angry young man. I don't think he was always angry with her, I think he was just angry. His father never gave him much emotional reward. He never gave him as much freedom in the business as my father would have liked. I don't think he was ever as comfortable as he would have hoped working for his father."

As was the case with many women of that era, Ann went from being a daughter to being a wife then immediately became a mother, with no time in between to be herself. The couple's social life consisted mostly of weekend house parties. "In those days, people of our age group drank a lot, and so did we," admitted Edgar Sr. in his autobiography, *Good Spirits: The Making of a Businessman*. Edgar Sr. described Edgar Jr. as the family member best able to cope. Wrote Edgar Sr., using a nickname Edgar Jr. acquired later: "As he was growing up, there was always something special about Efer—his calm in a crisis, his ability to deal with his mother's problems, his sense of responsibility for his siblings."

Outside the family circle, Edgar Jr. had trouble finding his rightful place. For classes in junior kindergarten through second grade he attended nearby Rye Country Day School. "Not for self, but for service" was the motto; development of the complete child was the goal. A good education was important, but community service and humanistic values were also stressed at the private school. Despite that breadth of possibilities, Edgar Jr. did not feel that he fit. "I remember being bored in second grade—it could have been first. We were reading from some book or other, some kids were really struggling to read. I don't really remember having a problem reading. I do remember feeling bored to death."

In 1963, Edgar Sr. bought an apartment in a New York co-op so the family could live there during the week while the children attended the proper prep schools. Edgar Jr. and Sam were enrolled in Collegiate School, the oldest independent school in the U.S. The Dutch West India Company and the Dutch Reformed Church established Collegiate in 1628 for the colonists of what was then called New Amsterdam, two years after the Dutch West India Company paid twenty-four dollars in beads for Manhattan. For two centuries the school was located on the southern tip of the island, before moving in 1892 to its present location on West Seventy-eighth Street, almost directly across Central Park from the family residence on the Upper East Side.

Edgar Jr. began in third grade at the elite day school where tuition today costs $21,000 a year for kindergarten through fourth grade and $22,300 for fifth through twelfth grade. "It was very established and preppy. We all loved it. We knew we were in one of the best schools in the city. There was a certain sense of privilege," says Alex Bernstein, who now runs the Leonard Bernstein Family Foundation in New York. The school demanded a high level of deportment and deference. The students wore jackets and ties and called their teachers Sir.

Not Edgar. He observed the dress code but refused to recognize the teachers' authority. "I remember being taken aback at how brazen he was with our teachers," recalls Bernstein. "He was able to talk back at them, which I found shocking. At the time it seemed arrogant. I was half envious and also not particularly approving. His family had a lot of money and they gave the school a lot of money. He felt he could do whatever he wanted."

To Edgar Jr., his teachers were lesser lights with no real power compared with his father. Edgar Jr. was thirteen when he overheard his father talking on the telephone one day. "I don't remember what he was talking about but I remember I must have been very impressed because I said to him: 'Dad, you're very powerful, aren't you?' He looked at me and said: 'Always remember, son, you never have any power if you have to use it.' That means if you walk into a room and you have to tell people who you are, you are not powerful." Edgar Jr. concluded he simply had to wait for his destiny to unfold and such power would become his.

Meanwhile, family wealth bought him access and friends. Four students—Tom Moore, Leslie Reif, Alex Bernstein, and Tony Hodes—created their version of the Beatles. The troupe was not just a celebration of popular culture but also a huge leap from the usual school pageants about the Pilgrims. When Hodes dropped out, Edgar Jr. replaced him. "He wanted to be in the group very much," says Reif. "His parents were willing to have us practise out at his country house and I think this was the main reason that he was in the group. I don't think too many other parents wanted four fifth-graders or sixth-graders practising at their homes." So generous were the Bronfmans that they bought Reif the set of drums he used as the group's Ringo Starr. Bernstein was John Lennon, Moore was George Harrison, and Edgar Jr. played Paul McCartney, complete with guitars. Edgar Jr. and Bernstein even wrote a pop song, just like their heroes. For two years the group appeared at school talent shows and lip-synched to Beatles tunes.

When Edgar Jr. was in sixth grade, Collegiate expanded with the building of the New School, renamed Platten Hall in 1983. The eight-storey addition included more classrooms, a library, science labs, and a gymnasium. The structure, completed in 1967, also had a professional theatre with sloped seating for 260, a raised and raked stage, as well as rows of spotlights that could be controlled from a booth in the balcony. A discreet plaque on the lobby wall honoured the donors who made it possible: *The Ann and Edgar Bronfman Theatre.*

In the seventh grade, Edgar Jr. played the devil in Stephen Vincent Benét's *The Devil and Daniel Webster,* a major production held in the Bronfman Theatre, complete with costumes, lighting, and stage props. "I liked the camaraderie of it. People came together towards a common goal. It was distinct, it was a project, it wasn't a lifetime, it was just *this,*" says Edgar Jr. His parents attended the performance, then took the young thespian out to dinner. He was in no mood to celebrate; he was sullen and depressed. "My great disappointment with it was that we only performed it one evening. It was wonderful and it was over."

Yet when there were more lasting activities available, Edgar Jr. did not stay involved. Teacher Colin Reed urged Edgar Jr. and his classmates to make a sixteen-millimetre documentary film called *A Day in the Life of the School.* "It had so much wrong with it that it was very good," recalls Reed. "Ultimately he was deeply involved in film. We like to think it started at Collegiate." That first film project spawned the Middle School Film Club and the Middle School Film Festival the following year. By 1970, the club had thirty members and was the largest in the school. As the founders moved into upper school, they stayed in the club and attained national attention. A film by Peter Grunwald was reviewed in the *Los Angeles Times.* Jonas Mekas, the respected film critic for *The Village Voice,* commented favourably on the Collegiate Film Festival. By the time Edgar Jr. reached his junior year, however, he had lost interest. He had moved beyond his peers and, with a helping hand from his father, was already working with professionals.

For Edgar Jr. the wider world was not a walled-off place. "We had real awareness. We were in the middle of New York City, the riots. There was a lot of discussion at Collegiate, so [we] certainly weren't hidden from it. Once middle school started, it never felt like an extremely sheltered, separate environment," says Edgar Jr. Protests were not squelched, they were welcomed. When the students staged a one-day sit-in against the Vietnam War, most faculty members participated. "Nearly everybody in the school felt the same way," says Colin Reed. "It was very frustrating for the kids. They didn't really like the reaction of the teachers, which was to be very sympathetic with them and agree with what they were doing."

Edgar Jr.'s liberal views were also formed by his father's socially responsible activities. Edgar Sr. helped the National Urban League in its efforts to empower African-Americans, and he was close to both Whitney Young and Vernon Jordan, successive executive directors of the organization in the 1960s and 1970s. Edgar Sr. was also a member of the Interracial Council for Business Opportunity, a business group that fostered economic growth for minorities. "You need to have a market economy, but you also need to have a system that preserves everyone's ability to get ahead," observes Edgar Jr. "Otherwise, when the division between the haves and the have-nots becomes too broad, the haves are as lost as the have-nots, maybe more so. Certainly I didn't feel we had a very equitable society in the middle sixties."

While Collegiate aimed to develop the "whole man" through sports and the arts, the school's main purpose was to prepare the students for admission to a top-ranked college. Edgar Jr. had no interest in continuing his education; by age ten he had decided that college was not for him. "He didn't seem to be the studious type. He gave the impression that he didn't feel the same need to be that way. He wasn't cocky, but there was more of a self-assuredness that permeated him and set him apart. Sometimes it did appear as the spoiled rich kid, slightly arrogant, but other times he was just different. He was more mature and more his own person. He was much more in charge at that age than the rest of us kids," says classmate Tom Moore, now a lawyer with Philip Morris in Lausanne, Switzerland. "Edgar was much more a phantom than he was anything else," says A. Edward Major Jr., a New York attorney. "I think he frankly considered himself a man of destiny. All of us rather marvelled at the fact that he could go through school without attending classes, or rarely attending class. He felt himself in a social class apart." That poor attendance record drove Edgar Jr. to take shortcuts. "We cribbed answers from much more scientifically oriented pre-med nerds in our chemistry class. The teacher knew about the whole thing and thought it was hysterical," says Andrew Wolfson, a journalist with the Louisville *Courier-Journal.*

Among the 41-member graduating class of '73, Edgar Jr. was the only one who did not go on to college. "That always absolutely amazed me. I would have thought he would have gone to college," says Colin Reed. "He was a bright, interesting person." Edgar Jr.'s decision was particularly unusual given the family's scholastic endeavours. Both of his parents attended college. So did his aunts Phyllis, who graduated from Vassar, and Minda, who graduated from Smith College then took her master's at Columbia. Charles went to McGill before quitting in third year to work at Seagram. Edgar Jr.'s brothers Sam and Matthew both graduated from Williams; Matthew went on to obtain his MBA from Harvard Business School. Adam attended Pomona College in Claremont, California.

Even Edgar Jr.'s farewell to Collegiate spoke to his disdain for the rites of student passage. Each graduate was given a full page in the yearbook, *The Dutchman,* to do with whatever he wanted. Edgar Jr.'s offering consisted of a full-page photo of himself and eight lines of plaintive poetry.

> *Into the air a wind that kills*
> *From yon far country blows.*
> *What are those blue remembr'd hills?*
> *What spires, what farms are those?*
>
> *That is the land of lost content*
> *I see it shining plain.*
> *The happy highways where I went,*
> *And shall never come again.*

The thoughtful Edgar Jr. was immediately recognizable, but not every reader would have identified the poetry, and there was no source cited. The melancholy lines were appropriated from *A Shropshire Lad,* written in 1896 by the English lyric poet Alfred Edward Housman. Edgar Jr. changed the spelling of "remembered" and altered two of Housman's lines. The original first line was, "Into my heart on air that kills." The last, "And cannot come again."

Did Edgar Jr. really believe that he could pass off such famous work as his own? Or was it just a harmless intellectual prank to see if some wiseacre would remember studying the poem? Whatever the motivation, when Edgar Jr. was with his family he knew his place, but elsewhere he seemed disconnected and purposeless. Some called that careless detachment arrogance; others dismissed him as a spoiled rich kid who didn't believe he even needed to be like the others or bother making an effort in order to succeed. Those differing perceptions of his personality haunt him to this day.

Edgar Jr. could turn his back on school or any of society's usual rules because of who his father was. But beyond the money and security, for Edgar Jr. the other allure of the family business was the fantasy life it allowed his father to lead. By the time he was in his early teens, he could see how his father's role at Seagram also permitted his active participation in the world of entertainment. Edgar Sr. began buying shares in Metro-Goldwyn-Mayer in 1968 and was named chairman of the movie studio in May 1969. The investment gave rise to the most famous of all Bronfman family anecdotes, when Mr. Sam asked his son: "Tell me, Edgar, are we buying all this stock in MGM just so you can get laid?" Came the reply: "Oh, no, Pop, it doesn't cost $40 million to get laid."

Whatever the real reason for his interest in Hollywood, Edgar Sr.'s reign was brief. During the summer of 1969, financier Kirk Kerkorian accumulated 40 percent of MGM, enough for control, and fired Edgar Sr. that fall. Soon after, comedian Don Rickles spotted Edgar Sr. taking his seat in a nightclub and quipped from the stage: "Hey look—here's Edgar Bronfman! He was chairman of MGM for five whole minutes!"

Edgar Sr.'s interest in entertainment was not quelled by the humiliation. He took his profits from the MGM shares, formed Sagittarius Productions, and set out to finance films and Broadway plays. He bankrolled *Jane Eyre*, a 1970 made-for-TV movie starring George C. Scott and Susannah York. In 1973 he was the producer on *Charlotte's Web*, an animated family film based on the E.B. White children's classic. On Broadway, Edgar Sr.'s most successful venture was *1776*, a patriotic musical that ran for three years. Other plays flopped. *Stages* closed after opening night in 1978. Edgar Sr. would rather make money than lose it, but fun was as important to him as financial returns. President of Sagittarius was Ron Kass, third husband of Joan Collins, who made her first film, *Lady Godiva Rides Again*, in 1951 and went on to star in dozens more. "We all became jolly buddies, double-dating with Samantha Eggar, Sue Lloyd or whoever was his lady of the moment, jetting in the Seagram private Gulf Stream jet to San Francisco, New York or Acapulco, where Edgar had a villa," Collins wrote in her autobiography, *Past Imperfect*.

For Edgar Jr., entertainment looked far more exciting than the family liquor business. Equally important, film and Broadway provided a ready-made opportunity for him to seek his father's attention and strive for his approval. Movie directors screened their work for Edgar Sr. in the family home. Sam was away at boarding school, so Edgar Jr. was the eldest child in residence. He sat with the adults, watched the shows, and participated in the discussions that followed. Scripts from producers seeking financial backing were stacked around the house. Edgar Jr. read one that he particularly liked and persuaded his father not only to invest but also to send him to London during the summer of 1970 to work on the film.

Melody was the first movie for director David Puttnam. The script by Alan Parker was about two eleven-year-olds who fall in love and want to marry. Edgar Sr. invested $450,000 and off went Edgar Jr., who had just completed ninth grade, to be a lowly tea boy on the set. He briefly lived with Collins and Kass, the latter representing Edgar Sr. and his money as executive producer on *Melody*. But Edgar Jr. was lonely living in the basement of their house in Mayfair, so Puttnam offered to let him stay with his family in Pimlico.

Patsy and David Puttnam had two children, Debbie, eight, and Sacha, four. Patsy, who was twenty-six, was a lively presence in a fun-filled place that was very different from Edgar Jr.'s home, where adults and children rarely spent much time together. Edgar Jr. quickly became closer to his adopted family than he had ever been with his own. David was "Da" (pronounced *Day*), the pet name Patsy used. Patsy became Patricia, as if Edgar Jr. had his own special relationship with her.

Edgar Jr. soon had his own affectionate nickname. London was plastered with posters that summer for an Egg Marketing Board campaign using the slogan "Eggs for Breakfast." The letters matched Edgar Jr.'s initials, so the Puttnam children began calling him "E for B," which soon became Efer (pronounced *Eefer*). "He didn't seem to be like most fifteen-year-old boys. He seemed to be old for his years. Efer was a romantic. He could be deeply touched by very simple things. Even being given the name Efer touched him. It meant that he found somewhere

where he belonged," says Patsy. "It gives you some idea what a gaping hole was in his heart by the time he got to us." Efer is what Edgar Sr. calls his son to this day, but the name has never been one that can be used by just anybody. A select few colleagues with whom Edgar Jr. later worked were permitted to use it, but there have been occasions when others called him Efer only to be told in no uncertain terms to desist.

Edgar Jr. worked conscientiously on the set of *Melody* during the daily filming at various locations in Lambeth, Hammersmith, and Trafalgar Square. "He wasn't one of those kids coming into a situation set up by his father and then you thought 'What a waste of time' or 'What a pain in the ass.' He was just the opposite. He was willing to do anything to get ahead and learn about filmmaking," says Sandy Lieberson, David Puttnam's business partner. Puttnam himself remembers, "He was a quick learner, very, very easy to work with. There are people in life that get it and people in life that don't. I remember telling his father, who at the time was worried about him, that he had absolutely nothing to worry about. Anything that he was asked that would help the movie, he would do. By the time we finished *Melody*, he'd pretty well decided that he wanted that to be his world."

In his American jeans and sneakers, Edgar Jr. looked different from others his age. "He had cameras and gadgets that we were all envious of," says Mark Lester, who played Daniel Latimer, the boy in the film who falls in love with Melody. "He ordered twelve Coca-Colas just for himself. It was extraordinary. He lined them all up and drank a few. He used to do quite a lot of things like that." For all his wealth, Edgar Jr. seemed to care little for worldly possessions. He paid twenty pounds for a pale blue tie-dyed cotton jacket that he wore daily for the next three summers.

Edgar Jr. enjoyed many points of connection with the cast, the characters they played, and the plot in a coming-of-age movie that exuded innocence. Tracy Hyde, who was appearing in her first movie, played Melody Perkins. In an unusual coincidence, Hyde's birthdate was four years to the day after Edgar Jr.'s. Jack Wild played Mark Lester's movie friend, Ornshaw. Both lads had appeared in the movie *Oliver*, in which Lester played Oliver, Wild the Artful Dodger. Edgar Jr. would have identified most closely with Daniel, played by Lester, whose parents pay him scant attention. At one point Daniel sets fire to the newspaper his father is reading. Ornshaw, a lower-class lad, is the movie's worldly-wise philosopher. "Some people are winners and some people are losers," goes one of his lines. "That's all decided before we get on this earth." Ornshaw conducts the marriage "ceremony" of Tracy and Daniel under a railway viaduct. Teachers and parents arrive to disrupt the occasion only to have dozens of students respond with fists and homemade bombs. The film ends with the newlyweds using the chaos as cover to escape on a railway handcar.

One of the successful ingredients in *Melody* was a soundtrack by the Bee Gees. The Gibb brothers, Barry, Maurice, and Robin, had begun singing in Australia and moved to London in 1967. Among their songs for *Melody* were: "To Love Somebody," "In the Morning," "Melody Fair," "Give Your Best," and "First of May." Also on the soundtrack was "Teach Your Children" by Crosby Stills Nash & Young. When *Melody* was released in 1971, *Newsweek* called it "a pure delight," but it did badly at the box office in the U.S. and Britain where it was renamed *S. W. A. L. K.* (Sealed With A Loving Kiss). The movie became popular in Japan, where readers of *Roadshow*, a Japanese magazine, named Tracy Hyde actress of the year.

Many of the movie's participants went on to fame. The Bee Gees hit it big with the 1977 soundtrack for *Saturday Night Fever*. Scriptwriter Alan Parker directed *Midnight Express* and

Angela's Ashes. David Puttnam produced *Chariots of Fire* and *The Killing Fields.* Hyde appeared in several made-for-TV movies and had a supporting role in a 1986 film called *Alice.*

By his own admission, Edgar Jr. was bitten by the entertainment bug. He returned to London in the summer of 1971, lived with the Puttnams again, and did odd jobs on another David Puttnam film, *The Pied Piper,* also paid for in part by Edgar Sr. The film was financially less successful than *Melody.* Its sole redeeming quality was music by Donovan, the Scottish folksinger. Edgar Jr.'s roles during both those summers were so modest that he was not listed on the credits of either film.

Among those in London who befriended Edgar Jr. was Andrew Birkin, who wrote the screenplay for *The Pied Piper.* Birkin was nine years older, eccentric, and widely read. His mother was an actress, his father was in covert operations for the British government, and his sister was a singer. (Birkin is probably best known for his film *The Cement Garden,* from the book by Ian McEwan, for which he was named best director at the 1993 Berlin Film Festival.) Among other adventures, the two travelled to Corsica to stay with Patsy Puttnam, who was holidaying in a cliffside dwelling with the children. Puttnam pleaded with the two to bring food. They arrived bearing a Fortnum & Mason hamper filled with foie gras and other exotic items of little interest to children.

Edgar Jr. and Birkin endlessly discussed projects. Edgar Jr. read a book called *The Silent People* and he wanted Birkin to write a screenplay. "It was very Efer. It was about the British exploiting the Irish and the Irish exploiting themselves," says Birkin. Commercial success was not crucial. "He never struck me as saying 'What does the audience want?' It was more what was right for the movie."

Birkin could sense Edgar Jr. struggling as he headed for a future on his own in film rather than joining the family business.

"Edgar certainly had the creative genes. It seemed to me that he wanted to make his way creatively and independently of his family. He was curious and adventurous. There was a Peter Pan element, a streak of irresponsibility." Edgar Jr. brought to Birkin's mind the lines written by Frances Cornford about another English poet, Rupert Brooke, who was killed during the First World War:

> *A young Apollo, golden-haired,*
> *Stands dreaming on the verge of strife,*
> *Magnificently unprepared*
> *For the long littleness of life.*

TWO

COMING HOME

IN MARCH 1971, on the occasion of Sam Bronfman's eightieth birthday, the entire family gathered together for what would be the last time. An official portrait of the three generations, the men in black tie and the ladies in evening gowns, commemorated the celebration held at 15 Belvedere Road in Montreal. Saidye and Sam sit on separate armchairs in the foreground. Saidye smiles serenely into the camera; a solemn Sam gazes intently at his wife of forty-nine years.

To their right are Charles and Barbara with their two children, Stephen and Ellen. Standing in a row against the wall, beneath a radiant canvas by French impressionist Claude Monet, are Alain and Minda de Gunzburg, Phyllis Lambert, Ann and Edgar Sr.; near Alain and Minda are their two sons, Jean and Charles. Perched on a sofa over Mr. Sam's left shoulder are Ann and Edgar Sr.'s five: Sam, Holly, Edgar Jr., Adam, and Matthew.

Mr. Sam was dying of prostate cancer. Saidye had kept the fatal diagnosis from him, but he probably suspected the worst. Whether that was the reason, or just because family get-togethers were rare, Mr. Sam proposed a toast at the dinner table. He spoke about the business he'd built, the wealth he'd created, and how he was passing along the responsibility to preserve the family dynasty.

Edgar Jr., who would turn sixteen in two months, wasn't sure he wanted such an onerous duty so soon, if ever. "I made a toast back to him that basically said, 'Thank you, Pappa, for all that you've done for us and for the family and for working so hard so that all of us can do with our lives what we would like to do with our lives, which is an extraordinarily great gift.' But it was also a way of saying to him, 'Not so fast. We'll decide ourselves what we're going to do with our lives.'"

Edgar Jr. did not have the last word. "When we left dinner and we were going to the library or the sunroom, which was where we would always go after dinner, he walked by me, and as he walked by me, he just looked into me and I remember he distinctly said, 'You're the one.'"

In June, Mr. Sam had a final conversation with Edgar Sr. about Seagram as well as Edgar Sr.'s investments in Hollywood movies and Broadway plays. Mr. Sam had never before approved, but now he said, "Well, at least it was something you really enjoyed doing." That was as close to his father's blessing as Edgar Sr. ever got. He was never to hear the three words he most desired: "I love you." On July 10, 1971, Mr. Sam died.

Edgar Jr. had already inherited his father's enthusiasm for the world of entertainment. Now he had also been handed the full burden of the family's financial future. Edgar Jr. told no one, not even his own father, that Mr. Sam had both chosen him and cursed him in the same breath.

From an early age, Edgar Jr. realized that the family name and fabulous wealth gave him unusual access. Unlike most young men, he could phone almost anyone, get a hearing, and more often than not find a willing mentor who would accelerate the pace of his life. Once such access was gained, he was sufficiently intelligent to impress his new acquaintance and easily persuade him to help out while at the same time coming along for a ride that might benefit the mentor as well. When he was fourteen, Edgar Jr. made one such approach to Porter Bibb, a documentary filmmaker at Maysles Films in New York. When Bibb, who was then in his thirties, learned that Edgar Jr. wanted to be a producer, he pointed out that his family fortune put him into an unusual category: he did not need to seek financial backing from others. But Bibb also warned him not to use his own money. He told Edgar Jr. he'd invested $1 million, all the money he had, in a film about Woodstock, the 1968 music love fest. The project subsequently became *Gimme Shelter,* the 1970 documentary about the Rolling Stones concert at Altamont Speedway where a fan was beaten to death. At the time when Edgar Jr. and Bibb talked, the film was not yet the critical or financial success it would become. Bibb worried that as associate producer he might lose everything. "I made the mistake of putting my own money into this, and now I'm up the creek because I may or may not get it back," Bibb told Edgar Jr. "You never want to spend your own money. If it's not an idea that you can sell to somebody else, it's probably not a good idea."

Easy money was also on the mind of Bruce Stark, producer of *Soon,* a 1971 rock opera bankrolled by Edgar Sr. that closed after a brief three-week run. A few months later, Edgar Jr. showed Stark a screenplay he'd written. Stark told him that his work wasn't good enough, but they went on to talk about other possibilities they might pursue together. Stark said he didn't want their relationship to be based on Edgar Sr.'s money. If Stark thought the idea had commercial merit, he would invest with

Edgar Jr. on a fifty-fifty basis. "I hadn't had a hit show yet, but I still had those hopes of having a hit show, and I didn't want to be seen as the guy that's sucking the money out of the Bronfmans," recalls Stark.

The partnership was unusual. At thirty-two, Stark regarded Edgar Jr., who was half his age, as a younger brother. "Even at that point Edgar's ability to schmooze up people in the upper echelons of the agent world and the film world was really good. People were very impressed with him," says Stark. "Edgar always had this ability to have a short learning experience and then jump right in. Adults loved him. It wasn't just me, they all loved him. He was a charming kid and way old beyond his years."

The two formed a company, Mileswade Enterprises Inc., a combination of their middle names. After school, Edgar occupied a desk in Stark's sixth-floor office in the Victoria Theatre Building, a structure filled with agents, publicists, and other theatrical types. (The building has since been replaced by a hotel, the Marriott Marquee.) Edgar Jr. paid for an ad in his high school yearbook. The Mileswade principals were not named, but the office address on Broadway and a phone number were listed. So were their four properties: *The Silent People, The Me Nobody Knows, Christian Rudis: The Life and Times,* and *Act of God.* During their three-year association, Stark and Edgar Jr. got no projects going.

The partnership ended in 1974. They had worked together on a film idea, but the director Edgar Jr. had in mind demanded $150,000 in a "pay or play" contract, which meant the director would be paid whether the film got made or not. Stark, who had a wife and two children, did not have $75,000 for his half. He backed out and took a salaried job he'd been offered as a Broadway stage manager. "Edgar got a little annoyed because he was impatient. I told him I couldn't sign the contract. I wasn't going to rely on his dad to put the money up for my end. The film didn't get made and [the director] did get his money and I felt somewhat justified as far as my position. I think [Edgar] got in with a bunch of sharks."

Edgar Jr.'s first screen credit—as producer—came on a film shot during the summer of 1972, when Edgar Jr. was seventeen and about to enter his final year of high school. *The Blockhouse* was a depressing Second World War story about seven men who became trapped in an underground bunker after German troops, fleeing the Allied invasion, blew up the entrance. During their six-year imprisonment, five of the men died. The other two died within days of being found and freed.

At this stage in his young life, Edgar Jr. was still wrestling with what stories would work and what stories wouldn't. When he read the script, which had been sent to Puttnam, Edgar Jr. told him it was the best story he'd ever read. Puttnam went through the script, said he wasn't interested, and told Edgar Jr. that if he liked it so much, he should produce the movie himself. "I can't," replied Edgar Jr. "Why not?" asked Puttnam. "Then it occurred to me that the right answer was 'I can.' And I did," said Edgar Jr.

There were two other producers on *The Blockhouse,* Kent Walwin and Antony Rufus Isaacs, both of whom were ten years older than Edgar Jr. Walwin was supposed to raise the money to cover production costs but came down with appendicitis and did not deliver. Recollections vary as to how Edgar Jr.'s involvement came about. According to Isaacs, Edgar Jr. was there because David Puttnam had asked Isaacs to give him a job. "Edgar engineered himself into taking a producer credit with a sort of understanding that he would bring the money in," says Isaacs. "The English are incredibly subservient when it comes to

American money. If you have somebody called Edgar Bronfman who's lurking about, this gawky kid, you tend to call him sir because he might write you a cheque." Director Clive Rees agrees, saying that Edgar Jr. joined the film by promising Antony money. "He had very little to do with the actual making of the film."

Puttnam, who encouraged Edgar Jr. to tackle the project, has a far different recollection. "The film was going absolutely nowhere. Without Edgar's energy and contacts and everything else, that film would not have been made. Without Edgar, there would be no movie. You're talking about a couple of people in the case of Clive Rees and Antony whose careers badly stalled. Had they had glorious careers, I suspect they'd be a lot more generous," Puttnam declares.

Who is right—Puttnam, or Rees and Isaacs—is irrelevant. What matters about the debate is that it typifies the problems that have plagued any project Edgar Jr. has undertaken or any deal Edgar Jr. has negotiated throughout his life. There would always be those on his side, such as Puttnam, who liked Edgar Jr. and sought to assist him but did not necessarily need him for their own success. And there would always be those, like Rees and Isaacs, who saw him only as a source of money or momentum to further their personal goals. While they might play along with his suggestions and pretend to do what he wanted, such people were seeking their own ends, not Edgar Jr.'s—and often at his expense. Edgar Jr. would never learn how to tell the two groups—friend and foe—apart on any kind of consistent basis. That failing has remained with him, unaffected by experience, maturity, or the passage of time.

The Blockhouse was shot in an actual underground cavern built by the Germans on the English Channel Island of Guernsey. Casting was unlikely. French singer/songwriter

Charles Aznavour played an Italian; British comedian Peter Sellers was a Frenchman. Sellers's career had faltered since *The Pink Panther* and *Dr. Strangelove,* both released in 1964. *The Blockhouse* was among three of Sellers's films from the early 1970s that were not released. (The other two were *A Day on the Beach* and *Ghost in the Noonday Sun.* His career was resurrected in spectacular fashion with *The Return of the Pink Panther* in 1975.)

The shoot took on a Monty Python madness. Participants still tell tales, some of which may even be true. Edgar Jr. and Isaacs once hid in a cupboard in the hotel meeting room where Rees conducted the daily meeting, then burst out in the midst of proceedings to the surprised amusement of the assembled. After the opening D-Day battle scene was filmed, one of the pilots stayed on, had a few drinks, and buzzed chimney tops in his Spitfire. When some of those on the set saw how relentlessly bleak the film was becoming, various new upbeat endings were proposed. One suggestion was for the men to hear tapping then discover a group of nuns who had also been trapped underground.

The most unlikely story that has survived involved an attempt by Edgar Jr. to fly to London. He is said to have climbed aboard a plane hoping to speak to the pilot about hitching a ride. Before he could make himself known, the doors closed on the Blackburn Beverly, a huge transport with fixed wheels. The craft took off with a stowaway Edgar Jr. jouncing in the cargo hold with tons of the hothouse tomatoes for which the island is famous. Upon landing, he found himself in the English Midlands city of Coventry.

There was a premiere, but the film was literally unwatchable, the underground lighting was so poor. "It has been my very good fortune that practically no one has ever seen the picture. But the incident taught me not to take for granted what is possible and what is not," Edgar Jr. said in a commencement address he delivered in 1989 at Pine Manor College in Chestnut Hills, Massachussets. "It taught me that maybe I could write on a blank page. The pages that had been written before certainly had me believing that sixteen-year-olds didn't produce major movies. Or even minor movies. But then somebody whose own life has been ruled by passion gave me the chance to stop and ask myself, 'Why not?' And it changed me forever, because it taught me that whatever limits existed were self-imposed."

Edgar Jr.'s role as a teenaged producer also brought him to the attention of *The New York Times*. On May 13, 1973, A.H. Weiler featured Edgar Jr. in his column under the headline "Ah, To Be 18 and a Movie Mogul!" Edgar Jr., who was at the time three days short of his eighteenth birthday, was described by Weiler as "a plucky lad." He told Weiler how he'd discovered the script for *The Blockhouse* while working in London. "Then, last summer, I joined Antony Rufus Isaacs, my co-producer, and we shot the movie—with Clive Rees directing—in the Channel Islands."

Weiler announced that Edgar Jr. was "rarin' to go" on his next production, a movie version of *The Me Nobody Knows,* a Broadway musical about ghetto life financed by Edgar Sr. that ran from December 1970 to November 1971. Concluded Weiler: "How you gonna keep Bronfman down on the school farm, now that he's seen the world of movie production? You're *not* gonna. There's no college in this young man's immediate future. 'I've fallen in love with producing,' he confesses, 'and I plan to make it my life's work.'"

Edgar Jr. had temporarily avoided the role given him by Mr. Sam when he called Edgar Jr. "the one," but the death of his grandfather affected the teenager's life in another, unpredictable way. In July 1971, Edgar Sr. succeeded his late father as president of Seagram and proceeded to run the company with a new-found freedom he had never previously known. But his marriage soon came apart. It was almost as if Edgar Sr. had been waiting for the old man to go.

According to Edgar Sr., Ann started a fight that September while they were visiting Israel. She threatened to go back to New York. He told her if she did, they were finished. Ann left anyway. Upon his return, Edgar Sr. moved into the Seagram suite at the St. Regis Hotel and launched divorce proceedings. Both Sam and Matthew were away at school. Edgar Jr. was left alone to deal with his mother as well as help Holly and Adam. "It was difficult because it was bitter. They were both angry. They were both intemperate," Edgar Jr. recalls. "My mother was really in a bad way. There was no one to take care of her. I asked her parents to help, but they didn't. I couldn't go to my father. I didn't know where else to go. I had to try and help her. I had to explain the fundamentally unexplainable to Adam. Your parents are, for most kids, your emotional ports in a storm. When they both go wobbly at the same time, it's disconcerting. For me it was a hard time." On several occasions Edgar Jr. arrived in tears at the apartment of Bruce Stark and his wife. He'd sleep on their couch because he didn't want to go home.

Ann's changed circumstances included moving to a condo-minium in Washington, D.C., and her own new-found free-doms. In 1985, she set out on a three-year round-the-world trip aboard her 38-foot sailboat, *Champagne*, accompanied by her friend Jane Hart. "She has five kids and I've got eight. We've each got four grandchildren, and here we go," Hart told the *Detroit Free Press*. Both women were sailors and shared similar experiences with the men in their lives. They both had been

raised by a powerful father and had married an equally dominant husband. Hart was the widow of U.S. senator Philip Hart,
who died in 1976, and the daughter of Walter Briggs, the auto
industrialist and owner of the Detroit Tigers.

For his part, Edgar Sr. wasted no time looking for love. His
quest, which ultimately lasted seventeen years, began on his trip
home from Israel after Ann left him. En route he stopped in
London and looked up Lady Carolyn Townshend, whom he'd
hired to do public relations for Seagram. Once the divorce was
final, they were married on December 18, 1973. Edgar Jr. was
sufficiently forgiving that he and Bruce Stark made a short film
for his father in which Lady Carolyn sang a tune from *Seesaw,*
that season's hit Broadway musical: "It's Not Where You Start,
It's Where You Finish."

The marriage lasted three months. Annulment proceedings, conducted in open court, filled the tabloids with titillat-
ing details about Edgar Sr.'s sexual performance. Edgar Sr.
next took up with Rita Webb, a barmaid at Ye Olde Nosebag,
a pub in Finchingfield, Essex, England. He called her George;
she changed her name to Georgiana. At twenty-five, she was
only five years older than Edgar Jr. when she married his
father on August 20, 1975. After they had two girls, Sara, born
in 1976, and Clare, born in 1979, Georgiana asked for a
divorce, which Edgar Sr. granted. He then remarried her and
divorced her again.

In 1988 he met Jan Aronson, an artist and former triathlete.
Jan was nervous as she dressed for their first date, trying to
decide what jewellery to wear. Naked, she put on a pearl neck-
lace and asked her roommate, "What do you think?" Came the
reply: "It's a start." Two months later, Aronson moved in with
Edgar Sr. He waited until 1994 before marrying her, bringing his
lifetime total to four wives and five marriages.

Angry over his parents' split, and embarrassed by his father's peccadilloes, Edgar Jr. turned inward and became rebellious. He put on weight and wore a gold medallion. Still, he missed his father even though he had been an absentee parent. "If you're given a piece of bread a day and it goes away, you can miss it as much as a steak. It wasn't really so much that Dad wasn't around a lot and therefore why would I miss him if he was around less. To me, he was around as much as he was, and then he wasn't."

As Edgar Jr. grappled with his parents' divorce and his father's marital shenanigans, his brother Sam suddenly became page one news after he was abducted by two men on August 8, 1975. At twenty-one, Sam was an intern for New York State senator Roy Goodman. In September he was to join *Sports Illustrated* as a marketing trainee. Because Sam was the eldest son in a wealthy family, his disappearance was the focus of intense media coverage. After he disappeared, early reports said he was buried in an isolated location with a ten-day supply of air and water. The kidnappers demanded ransom of $4.6 million, then inexplicably cut that amount in half. Edgar Sr. paid, but Sam was not released. Finally, more than a week after the abduction, the FBI burst in on Sam and one of his kidnappers in a Brooklyn apartment. Mel Patrick Lynch, thirty-seven, a fireman, and Dominic Byrne, fifty-three, a limousine service operator, were arrested. The money was recovered.

During the eight-week trial that began in October 1976, Lynch claimed that Sam was an accomplice in the crime and that the two of them had a year-long homosexual relationship. Sam denied the allegations, saying that he feared for his life, was constantly kept bound and gagged, and had never seen either man before his capture. The jury acquitted Lynch and Byrne on the kidnapping charge but found them guilty of extortion. (Byrne, sentenced to three to nine years, was released in December 1980. Lynch, sentenced to four to twelve years, was released in August 1981.) Some of the jurors said that they did not find Sam's story credible. At six foot four and 185 pounds, they wondered why he'd never tried to overpower his captors since there were long periods when only one of them stood guard. The rope used to bind Sam was so frail that it broke when jurors examined it. The family supported Sam and believed his version of events. Edgar Jr., who was living on his own, helped out as best he could by staying strong, answering phones, and relaying information. Sam's kidnapping took on a particular significance in Edgar Jr.'s life; he has never talked publicly about the incident. It was as if he bottled up that event along with the pain of his parents' divorce and buried everything underground, where Sam was said to have been held.

Through all the tribulations of divorce, kidnapping, and courtroom drama, Edgar Jr. struggled to find his place in show business. In 1976, his father's money again presented an opportunity, this time in another medium, television. The idea for a children's program about the history of jazz originated with producer and writer Gary Keys. Twenty years older than Edgar Jr., Keys had lined up Dizzy Gillespie, Gerry Mulligan, Count Basie, Stan Getz, Herbie Hancock, and Dionne Warwick, among others. Keys knew Ron Kass, Edgar Sr.'s partner in Sagittarius Productions. Sagittarius agreed to invest $350,000 in the one-hour CBS show that aired on an afternoon in April 1976. The program, shot at the Ed Sullivan Theater, was originally to be called *Once Upon a Groove*, but the title was changed to *The Original Rompin' Stompin,' Hot & Heavy, Cool & Groovy, All-Star Jazz Show*.

This time, his father's money meant a major role for Edgar Jr. He had gained confidence since his time on *The Blockhouse.* As executive producer, he threw his weight around with such force that he caused ructions on the set. "Kass was a pussycat, Edgar wasn't. Edgar had opinions: 'I want this director and I want that and I want this,'" says Keys. "I went along with that up until it really started running over budget, and then I put an end to it and told the director what was really going to happen. It was turning into a disaster."

Relations between Edgar Jr. and Keys grew tense. Because the taping involved many artists and numerous scenes, it was already complicated enough. Any changes added to production costs and reduced eventual profits. Keys can no longer remember the precise demand Edgar Jr. made, but whatever it was, Keys refused. Keys does, however, recall very clearly what Edgar Jr. then said to him: "You know, in my grandfather's time, we'da killed you." Keys's response was equally direct: "Fuck you."

The moment passed, tempers cooled, the taping was completed, and the show was nominated for an Emmy in the daytime children's category. Edgar Jr. even appeared in the final version. Bodies were needed for a bar scene when Joe Williams sang, so Edgar Jr. was conscripted as one of the happy patrons.

The show also yielded the love of Edgar's young life. Although she wasn't part of the production, a young black woman stopped by the theatre because she knew many of the participants, including George Faison, the show's choreographer. After Faison and the visitor had chatted and Faison was again alone, Edgar Jr. hurried over to ask: *"Who was that?"*

Her name was Sherry Brewer, but everyone called her Peaches. The young actress and dancer had studied at the Goodman Theatre in Chicago. She'd played Marcy, the kidnapped teenaged daughter of Harlem crime boss Bumpy Jonas, in the 1971 movie *Shaft*. (In the credits for the non-speaking role her first name was spelled Sherri.) She had also appeared as Minnie Fay in the all-black 1974 Broadway revival of *Hello, Dolly!* starring Pearl Bailey.

After talking with Faison, Brewer went to see Dionne Warwick in her dressing room. Edgar Jr. made some excuse to visit the singer so he could be introduced to Sherry. "She was absolutely radiant, a breath of fresh air. She looked like the Barefoot Contessa," says Faison. "Those were wild, crazy days, a whole world away from where we are now. They were young and he was enamoured of her and she of him. They had come from two different worlds and they fell in love."

That May, a month after the TV show aired, was Edgar Jr.'s twenty-first birthday. Edgar Sr. decided that his son deserved a proper party to mark his coming of age, an occasion that might also advance his career in show business by allowing him to meet the Hollywood crowd. Kass ran the Los Angeles office of Sagittarius, so Edgar Sr. asked Kass and Joan Collins to hold the celebration at their home. Edgar Sr. was close to the couple. He was godfather to their daughter Katy. When Sam was kidnapped, Kass flew to New York and stayed by Edgar Sr.'s side throughout the ordeal, then was best man when he married Georgiana Webb a week after Sam was rescued. Collins almost felt sorry for father and son and their apparently perfect lives, saying, "Rich men's sons have a hard row to hoe. It is almost the equivalent of being a beautiful girl. You are born with everything. You don't have to do a thing for yourself. It's all there: the money, the power, the girls, the fast cars and the fast life."

Such pampered men were not to be fully trusted, Collins thought, but she went ahead with the party as requested. Edgar

Jr., accompanied by Sherry, was feted that warm May evening by Dani and David Janssen, Audrey and Billy Wilder, Dionne Warwick, Tina Sinatra, Susan George, George Segal, and many others. The next day, without warning, Edgar Sr. fired Kass. After that, Kass only worked sporadically. Collins briefly fell on bad times herself and at one point applied for unemployment benefits. Her career took off again in 1981 when she joined the TV soap opera *Dynasty* in the role of Alexis, the ex-wife of John Forsythe, the woman America loved to hate.

With Kass unceremoniously tossed overboard, Edgar Jr. now had more powerful roles available to him on those projects that depended upon his father's largesse. In April 1977, he was the producer of *Ladies at the Alamo,* a five-woman show backed by Edgar Sr.'s money. The show was a flop; it closed after only three weeks. "I learned about theatre with *Ladies at the Alamo,*" Edgar Jr. told John Corry of *The New York Times.* "First, I learned about the personality question. I'm a spoiled, rich kid and people always had to deal with my personality. But as a producer, I had to deal with the author, the director, the stars and their personalities. Second, I was surprised at the variance of the critics. I thought you presented something, and there it was, and everyone agreed on it. Instead, the critics had twelve different responses. I was Mr. Know Nothing."

Edgar Jr.'s next production was *Broadway, Broadway,* starring Geraldine Page and James Coco. He tried to keep costs down by taking the show first to Cape Cod and Long Island prior to previews in Philadelphia before the New York opening scheduled for September 1978. "Because of the lower salary scale for summer stock we have three weeks to get the show in shape in front of an audience practically for free," said Edgar Jr. "It can be terribly expensive to open a show in Philadelphia or Boston. The only other show I've produced, *Ladies at the Alamo,* and the first show I put money into, *I Love My Wife,* each lost $75,000 in Philadelphia." *Broadway, Broadway* never made it to Broadway. One night in Philadelphia, Edgar Sr. arrived in a black limousine. After the two talked in the limo outside the theatre, Edgar Jr. closed the play.

Bruce Stark, Edgar Jr.'s former partner, knew exactly what was going wrong. Edgar Jr. might have been born with a silver spoon in his mouth, but he was not blessed with good gut instincts. "Edgar was a theatre idealist like I was a theatre idealist. We didn't do things that were necessarily overtly commercial. Both of us had one fatal flaw: we couldn't pick a show that people wanted to see. That's why I got out. I put on a show just the way Edgar did. They came in on budget, they looked good, they had excellent casts, they were well performed, but the critics and the audiences wanted something else," says Stark. When Edgar Jr. listened to his inner self, things turned out poorly. Edgar Jr. was making the very mistake that he had been warned about by both Porter Bibb and Bruce Stark. Instead of following the advice he had taken the trouble to seek, however, Edgar Jr. bulled ahead on projects, spending Daddy's money rather than test his ideas in the crucible of the search for financial backing from others.

As if Broadway weren't bedevilling enough, Hollywood beckoned. Edgar Jr. first heard about Thom Mount through David Puttnam. Mount, seven years older than Edgar Jr., had joined Universal Pictures in 1973 and was named president in 1976. During his eight years as president, Mount, known as one of Hollywood's "baby moguls," was responsible for 150 movies, including *Car Wash, Smokey and the Bandit,* and *Animal House.* "The content needed to change and we needed people who could deliver that content," Mount says. "Edgar seemed smart, aggressive, young, and focused." Edgar Jr. had already acquired rights for *A Place to Come To,* a novel by Robert Penn Warren.

In 1977, Universal signed Edgar Jr.'s Efer Productions to a three-year contract to produce two movies and develop four others. The deal consisted of a low six-figure sum that Edgar Jr. could use however he saw fit to buy movie rights, hire screenwriters, cover development costs, and draw a salary. The contract with Universal finally allowed Edgar Jr. to break free of family. If he needed more funds than his contract provided for, he could turn to Universal. If the studio bosses liked the idea, money would flow. The change in his life was significant. "That was a very tough period for Edgar. He was unplugged from the family support system. It was a little terrifying," says Mount. Because Universal had New York offices at 445 Park Avenue, he no longer needed to work out of the Seagram Building.

In 1978, Edgar Jr. took another step towards independence. He moved to Los Angeles, where he was assigned a bungalow on Universal's back lot in a glade of similar structures occupied by the likes of the legendary Alfred Hitchcock. At first Edgar Jr. rented a small house in West Hollywood, then moved to Escondido Beach, where the ocean views were as good as Malibu but the rents were more reasonable. Sherry had dance commitments in New York, so they commuted to see each other.

Racially mixed relationships were unusual. Until a Supreme Court ruling in 1967, sixteen Southern states did not permit marriage between races. Although the law had changed and the number of mixed couples was increasing, some Americans held on to their racist views. "I didn't think twice about it, but then you know, the theatre world is a little bit less tied up with that kind of thing than mid-America," says Stark, who, along with his wife, entertained them at dinner. "She was a very attractive, very sweet, funny, bright woman and Edgar was a funny, bright man, and it didn't strike me besides the fact that I knew it would probably kill his parents."

Stark was right. When Edgar Jr. announced that he planned to marry Brewer, his parents were opposed. "I very much wanted for him to end the relationship, because, I told him, all marriages are difficult enough without the added stress of totally different backgrounds. His children, I said, would have problems being accepted by either black or white society," said Edgar Sr. "Sherry offered to convert, which, though well intentioned, was not the point." (Brewer was a Buddhist.) Ann persuaded her son to postpone the wedding for a year. But Edgar Jr. was not about to change his mind. This was a different era than the 1940s, when his father was at Williams, had proposed to a co-ed, but called off the wedding at his parents' request.

Six months before the wedding, Edgar Sr. sent Edgar Jr. a handwritten eleven-page letter that he showed to Seagram president Phil Beekman. "It was a very thoughtful, well-written letter. It went into great detail as to what he should expect, [saying] in my opinion this is going to happen, you have to be happy and be prepared for it," Beekman remembers. Although Edgar Jr. has since been portrayed as something of a rebel for going ahead with his mixed marriage, he was shrewd enough to ask his father if marrying Brewer would end his chances of becoming president of Seagram. "Being a closet liberal, and having respect for the optimism of youth, I told him that one had nothing to do with the other," said Edgar Sr.

In 1979, Edgar Jr. and Sherry eloped and were married in New Orleans. Edgar Sr. was slow to warm to the union until his then wife, Georgiana, said to him, "Don't be an a——. You wouldn't want him to marry anybody. Give them a cocktail party." The marriage was belatedly celebrated at Edgar Sr.'s Fifth

Avenue apartment, but no soiree could repair the rift. Father and son remained alienated.

In addition to his contract with Universal, Edgar Jr. had income from a trust fund. In 1976, during the trial of his kidnappers, Sam testified he would receive half the capital of a $20-million trust fund at thirty-five, the other half when he turned forty. Meanwhile, the fund established by his grandfather paid Sam $32,000 a year as soon as he turned twenty-one. Edgar Jr.'s similar annual stipend would be the equivalent of $110,000 today—but there he was, going from studio to studio, pitching ideas.

Among those Edgar Jr. knew in Hollywood was Barry Diller, chairman and CEO of Paramount Pictures. Edgar Jr. had first met Diller in 1974, after an introduction by Tom Lewyn, a lawyer with Simpson Thacher & Bartlett, who acted for both Diller and the Bronfman family. Although Edgar Jr. was only nineteen at the time and Diller thirty-two, they got on. "I thought he was smart and energetic. Given his circumstances, he really wanted his own life, and I liked that," Diller recalls. "We talked about all sorts of things. He and I talked many times during that period at certain points, about the ambitions and what the possibilities were." Diller's advice and friendship included no film deals, but Diller did present a role model for the kind of success in movies that Edgar Jr. sought.

The film based on the Robert Penn Warren novel was going nowhere, so Edgar Jr. began developing *The Border,* a movie about corrupt border guards in Texas. He hired Deric Washburn to write a screenplay for Robert Blake, star of the popular TV police show *Baretta,* who was to play the lead. When an opportunity arose to get Jack Nicholson, Edgar Jr. bought out Blake's contract and signed Nicholson. "He didn't hesitate, he stepped right up," says David Freeman, the next screenwriter involved.

"He saw a chance to improve the picture. I was impressed by that." Edgar Jr. also lined up the brilliant but difficult British director Tony Richardson, whose previous work included *Tom Jones* and *A Delicate Balance*. As shooting started in El Paso, Edgar Jr. hired a third screenwriter, Walon Green, who had co-written Sam Peckinpah's *The Wild Bunch*. Says Green, "Even though he was young, he'd been around. He liked movies. He liked talking about them. He was interested in war stories about Hollywood. He was savvy. I thought he got it pretty good. He was irreverent, he was not particularly star-struck."

Shooting had barely begun in July 1980 when the Screen Actors Guild went on strike, shutting down all productions. Not knowing how long the work stoppage would last, Edgar Jr. remained in El Paso through the torrid summer heat, trying to keep the idled crew together. Sherry and their newborn first child, Vanessa, sweltered along with him.

When the strike finally ended in October, much had changed. Cinematographer Vilmos Zsigmond, who shot the first few scenes, had moved to another project and was replaced by Ric Waite. The school used for interior scenes was again filled with students, so sets had to be constructed Friday night then torn down Sunday. As the weather turned colder, the crew buried in the ground plastic pipe carrying propane, which escaped through holes. They lit the gas so that long shots included what looked like the distorting heat waves of a desert summer. "What's pertinent is that Edgar, with Tony, worked things out," says Freeman. "Movies can collapse over things like that."

Once a film shoot is underway, the director is in charge; the producer's role ranges from averting large crises to putting out small fires. Edgar Jr. learned how to work with Richardson, who gave producers a hard time just for the sport of it. "Nobody ran one of Tony's sets but Tony," Freeman says. "Edgar worked his way through that and got some of what he wanted. What Edgar knew was to deal with the important issues and leave lesser matters to someone else. He had good instincts. Producing a picture is a combination of scutwork and big thinking. Edgar wore that part of himself well. He knew that if he wanted to be a producer he'd have to get his hands dirty, and he did."

In the movie, Jack Nicholson plays border guard Charlie Smith, whose never-ending task is to catch "wetbacks," many of whom have previously been captured and returned to Mexico. His wife, Marcy (Valerie Perrine), persuades him to buy a dream home that she fills with furniture, beginning with a waterbed. "We don't have to worry about paying for it," she says. "I opened up a charge account at the Galleria." Nicholson reluctantly joins his fellow guards in taking bribes from local businessmen to allow uninhibited passage of illegals who will work for low wages. Nicholson soon regrets his decisions and gives money to Maria (Elpidia Carrillo) so she can pay the "coyote" who will guide her to a better life across the Rio Grande. Charlie's reasoning: "I want to feel good about something sometime."

Most everyone on the set was well aware of Edgar Jr.'s family wealth. He was not only generous, but he also took care to give presents with individual significance. Production manager Michael Maschio received a bottle of his favourite Chivas Regal as well as a book of cartoons by Charles Addams, an artist Maschio's parents collected. Edgar Jr. had a vision beyond this film and talked about the day when actors would be paid, not in salary, but in ownership positions. "I joked with him that only a rich kid would think like that," says Freeman. "He was open to new ideas and looking for something to do. He was looking at movies in a larger sense, not the way some producers just go picture to picture."

That larger world intruded one strikebound summer's day when Edgar Sr. phoned to say that he had just left San Francisco aboard the Seagram corporate jet en route to New York. "I want to see my granddaughter," he said. "If you and Sherry will come out to the airport, I will meet you in an hour and fifteen minutes." Edgar Jr. said he'd think about it and call his father back. Thom Mount, who was having dinner with Edgar Jr. and Sherry when the call came, realized that a historic rapprochement was possible. "Not only was the mountain coming to Mohammed, the mountain had an agenda. This was the first time Dad had reached out. This was a big deal for him." Father and son had not spoken for more than a year. Mount encouraged a meeting, saying, "Let him have a little dignity. It ain't going to kill you and it'll be good for Sherry. There are few men, no matter how hardened they are, who can resist the sight of their grandchild and that child's mother."

During the reunion aboard the plane sitting on the Tarmac, Edgar Sr. held Vanessa and was charming to Sherry. Before take-off, he told Edgar Jr. that he wanted to have a more serious conversation with him in New York at some point. Edgar Jr. said he would be open to such a discussion, but first he had to finish the picture. Edgar Sr. made another flying visit a few weeks later, this time with Seagram president Phil Beekman in tow. Family relations were returning to normal.

Filming, editing, and post-production work took more than a year. Audiences at test screenings did not like the original ending. They wondered what happened to the baby stolen early in the movie from the mother who had been helped by Nicholson. Everyone returned to El Paso to shoot a new, more upbeat finale where Nicholson rescues the baby and returns it to its mother.

Finally, on January 29, 1982, *The Border* opened in twenty major markets, then spread to an additional sixty markets the following weekend. The movie was far from Nicholson's best work. "He slouched and muttered his way back and forth across *The Border*," wrote David Thomson in his definitive *Biographical Dictionary of Film*. Nicholson certainly was capable of better: He was nominated for an Oscar as best supporting actor that year for his role as Eugene O'Neill in *Reds*; he won best supporting actor a year later as Shirley MacLaine's neighbour and love interest in *Terms of Endearment*.

Audience interest quickly faded. After four weeks, *The Border* closed. Box office receipts amounted to a meagre $6.1 million, compared with $143 million for *Terms of Endearment*. "It was the wrong movie at the wrong time," says Ned Tanen, the senior studio executive who had given the green light. "I thought it was a subject that should be brought to people's attention. Even I looked at it when it was over and worried no one was interested. We shouldn't have made it. It was my fault."

After the New York premiere of *The Border*, Edgar Jr. and his father had dinner at La Côte Basque on West Fifty-fifth Street, a formal French restaurant famous for its haute cuisine. "Though the movie was a critical success," said Edgar Sr., "it left him frustrated with the film industry. From his standpoint, it wasn't a 'business.'" Edgar Sr. sensed the time was right to draw his son back into the family fold. At fifty-two, he had his own compelling reasons to begin the process of orderly succession. The previous year he had been elected president of the World Jewish Congress, an organization representing Jews in sixty-six countries, and he wanted to immerse himself in that role. Edgar Sr. invited his son to visit him at the Seagram Building the next day.

During their meeting, Edgar Jr. admitted that he was "fed up" with Hollywood. Edgar Sr. seized the opportunity to ask: "Will you join the company with a view to eventually running it?" Edgar Jr. was both surprised and secretly pleased. "It was a great personal victory to be asked. In a sense, it was like having approval bestowed on you."

Edgar Jr. did not give an immediate answer. He said he'd think about the offer, then returned to Los Angeles to consult family and friends. Edgar Jr. worried that by joining Seagram he would be forever giving up his right to say that he had done something on his own. Sherry was in favour of him taking the job, an endorsement that surprised Edgar Jr. Sam also urged him to join. In fact, everyone said he would be an idiot not to accept.

Even his dashed hopes for the next project pointed him back to New York. Edgar Jr. thought he had Sydney Pollack lined up to direct Robert Redford in *A Place to Come To*. Pollack and Redford changed their minds; they decided to make another picture. Five years had gone by since Edgar Jr. signed his deal with Universal. In that entire time he had completed only one movie, and a commercially unsuccessful one at that. He had tried to break free from his father's grip, but he could not seem to make a go of it on his own.

Edgar Jr. phoned his father to say he was flying to New York to deliver his answer. When they met and Edgar Jr. told him he had decided to accept the invitation, Edgar Sr. said: "I knew that's what you'd say. I knew it when you said you were flying back." Edgar Jr. was upset to be seen as so transparent. "We've got some people-learning to do about each other," said Edgar Jr. "I'd certainly have flown back to say no. But I might have said yes over the telephone."

When Patsy Puttnam heard what had happened, she concluded that Edgar Jr. was fulfilling his destiny. "He was being the peacemaker once again. He'd been chosen over his brother. That was a way of keeping it together. He wanted to be back with the family. He clearly did not like being on the outs. It didn't suit his personality at all."

Edgar Jr. told his father that if he didn't like working at Seagram, he wouldn't stay. Thom Mount assured him that Universal would offer another multi-year production deal on better terms than before. Edgar Jr. needn't have worried; he required no fallback position. "The day I joined—literally the day—was like coming home. It was uncanny, *uncanny.*" Of course it was like coming home; it *was* home. His corporate position was simply a continuation of his earlier role in the family: to look after Holly, to achieve consensus among the inheritor-siblings, to accept the mantle bestowed by Mr. Sam. The difference was that for the first time Edgar Jr. felt affirmed by his father. He was ready to follow him anywhere.

THREE

UP THROUGH THE RANKS

EDGAR JR. WAS NOT THE first Bronfman who tried to flee the family's clutches only to be lured back. His aunt Phyllis suffered nightmares as a child because of the dark décor of the family mansion. In 1949 she married Jean Lambert, an economist and consultant with offices in New York and Paris. The marriage soon ended in divorce, and by 1952 Phyllis was living the bohemian life of a sculptor in Paris. By her own vivid description, if she were a cat, the family money was a tin can tied to her tail.

Montreal was Seagram's head office, but New York was where Mr. Sam had built the business. Beginning in 1934, he'd lived during the week in a suite at the St. Regis Hotel and had an office in the Chrysler Building, commuting to and from Montreal by train every weekend. In 1954, he bought land on Park Avenue between Fifty-second and Fifty-third Streets to serve as the site for Seagram's U.S. headquarters. Sam wanted something conservative, a tower with three entrances, one for each of the sales divisions, Seagram, Calvert, and Four Roses. Saidye suggested he send the plans to Phyllis, who had studied architecture, as a way of bringing her back home. In a letter to Sam dated June 28, 1954, Phyllis declared herself to be adamantly against the proposed plans. "This letter starts with one word repeated very emphatically: No, no, no, no, no. You must build a building which expresses the best of society in which you live and at the same time your hopes for the betterment of the society."

Phyllis offered to help him find an architect worthy of the project and Sam accepted. "He must have seen himself in me. His children were a projection of him." Aided by Philip Johnson, chairman of the architecture department at New York's Museum of Modern Art, Phyllis spent three months interviewing architects such as Walter Gropius, Frank Lloyd Wright, and I.M. Pei, before choosing Ludwig Mies van der Rohe. Mies's design for a 38-storey building, done in bronze- and amber-tinted glass, was both delicate and powerful. As one of the first Manhattan office towers set back from the street, the one-hundred-foot plaza not only drew in the observer but also provided an appropriate distance from which to admire the creation.

The Seagram Building, completed in 1958, cost $41 million. Ceiling heights were a gracious nine feet, hardware was specially designed, Roman travertine was used for the elevator core, Swenson pink granite for the plaza. Seagram's took seven floors and rented the rest out to tenants. "The day we moved in, I was with Father in his corner office on the fifth floor," said Edgar Sr. "I greeted all the employees one by one and introduced each to Mr. Sam. We were so proud of our Building. Company stationery, calling cards, even interoffice memos bore its image."

Edgar Jr.'s arrival at the Seagram Building in 1982 connoted a regal continuity every bit as significant as the investiture of

Charles, Prince of Wales, at Caernarvon Castle in 1969. Succession to the Seagram throne was now just as secure as in the Royal House of Windsor. Seagram was the world's largest producer of beverage alcohol, with annual revenue of $2.8 billion from the sale of three hundred brands of distilled spirits and four hundred different wines, champagnes, ports, and sherries in Canada, the United States, and 150 other countries. Seagram's twelve thousand employees didn't feel as if they toiled for some faceless corporate entity; they proudly served a regal family. They offered respectful deference and tried to anticipate their rulers' every desire. Decrees from on high gained a meaning and momentum among the dutiful that were never dreamed of by those who issued the order. At most companies, an ability to follow instructions might be sufficient; at Seagram, on-your-knees obedience by supplicants was rewarded above all.

The Bronfmans were all-powerful because family control of Seagram was indisputable. CEMP Investments owned 10,808,090 shares, or 35.9 percent of Seagram's 30,077,400 issued shares. CEMP was in turn 100 percent owned by four family trusts created for the benefit of the descendants of Mr. Sam. (The name came from the first initials of the four members of the second generation: Charles, Edgar, Minda, and Phyllis.) If all the shares owned by Seagram directors and officers were added—and their voting support was unquestioned—the control block rose to 39.4 percent, enough to easily stave off any hostile takeover attempt.

Edgar Jr.'s first role was assistant to president and chief operating officer Phil Beekman. Edgar Sr. had held a similar staff role, but he'd also studied production methods and procedures at the plant in LaSalle, Quebec, and spent two years learning various administrative duties before being appointed treasurer in 1956. Charles worked mostly on the sales and marketing side.

He became head of Canadian operations in 1958 and lived at home until he married at thirty-one in 1962. Beekman took it as a sign of his own value to the family that he had been given the task of grooming the next generation's leader. Of Edgar Jr., Beekman says, "He worked very hard at learning the business, he worked long hours, and was not afraid to take on anything I gave him to do. He was very quiet, very laid-back, and very thoughtful. We tried to get as much into him as he could absorb. It was an ideal job to bring him into because he got exposed to the entire scope of the company rather than just one specialty, such as marketing, manufacturing, or administration."

Nevertheless, Edgar Jr.'s exposure to the business was cursory by comparison with the hands-on experience gained by his father and his uncle Charles. Moreover, he couldn't seem to forget the entertainment world. "He wrote songs and he kept up all his West Coast contacts," says Beekman. Edgar Jr. had been writing lyrics since his teen years, when he sought to impress a woman who was a songwriter. Edgar Jr. and Bruce Roberts began collaborating in the 1970s, with Roberts playing the piano in his New York office at Fifty-first and Broadway. The first song Edgar Jr. wrote with Roberts, "Sunshine," was recorded in 1975 by Australian pop-country singer Diana Trask. Now that Edgar Jr. had an office job, their methods altered. They would exchange ideas for lyrics or music by fax or phone.

Songwriting helped Edgar Jr. pass the time on business flights. He'd put on his earphones, listen to the music, and jot down lyrics on a yellow legal pad, a dictionary close at hand. Colleagues aboard the corporate jet knew well enough to leave him alone. Except for some tennis and the odd game of golf, songwriting was his only hobby. Using pen names Sam Roman and Junior Miles, he'd write to relax or to commemorate special occasions. In 1985, he and Roberts wrote "Whisper in the Dark" for Dionne Warwick as a thank you for introducing him to Sherry. *Friends,* the album on which his song was included, reached number seven on the charts. Reverently, Edgar Jr. hung a copy of Warwick's gold record in his office.

A little songwriting on the side was distracting enough, but as a Seagram executive Edgar Jr. also continued to invest in Broadway in spite of his proven incapacity to pick a winner. He had earned such a reputation for backing unpopular and money-losing plays—*Ladies at the Alamo, I Love My Wife,* and *Broadway, Broadway*—that his participation had become unwelcome. In 1985 he called producer Jim Walsh and said, "You're in real trouble. I like the play, and I think I'm going to jinx it for you." Not even Edgar Jr.'s bad karma could hurt *I'm Not Rappaport,* which ran for more than two years and won three Tony Awards.

Because Beekman had been put in charge of the heir apparent, he had every reason to praise the results achieved, but other executives doubted the sincerity of Edgar Jr.'s enthusiasm for Seagram. The family business couldn't seem to match the pleasure the entertainment industry gave him. "He was a very aloof young guy. It didn't seem to me that his heart was really in the business. I don't think he liked the business," says Jim McDonough, who joined Seagram in 1955 and pioneered the sale of Seagram products in China. McDonough concluded that Edgar Jr. joined Seagram only because he felt the pressure of family tradition. "I found it very hard to have a conversation with him. I was probably pretty boring. All I wanted to do was talk business or answer questions, but he never had any questions. Edgar Jr. was not my cup of tea, and he was not the cup of tea of a lot of people."

After three months of showing Edgar Jr. the ropes, Beekman decided that he was ready to become managing director of

Seagram Europe, a job that happened to be vacant. Edgar Sr. agreed and dispatched Beekman to convince Charles, who also gave his blessing. When Beekman broached the subject with Edgar Jr., his response was: "I'd kill for that job." Beekman allowed that homicide was not necessary.

Seagram Europe comprised the United Kingdom, France, Germany, Italy, the Scandinavian countries—everything except the Soviet Union. For almost fifty years Seagram had been exporting beverage alcohol to the region and acquiring businesses that included premier brands of Scotch such as Chivas and Glenlivet, Mumm and Perrier-Jouët champagnes, wines from Barton & Guestier, as well as ports and sherries by Sandeman.

On his next trip to London, Edgar Jr. invited Ed McDonnell, vice-president of international marketing, to dinner. McDonnell tried to beg off, saying he was too busy interviewing candidates for the job of running Europe. "Didn't anyone tell you? I'm going to be running Europe," said Edgar Jr. McDonnell cancelled the search but worried about working with the prodigal son, telling him, "It'll probably cost us a few million dollars until you learn what the hell you're doing." Edgar Jr. banned all official visits by executives based in New York, and set out to prove he could accomplish something on his own. "Edgar really got his back up and he worked like hell. He was really a very bright, hard-working guy that knew he didn't know all the answers," says McDonnell, who had joined Seagram two years earlier after working at Pillsbury and General Foods. In return for helping the scion, there was a payoff for McDonnell. "There were a lot of things I wanted to get done that Phil Beekman was opposed to. Having both Junior and myself make presentations on acquisitions and on strategies for running particular brands and investing was pretty tough to beat."

Edgar Jr. and Sherry moved into the Knightsbridge area of London, where they lived in a Georgian townhouse covered in climbing roses. Porter Bibb, who had not seen Edgar for ten years, lived around the corner on Hasker Street. "I was dumbfounded at the transformation that had come over Edgar. He had been a roly-poly, cherubic, big teddy-bear-like teenager. All of sudden he was a tall, slim, very sophisticated-looking businessman. His whole demeanour had changed. He was decisive. I started following what he was doing and I was impressed."

The career change came with a cost. Sherry was unhappy in her new role as a corporate wife. "He chose a very nice house in Walton Street, near Harrods, so that all Sherry needed to do was walk a few paces and she could get almost anything she wanted. So that wasn't what we would call heavy lifting," says Patsy Puttnam. "She'd lost her playmate. This wasn't playing any more. She had two children and Efer was being seduced or encouraged back into the family fold. She's already flagged up that she didn't care about the family. She just wanted to be with Efer. He was working like mad to prove himself to the family. The ground was moving beneath her feet."

Edgar Jr. forged ahead anyway. He awarded an advertising contract to John Bernbach, who had been in London since 1978 as CEO for the European division of ad agency Doyle Dane Bernbach. The two men were kindred spirits. Bernbach was also working for a famous father, William Bernbach, whose campaigns with Avis and VW had redefined advertising. John Bernbach had just started on the Seagram account when Edgar Sr. asked him to rate his son. Although it was too soon in their relationship for Bernbach to have a fully formed opinion, he spoke favourably about Edgar Jr.'s sensitivity and how well he worked with creative people. Edgar Sr. pushed to hear more.

"Is he the best client you've got?" Bernbach replied, "Well, if he's not the best, he's certainly the second-best." A year later, when Edgar Jr. gave a speech at a party to celebrate Bernbach's birthday, his opening line was: "Let me speak as John's second-best client."

"That competitive nature came out. I'd even forgotten that I'd put it that way," recalls Bernbach. "It was clear that he wasn't going to be in Europe for very long. He was more or less impatient to get back to the United States. I don't know what flicked that switch, but by the time I got to know him it was clear that he intended to be the top person."

Of Edgar Jr.'s three major initiatives as president of Seagram Europe, two were resounding failures, a poor performance ratio given the company's successful history. Beekman counselled Edgar Jr. against buying Oddbins, a wine retailer with outlets in the U.K. and France, but he went ahead anyway. "It didn't amount to anything as an operational vehicle. Those things happen, that's experience," says Beekman. "I think we gracefully stayed away from the subject."

Edgar Jr. did well when he bought Matheus Müller GmbH, a German sparkling wine, but fumbled on making changes at Geo. G. Sandeman Sons & Co., makers of ports and sherries, acquired in 1980. "The acquisition of Matheus Müller has to be regarded as an extremely successful acquisition at a great price. That really leveraged the German business. Sandeman didn't have the right demographics. He thought that there was some potential to spruce up the consumption profile and get young people to drink it, and they didn't bite," says John Preston, who headed international financial planning for Seagram in the 1980s.

Overall, Edgar Jr.'s two years in London were successful. Sales in the division rose 20 percent, profit 200 percent, but his most notable coup came simply by giving away money. The

Grand National steeplechase was in financial trouble and Edgar Jr. offered a donation of $500,000 to save the storied event. When the owner of Aintree, where the race was held, asked for another $100,000, Edgar Jr. agreed. The $600,000 gift raised Seagram's corporate profile and led to what Edgar Jr. wryly called an "expensive introduction" to the Queen Mother.

When Edgar Jr. returned to New York in August 1984, he was named president of the House of Seagram, the U.S. marketing arm and the company's largest division, with about 40 percent of total sales. Edgar Sr. had decided he was not going to be the same kind of controlling boss his own father had been. Instead, Edgar Sr. vowed to give Edgar Jr. his head in business just as he had indulged the teenager when he wanted to work in film.

Edgar Jr. received different treatment than his brother Sam, who seemed to have less interest in larger roles. Sam joined Seagram in 1979, three years before Edgar Jr., but followed a more confined path as executive vice-president of sales in the Seagram Wine Co., then president of the newly created Seagram Classics Wine Co. in June 1984. Sam was offered a role in Australia but, unlike his younger brother, declined the foreign posting. The disparity between Edgar Jr.'s career and his father's was even more pronounced. Where Edgar Sr.'s promotions had been measured, Edgar Jr.'s rise was meteoric. Both were the same age, twenty-nine, when they were named to head the House of Seagram. But Edgar Sr. had seven years of experience by then and was given the job by Mr. Sam only after threatening to quit. Edgar Jr.'s arrival at the same place took only two years and was tantrum-free.

Among Mr. Sam's credos there was one in particular that Edgar Sr. had taken to heart: "Distilling is a science; blending is an art." Edgar Sr. learned the intricacies of blending from the master, Roy Martin, who had joined Seagram in 1927, became chief blender, and stayed more than forty years. Edgar Jr. had no interest in either production or tasting; he just wanted to run the show. He moved into an office on the sixth floor of the Seagram Building, one floor above the senior executives. He hung a portrait in pastels of Sherry, then set out to solve the dilemma of declining markets.

U.S. consumption of distilled spirits had peaked in 1978 and had been falling ever since. The cause was a combination of higher excise taxes, responsible drinking, and changing consumer tastes. Seagram's share of the business was shrinking at an even faster pace than the overall market. Seagram products were mostly "brown goods"—as blends, whiskey, and bourbon were called. Seagram had been slow to respond in "white goods"—vodka, gin, and rum—where there was growing consumer demand. As a result, six of Seagram's top ten U.S. brands had seen sales fall by an average of one-third during the previous decade. For example, 7 Crown, a blend of American whiskeys, had been the most popular brand of spirits in the 1960s but was now third. V.O., a Canadian blend introduced in 1913, had also fallen from top spot in its category. Of the four Seagram brands in the top fifty globally, only Chivas Regal—in twenty-fourth place—could be considered an international success.

In response, Edgar Jr. went on a cost-cutting spree. He fired 200 of the 750 employees in marketing and sales. He consolidated advertising by reducing the number of ad agencies from seven to three, and eliminated some poor-performing distributors. Edgar Jr. also decided to reorganize the divisions so that Seagram's marketing campaigns were aimed at competitors rather than at other Seagram brands, as they had previously been. "That works in a growing market," he said of the former strategy. "But when the market stagnates or slightly declines, the [Seagram] companies were fighting with margins to gain market share. We will be putting major marketing emphasis on fewer brands, but marketing those with greater intensity."

Edgar Jr. called his plan Project Alpha and set a date of January 15, 1985, to unveil the four new operating companies, each with its own president who would report to him. On the designated day, Edgar Jr. called the executives to his office one at a time. He revealed their new roles, the new name for the division they would head, and the brands for which they'd be responsible. One division, called Seagram Distillers, had high-volume products such as V.O., Crown Royal, and 7 Crown; 375 Spirits Company was to handle premium brands such as Chivas Regal, Glenlivet, and Myers's rums; Perennial would have Wolfschmidt vodka, Passport Scotch, and other brands that sold well in specific regions; Summit Sales got the leftovers.

His instructions were delivered with military precision, but the result was a fiasco in the field. Some distributors wasted time worrying needlessly about the impact when there was none. Other distributors, forced to give up good brands, suffered a drop in sales and sued Seagram. "I suppose you always can find something better in the way you do things," said Edgar Jr., commenting on the outcome in 1986. "But any mistakes that I've made have been executional in nature, not fundamental." That explanation offered a neat, but irrelevant, distinction. The plain fact was that he'd made a disruptive blunder that raised questions about his skill as a manager.

Rather than seek help and craft a consensus with those colleagues who would be directly involved in implementing the next round of changes, Edgar Jr. hired McKinsey, the consulting firm, to develop new procedures. Dependence upon outside advisers became a hallmark of Edgar Jr.'s management style that irked senior executives who believed such firms brought nothing to the table. "I find them not useful at all," says Phil Beekman. "Highly impractical, highly expensive, and a lot of stuff that you should know yourself without having to have them tell you." For Edgar Bronfman Jr., such assessments of his decisions didn't matter, even from his former mentor. Bad reviews could kill a Broadway play, but in a family-run company like Seagram, no amount of negativity about poor performance could hinder the inevitability of Edgar Jr.'s upward progress.

"Capitalist Dynasties," declared the cover line on the March 17, 1986, edition of *Fortune.* The photograph showed Edgar Jr. on the right, his father on the left. The reason for Edgar Jr.'s smug look was revealed in the caption below: "Seagram Chairman Edgar Bronfman Sr. and newly chosen successor Edgar Jr." Trumpeted the headline inside: *The second son is heir at Seagram.*

Edgar Sr. once boasted that the grooming of Edgar Jr. as heir apparent had begun at the time of his birth. Nothing he saw along the way deterred him from designating Edgar Jr. over Sam, the first-born. "It was clear even when they were teenagers that the brilliant, tough-minded businessman in our family would be Efer," said Edgar Sr. "He is one of those rare individuals who instinctively understands the business world and always has his priorities in order." Sam, on the other hand, he called "truly the nicest man I know." For Edgar Sr., the defining moment came during a game of doubles tennis with a teenaged Sam as his partner. Edgar Sr. had spotted a weakness in one of their opponents. "The man had a slight disability making it hard for him to shift positions easily. Noticing this I said to Sam: 'You can afford to poach at net.' He reprimanded me with his eyes and said, 'Oh, Dad.' If Efer had been playing, he would have noticed immediately and moved nearer the center of the court."

Edgar Jr. has a very different recollection of Sam's intensely competitive style. "Sam had a bad temper and he would throw his racquet. He was a great guy, but not a good sport," says Edgar Jr. In the summer of 1967, when Edgar Jr. was twelve, he finally began winning the occasional set from his older brother, who was a much better player. On one memorable day, when it was 4–4 on a set, Sam motioned for Edgar Jr. to meet him at the net. As they stood inches apart, Sam looked his little brother in the eye and said, "I just want you to know, if you win this set I'm going to beat the shit out of you."

Edgar Jr. said nothing. He returned to the baseline and threw the game, letting Sam win easily.

Edgar Jr. then quit tennis outright and took up golf, a sport he'd never before played. He was furtive about his new interest, storing his clubs at the pro shop in the hope of keeping Sam in the dark. Sam found out and, as Edgar Jr. had feared, took up that game as well. Edgar Jr.'s aversion to playing either tennis or golf with Sam has never faded. "I love my brother to death and I have been his best man at both his weddings. We're very close and I think we know a lot about each other, but to this day I'd be happy to find other things to do with him than play sports."

How Edgar Sr. could so misjudge the tennis styles of his sons cannot be explained. What is certain is this: Edgar Jr.'s milquetoast manner on the court showed that he was nothing at all like his brother or his father, both of whom could be bullies. Edgar Jr. was more like his uncle Charles, seeking to avoid confrontation at any cost. Faced with an ultimatum, both Edgar Jr. and Charles were willing to back off and lose whatever was at stake rather than fight hard to win. Maybe Edgar Sr. fabricated the anecdote about Sam, fearing that if Sam became

CEO, every mention of him in the media would revisit the kidnapping incident. By comparison, how much better to have a Bronfman at the helm who was so passionate about the company that he'd left the glamour of Hollywood behind. But maybe there was another motivation. While Edgar Sr. intended to back off his corporate duties in favour of other pursuits, he also planned to keep a fatherly eye on the firm. Who better to have at the helm than Edgar Jr.? He was the more malleable son, the one who would take seriously his responsibility, be respectful of where the power came from, and try to figure out what his father wanted in order to please him.

For Edgar Sr. it was business as usual, designating his successor, doing exactly as he liked without bothering to consult anyone else. "There were a few raised eyebrows at the speed with which the young man was rising to the top. The way the company operated in those days, you didn't question Edgar very much. When he made up his mind to do something, he didn't take kindly to advice pro or con," says Mel Griffin, executive vice-president of manufacturing at the time. Directors grumbled but did little. "When Edgar Jr. was appointed, I said I don't know him very well," says Jean de Grandpré, a Seagram director since 1972 and chairman of BCE Inc. "He had been operating in New York for a very short time. He'd had a stint in Hollywood circles for a while and musical circles. I said it's difficult for me to pass judgment, but I think he's being promoted too fast. It surprised me that he was given so much latitude, so much authority. You have to bear in mind that a board where a family controls 35 percent of the shares is not an ordinary board. It's not an easy board to be on for that reason. Maybe wrongly, you have the impression that some of the decisions are already taken by the family, which doesn't prevent you from expressing your views, but if they feel strongly about a particular suggestion or position, either you step down, you resign, or accept the decision of the family."

Edgar Sr. was so indifferent to Charles's views that he said in that same *Fortune* interview that Charles's children, Stephen and Ellen, then twenty-two and seventeen respectively, would never work at Seagram, citing an unwritten tradition that only two of any generation could be involved. He had unilaterally decided that Edgar Jr. and Sam were the next two, just as Edgar Sr. and Charles had been the two from the second generation. Mr. Sam had needed to be more brutal in order to achieve the same results. After fighting with his brother Allan for years, he bought Allan out in 1960, thereby ending any hopes of a future at Seagram for Allan's two sons, Peter and Edward. Peter and Edward took their share of the $15-million payout and created Edper Investments. By the 1980s, Edper was Canada's largest conglomerate with assets of $30 billion and 350 companies, including Trizec, Royal Trust, Noranda, and London Life. Unlike their Seagram cousins, the Edper Bronfmans always employed professional management.

Charles offered a mild protest to Edgar Jr.'s succession and the elimination of his own two children from the race. In an interview with the Montreal *Gazette,* he said that the *Fortune* article presented "one man's view." Charles noted that the board should be involved in designating the next CEO, but then his comments turned conciliatory. "I don't want to say I am in violent disagreement with my brother, because I'm not. I just think it needs a little more explaining. I think it's probable it [the next CEO] could be a family member if he can cut it, but in a publicly held corporation, I don't think we should try to tell the board what to do."

Seagram director Leo Kolber, Charles's business associate and best friend since they met at McGill, urged Charles to oppose the appointment of Edgar Jr. "He seems like a nice young man," Kolber told Charles. "But he is a high school dropout and has no college education for the very kind of complex world we now live in. To the best of my knowledge, he knows nothing about finance or money, and if you allow this to happen, you will look back someday and say it is the biggest single mistake you ever made in your life."

Charles did nothing. Charles, who had been deputy chairman since 1979, was mollified with the slightly more elevated title of co-chairman. Edgar Sr.'s title remained the same—one important notch higher—chairman. Says Phil Beekman of Charles: "He's a guy that would rather run than fight."

At the annual meeting later that same month, Edgar Sr. said things had been "blown out of total proportion" and that his relationship with Charles was "stronger than ever." Ever the second banana, all Charles would say to reporters after the meeting was, "I agree with him." Edgar Sr. had got his way again. His boy need not fear any pretenders to the throne.

Coincident with Edgar Sr. setting the future direction of succession, Minda, the Baroness de Gunzburg, died of liver cancer on July 1, 1985. Her death precipitated a major reorganization of the family trust arrangement established by Mr. Sam as CEMP Investments. Minda's sons, Jean and Charles, wanted to sell a large portion of the Seagram shares in their mother's estate. Edgar Sr. and Charles agreed to buy the shares in order to retain family ownership, but they needed cash to carry out the transaction. Cadillac-Fairview, the successor company to a real estate investment set up by Mr. Sam, had built shopping malls and office towers across Canada. When Cadillac-Fairview was sold in 1987, the family's stake yielded $1.2 billion. CEMP was dissolved.

Charles and Edgar paid $95 million to Minda's estate for 1,650,000 shares, thereby reducing to 5 percent the total number of Seagram shares still held by Phyllis and Minda's estate. Charles moved out of Seagram headquarters to offices in the former Windsor Hotel, also on Peel Street, the location of his own investment firm, Claridge Inc.

That accomplished, Edgar Sr. juggled the upper ranks of Seagram to prepare for Edgar Jr.'s next move up. In July 1986, Phil Beekman was replaced as president and chief operating officer by David Sacks, who had joined Seagram three years earlier as executive vice-president for administration and finance. Sacks had spent the previous twenty-five years as a lawyer at Simpson Thacher & Bartlett, where he'd counselled Edgar Sr. about corporate matters, Sagittarius, and marital issues. The choice of Sacks also showed an evolution in how Seagram would be run. Edgar Sr. had not consulted Charles about Edgar Jr.'s future role. He did not ask Charles for his opinion about Sacks, either. This time, father and son collaborated on the way ahead and only then informed Charles. Edgar Sr. would continue to be chairman and chief executive officer, but the choice of Sacks as president was crucial. At sixty-two, David Sacks was seven years older than Beekman and just three years away from normal retirement, so he was clearly a transitional figure.

Although everything was aligned for the next step in Edgar Jr.'s ascension to the throne, the young king-in-waiting seemed oddly lacking in self-confidence. His very name, Edgar Bronfman *Junior*, captured the dilemma of his life as a son trying on his father's robes. At a Seagram sales meeting in Dallas in 1987, Edgar Jr. stepped to the microphone, then stumbled through an introduction. "I could call him father," he began. "I could call him chairman. Or I could call him the other Edgar, which, even for me, is a little much." At last Edgar Jr. settled on some awkward terminology, telling the gathering that he would call his father "Edgar World" while he would be known as "Edgar U.S.A." That Edgar Jr. would still be struggling with his name and his father's name at the age of thirty-two, fully five years after joining the firm, was telling. At the office, to differentiate one from the other, executives called the father "Senior" or "the Chairman" while the son was "Edgar" or "Junior." But "Senior" was not a term anyone used in the presence of the father. "He resents the senior. It's Edgar M. Bronfman," Edgar Jr. once said. "He made it clear to me that I'm junior and he is not senior."

Such a distinction made *Junior* nothing more than a control device, a means of keeping him in his proper place—beneath or behind, or both. In that context, Edgar Sr. was no different from his own father. Being called Junior in and of itself carries a pejorative tone. *Junior* sounds wet behind the ears, not yet fully a man, like Junior G-man. When it comes to perpetuating a family name, the member of the next generation in the line is better off. If there had been a third male with the identical name, he would be Edgar Miles Bronfman III, a designation that at least has a classy look in print. Edgar Jr. will always carry that diminutive, even after his father is dead and gone, a reminder to one and all of the man he could never be.

Sales growth in both Edgar World and Edgar U.S.A. was stalled or falling. The only way to increase market share was by acquisition. Seagram's competitors had been following that strategy, and by 1986 Guinness had replaced Seagram as the largest spirits and wine company. Edgar Jr. decided not to worry about Seagram's rank among competitors but to focus instead on premium brands where profits were higher, so he sold off some poorly performing brands at the lower end of the price range.

He also set out to win over the younger crowd with wine coolers, carbonated drinks made with fruit juice and wine. E. & J. Gallo Winery was the market leader, with its Bartles & Jaymes line. Gallo's TV ads featured two country gents, Frank Bartles and Ed Jaymes, extolling the virtues of Gallo coolers with their down-home charm. The commercials always ended with the chatty tag line, "Thank you for your support."

Edgar Jr. wanted a hipper, more urban image for Seagram's Golden Wine Cooler. At a meeting in the fall of 1985 with the ad agency handling the account, Ogilvy & Mather, a number of names were being discussed for the role of TV spokesperson when Edgar Jr. suddenly said, "Get me Bruce Willis." Most of the people in the room probably had no idea whom Edgar Jr. was talking about. Willis had just made his TV debut in *Moonlighting,* a crime and comedy show in which he and Cybill Shepherd played private detectives. Within days, Willis had signed a three-year, $7-million endorsement deal. Edgar Jr. was so involved in the campaign that he had a hand in picking Willis's wardrobe and choosing the colours for some of the coolers.

Seagram soon attained a 24 percent market share, topping Bartles & Jaymes as the best-selling brand. But annual sales of Seagram's coolers peaked at $200 million, then began falling despite continued advertising that cost $25 million a year. The business was modestly profitable but did not raise total consumption; coolers simply stole customers from other beverage alcohol categories. Men avoided the product, while most women preferred Chardonnay. The main buyers for coolers turned out to be blue-collar women, not the most desirable of demographic groups.

Edgar Jr. had always fancied himself as something of a marketing expert. He left the entire production and quality control side of the beverage alcohol business to others. For all his supposed skill at appealing to public sensibilities, however, he had been unable to pick Broadway winners or to widen the appeal of the Sandeman line of ports and sherries. With coolers he again demonstrated no particular insight into consumer tastes. Under Edgar Jr.'s guidance, Seagram had bought leadership in a fad category with few prospects. Although Edgar Jr. acknowledged that the time and money spent on coolers wasn't worth it, he continued to introduce new flavours. There was a last-gasp tone to Seagram's ads that announced, "Reports of the death of coolers have been greatly exaggerated." Edgar Jr., no marketing savant, needed to find someplace where he could earn his stripes–and soon.

FOUR

AT THE TOP

THREE ACQUISITIONS DURING the late 1980s—Martell, Tropicana, and Soho Natural Soda—demonstrated Edgar Jr.'s ability to negotiate deals. But the transactions also showed how difficult it was for him to hold on to any ground he gained.

When Martell, the French cognac maker, came up for sale, the most likely buyer appeared to be Grand Metropolitan, the British beverage and hotel group that already owned shares in Martell. Founded in 1715, Martel had reached the ninth generation of family ownership and had 18 percent of the world cognac market. While sales of other spirits were levelling off or even falling, cognac was growing in popularity, particularly in Asia. Edgar Jr. and Steve Banner, a mergers and acquisitions specialist with law firm Simpson Thacher, scooped Grand Met's position and negotiated directly with family members: René Martell, the chairman, and Patrick Martell, the general manager. In December 1987, Edgar Jr. offered $454 a share for the family's 41 percent holding. Add that to the 12 percent stake that Seagram had acquired on the open market, and he had control.

The French government intervened and declared that one bidder was not enough; Martell must be sold by auction. On January 6, 1988, Grant Met offered $514 a share—and also said that bid was the firm's final bid, an unusual admission in an auction situation. At a Friday lunch meeting in New York, Edgar Jr. told his father and other executives that Seagram should not bid again, even though any offer that topped Grand Met's might very likely be declared the winning bid. As far as Edgar Jr. was concerned, Martell wasn't worth any more than Seagram's first bid. He was supported by Ed McDonnell, president of international, and by treasurer Richard Goeltz. Edgar Sr. was in a musing mood. He asked what would happen if he used his chairman's prerogative, overruled the others, and ordered another bid by Seagram. Said McDonnell: "That would be foolish." The meeting ended inconclusively.

Two days later, the seed of his father's question had sprouted in Edgar Jr.'s mind. Edgar Sr. held such power over his son that, merely by raising the possibility of using his chairman's prerogative, he caused Edgar Jr. to reconsider his decision and reject the advice of his colleagues. On Sunday, Edgar Jr. spoke by telephone to his father, who was in California, and told Edgar Sr. that he had concluded Seagram would never be anything more than a bit-part player in Asia unless he bid again and bought Martell.

Charles now had to be included in this abrupt shift in strategy. Seagram's earlier offer wasn't as final as he and the board had previously been led to believe. On Wednesday, Charles, Edgar Jr., Edgar Sr., Banner, and Goeltz met in Edgar Sr.'s office to hear Edgar Jr., the sudden convert to the cause, argue why Seagram should bid again. "Efer was brilliant in making his case, and Charles was convinced," said Edgar Sr., who thanked Charles for agreeing. "Not at all," said Charles, according to

Edgar Sr. "Thank you for making us do the right thing." With Charles onside, board approval for the winning $800-million bid was a breeze.

Edgar Jr.'s acquisitions while he was stationed in London had been modest by comparison. Buying Martell made him look like a bold player who was able to seize opportunities that increased market share. Edgar Jr. recruited Hubert Millet, former CEO of Cointreau, to be president and CEO of the renamed Mumm-Martell Group. Millet cut the number of employees and worked with the unions to reduce the frequency of strikes. In 1990, Martell launched a new ad campaign with the slogan *The Art of Martell.* "Edgar was very involved in advertising and brand recognition. He loved marketing and he loved the products. We revamped the Martell line totally," says Millet. By 1994, sales in Asia—led by cognac—were $305 million annually, a massive increase from $28 million in 1988. Martell was the best-selling cognac in Singapore, Malaysia, and Hong Kong. Nightclub revellers would pay $2,000 for a bottle of premium sixty-year-old Cognac Martell L'Or.

But increases in one brand in one region could not reverse years of declining beverage alcohol sales. In his search for new consumer categories that might provide growth, Edgar Jr. was attracted to a product only marginally related to booze as a mixer. According to consumer surveys, the Tropicana brand of orange juice was better known than Seagram's 7 Crown. Markets were well developed in Florida and New York City but not in the rest of the country, where higher sales only required better distribution and marketing—or so went Edgar Jr.'s thinking.

Anthony Rossi, an Italian immigrant, had founded in 1947 the company that became Tropicana Products Inc. By 1988, Tropicana was owned by Beatrice Foods, which was in turn controlled by Kohlberg, Kravis, Roberts & Co., the leveraged buyout firm that specialized in acquiring companies that had fallen on bad times, whipping them into shape, then selling them for a quick profit.

Seagram bid $1.2 billion, $400 million more than the Tropicana managers were willing to pay in the auction. Coming up with more money was the easy part for Edgar Jr.; actually running Tropicana proved to be more troublesome. In his rush to find a growth industry, Edgar Jr. had invested in a business neither he nor any of his Seagram colleagues knew anything about. Spirits are distilled, then aged for years before being brought to market. Orange juice is a commodity that involves carefully timed picking, immediate packaging, and efficient shipment. A surprise freeze can devastate the crop, limit supply, and cause wild price fluctuations. Rather than plunge in and learn about the business himself, or hire executives with experience in consumer products, Edgar Jr. took the easy route and left senior management at Tropicana in place, a decision that turned out to be a mistake.

An audit in 1991 uncovered cost overruns that had not been properly disclosed on new facilities under construction in California and New Jersey. It fell to Edgar Jr. to inform the audit committee of the Seagram board that his trust in previous management had been misplaced. "Edgar had been very self-assured up to then. In that meeting, he started off a little nervous," says Donard Gaynor, an auditor with Price Waterhouse who had been called in to confirm the problems at Tropicana. Edgar Sr. was quick to support his son and deny any family responsibility. He reminded everyone that leaving management in place at Tropicana had been someone else's idea, not his and not his son's. "They all counselled hands-off," said Edgar Sr. "The Bronfmans don't buy companies and not put their own people in. We made a mistake and we won't make that mistake again."

After Tropicana's two top officers took the fall and departed, Edgar Jr. asked Willie Pietersen to clean up the mess. Edgar Jr. had recruited Pietersen, a Rhodes Scholar raised in South Africa, to replace him in 1988 as president of the House of Seagram. Pietersen cut about 225 jobs at Tropicana, more than 5 percent of the workforce, improved contracts with fruit growers, and reduced retail prices to increase market share. Says Pietersen: "Edgar relished deals. He found the day-to-day running of an operation less appealing. It was the creative side that always enthused him: the advertising, the label design, the aesthetic elements of what we were doing, deals, combinations, acquisitions, plotting on a grander canvas."

Pietersen's family contacts weren't always so rewarding. Edgar Sr. would regularly invite one of the senior executives to brief him on what was happening in that person's orbit. No one knew if he was checking up on Edgar Jr., or just staying connected. Sometimes it wasn't clear if he was even listening. Pietersen had one early afternoon session with Edgar Sr. during which he fell asleep. "I had a couple of my people there who'd known him for years, and I stopped and I said, 'What happens now?' 'You carry on.' So I carried on. I'm speaking to a sleeping man. He woke up in due course and began to ask questions, and it was as if he had not skipped a beat. They said, 'Be very careful about assuming that he doesn't know what's going on if he falls asleep after lunch. If you don't want him to fall asleep, have pre-lunch meetings.'"

Edgar Jr. asked Pietersen to relocate to Tropicana's head office in Bradenton, Florida. Pietersen reluctantly agreed, unhappy with what he called Edgar Jr.'s "imperial sense of managing, of leading, and that sense of entitlement, if you like, that comes from owning that much stock in a company." After a year, Pietersen moved back north because of family circumstances. Now it was Edgar Jr.'s turn to be unhappy. While the two men were negotiating Pietersen's departure, Pietersen received and accepted a job offer from Sterling Winthrop Inc., a pharmaceuticals firm. As if to show there were no hard feelings, Edgar Jr. on several occasions invited Pietersen into his office, where they spent hours talking about business matters and their families.

The gentle way he handled Pietersen was typical of Edgar Jr.'s laid-back management style. "He was not too interested in getting his hands dirty. It would take him a long time to bite the bullet and say, 'This is no longer working.' He didn't like to do things that weren't fun to do—like fire people," says Jeananne Hauswald, who started at Seagram in 1987 as treasurer, then later served as head of human resources followed by another stint as treasurer. Ellen Marram, who was hired to run Tropicana six months after Pietersen left, agrees: "I don't think Edgar is a very good judge of people. He hung on to people that weren't very good too long. I'm not sure that he evaluated how good they were very well. His strength is strategic, his strength is not executional. Execution is everything. You can have a great strategy, but if you have lousy execution it doesn't make a difference what your strategy is. Edgar was not as good at assessing somebody's managerial abilities as he might have been at just knowing if they were bright."

After Pietersen but before Marram as head of Tropicana came Myron Roeder, an eleven-year veteran of Seagram. He lasted long enough to discover that Tropicana's problem was in large part due to the paternalistic corporate culture created by the company's entrepreneurial founder. Roeder hired a New York consulting firm, Swain & Swain, for help in surveying the 3,500 employees. "Tropicana reminded me of Sicily, it had been occupied by everybody," says Robert Swain. Middle management resisted change by every invader. "If they didn't care to listen, they didn't, and there were no consequences."

In April 1993, Edgar Jr. hired Marram, former president and CEO of Nabisco Biscuit Co., to run Tropicana. Marram was the right person, but she was the fourth CEO at Tropicana in Seagram's five years of ownership. Edgar Jr.'s solution to poor performance had been to keep adding another executive log until the fire finally lit. "It sounds like a funny thing to say, because it was a $1.5-billion company when I joined, but it was like a mom-and-pop. It wasn't a professionally managed company," says Marram, who immediately replaced the top three officers. Domestic deliveries were unreliable and retailers regularly ran out of product, so Marram also created a new position, head of customer service. "Our joke, which wasn't very funny within the company, was that the product must be extraordinarily good because we certainly weren't doing anything to encourage our retailers to buy it."

Exports were equally disorganized. Tropicana had been trying to increase sales in France by sending Pure Premium not-from-concentrate orange juice from Bradenton, but the packaged product had a shelf life of sixty-three days. Almost a quarter of that time was taken up by shipping. There was either too much product available, resulting in spoilage, or too little, so retailers ran out. To improve the situation Seagram paid $276 million in 1995 for Dole Food Co. The acquisition included production facilities in Europe and Asia that were closer to those potential new markets. By 1996, international had grown to 20 percent of total sales from 5 percent in 1991. Marram added vitamins and calcium in response to growing consumer health concerns, and focused on the not-from-concentrate product, where there was more demand and more profit than with frozen juice. Tropicana attained a 42 percent share of the chilled ready-to-serve orange juice market in the U.S. and 50 percent in Canada.

No sooner had Edgar Jr. concluded those two deals, Martell and Tropicana, than he bought another company. This time he acted almost on a whim, as if he believed his recent acquisitions had rendered him invincible. In 1989, while visiting the farm where his father raised bison near Charlottesville, Virginia, Edgar Jr. tasted Soho Natural Soda. He liked the soft drink so much that he bought the company.

Founded in 1977 by Sophia Collier and Connie Best, American Natural Beverage Corp. had annual sales of $25 million. Soho was distributed by beer and soft drink wholesalers to corner stores and grocery outlets where consumer traffic was high. Edgar Jr. changed the delivery system so that Soho was handled by Seagram distributors and sold in liquor stores. However, consumers who bought an alternative soft drink were not necessarily the same demographic group who shopped for whiskey. Soho's sales and profits plunged. "Running a brand does require a lot of TLC. When Häagen-Dazs went to Pillsbury, it was really never quite the same. The lesson I learned is that large companies are not as well suited to running these special brands," says Collier, who is now chair of Citizens Advisers Inc., a fund management firm in Portsmouth, New Hampshire, with $1 billion under management.

After paying $14 million for Soho in 1989, Seagram dumped the company three years later for $2 million. The brand never did regain its previous popularity, and eventually disappeared.

෴

Edgar Jr.'s inability to produce sustained results at work was matched by difficulties at home. Edgar Jr. and Sherry lived in a restored Victorian townhouse on New York's Riverside Drive with seven fireplaces and twenty rooms. The historic exterior had been retained, but inside was sleekly modern, done in coral and peach. The couple had three children: Vanessa, born in 1980, Ben, born in 1983, and Hannah, born in 1987. But the enchanted family life was not all that it seemed.

Edgar Jr. did not want a marriage breakdown, because he had fought so hard for Sherry, but he finally decided, during a business trip to Asia, that the differences that had grown between them were irreconcilable. They separated in the fall of 1989 and were divorced in 1991. "I will always be there for her. They will always be my children. I'm physically leaving them, I'm not mentally leaving them," Edgar Jr. told Patsy Puttnam. Says Puttnam, "I knew what was in his mind. What had happened to his parents was now happening to him. And I bet it's something he promised himself [was] never, ever going to happen. Here he was having to admit it had happened."

Yet divorce was more the norm than not in the Bronfman family. Charles divorced his first wife, Barbara Baerwald, and married Andrea Cohen in 1982. Andy, as she is called, and her first husband, David, had been close friends of Charles and Barbara in Montreal. Charles had been a groomsman at their wedding. Andy, who is fourteen years younger than Charles, is strong-willed, smart, and aggressive to his passive. Edgar Sr. had been through four divorces, Phyllis one. In the second generation, only Minda, who married Baron Alain de Gunzburg in 1953, remained with her first spouse. In the third generation, Holly has been married three times. Matthew's two marriages have both failed. Sam's first wife died of breast cancer; he has since remarried. Adam, who owns a construction company in California, is still with his first wife.

After his marriage came apart, Edgar Jr. was as good as his word. Whenever he was not travelling, he would pick up the children and drive them to school. On alternate weekends he took them to his country property in Dutchess County, an hour-and-a-half drive from Manhattan. The 12,000-square-foot Georgian mansion sat on a 125-acre estate near Pawling, a town of five thousand founded in 1788, which had long been popular with the wealthy. Famous residents of the community included journalist Edward R. Murrow, Rev. Norman Vincent Peale, and actor James Earl Jones. Edgar Jr.'s place had its own particular pedigree. He'd bought the house from filmmaker Dino De Laurentiis; it had once been owned by broadcaster Lowell Thomas. Edgar paid $3 million for the property, which included an eleven-acre lake, tennis court, golf course, and indoor swimming pool.

Edgar Jr.'s unhappy home life could not help but have an impact on his business performance. In the question-and-answer session that followed a 1990 speech to the Advertising Club of New York, he was asked about teachers who were upset because they thought that coolers were being marketed like soft drinks to the impressionable young. "I don't mean to be flippant," he replied, "but educators don't know a lot about advertising." It was a ridiculous remark, a thunderbolt tossed from on high.

At that same event he also showed his insecure side. During the introduction Edgar Jr. was described as having achieved success in the movie industry. "My success has been greatly overstated even by that brief sentence," he said. Flagellating himself further about *The Border,* he quoted Sam Goldwyn: "If the people don't want to come, you can't stop them." Who was this man? Was he an all-knowing industry leader so comfortable in his own skin that he could denounce teachers? Or a defensive misfit ashamed by his lack of accomplishment? On any given day, evidently, he could be both.

Those two divergent personalities would also show up at the office. He could demonstrate a distant and imperial style as the reigning monarch or he could be close, caring, and creative. Those who regularly dealt with him could never predict which side would assert itself. "He'd be pretty short with people who worked for him, people who worked with him, his equals. He had a touch of arrogance later on," says Phil Beekman, Edgar Jr.'s first boss. At one sales meeting Edgar Jr. was asked about plans to introduce a gin-and-orange-juice drink. The questioner worried that the new product would simply steal Seagram's gin sales and asked if there had been adequate research. "Let me put it this way," replied Edgar Jr. "One of us is right."

The abrupt boss could also turn on the charm when he so chose. Ellen Marram once asked him to meet someone she was considering for a job at Tropicana. When the candidate arrived for his appointment, Edgar Jr. didn't wait at his desk for the man to be presented. "To this day this guy has never forgotten that Edgar Bronfman came out of his office, walked into the reception area to say hello to him. Edgar did those things very consciously," says Marram. "This goes back to the sort of royalty, celebrity quality he had. Somebody else once told me that the highlight of his life was because Edgar called him on his twenty-fifth wedding anniversary. You would have thought the highlight of his life was that it *was* his twenty-fifth wedding anniversary, but it wasn't, it was that Edgar called. He was aware that he could be quite charming and quite persuasive. He knew how to use that."

Edgar Jr. exploited that quality to the fullest when he was glad-handing employees on a plant tour or speaking to them extemporaneously. Valerie Hendy, who worked in corporate communications from 1988 to 1995, accompanied Edgar Jr. on a trip to the Seagram distillery in Relay, Maryland. In the cafeteria, a female employee told him that she had worked for Mr. Sam. "He was actually flirting with her. He took her hand and was Prince Charming. He didn't need to do that. I've worked for executives who don't even make eye contact with their employees." During a question-and-answer session that same day, an employee reminisced how during Prohibition his family had made money selling homemade moonshine. Quipped Edgar Jr., "My family made a lot of money during Prohibition too."

Compared with his father's blustering and autocratic style, Edgar Jr. could be more low-key and inclusive—in the right circumstances. "He is actually more comfortable in groups of one thousand than he is one-on-one. He's much less self-conscious. He used a conversational tone that was very open, very friendly. He would lower his voice to almost be gentle," says Jeananne Hauswald, vice-president of human resources at Seagram in the early 1990s. As a royal, when his subjects' eyes gleamed in his presence, he could be in top form, feeding off their adulation.

More difficult for Edgar Jr. was sorting out his management team, trying to blend those he inherited from his father with the new blood he brought in. During one management meeting Edgar Jr. was questioning Richard Goeltz, executive vice-president of finance. Edgar Jr. seemed unhappy with what he was hearing and twice rephrased his question. Finally, Edgar Jr. leaned forward, smiled, and said, "You know, Richard, that's a very good answer to which I haven't yet found the right question." Goeltz eventually retired and was replaced.

Through all the management change, the tightly linked father–son relationship was ever-present. "You never knew whether it was his skill or whether it was his father's skill, because everything was probably filtered beforehand. It was very difficult to judge him as an individual in such a short period when you had a dominating father right next to him," says Jean de Grandpré, who retired as a director in 1992, four years after Edgar Jr. joined the board.

Edgar Jr. established the Office of the President in 1991 to deal with policy items such as long-range strategy, business opportunities, and cross-fertilization of global resources. In addition to top executives already working at Seagram, the newly formed inner circle included Steve Banner, hired by Edgar Jr. to be senior executive vice-president in charge of finance and strategic planning. In his previous incarnation at Simpson Thacher, Banner had advised Edgar Jr. on the Martell acquisition, but Banner also had experience with entertainment deals. He'd helped Paramount with its hostile bid for Time Inc. in 1989, and had acted for Matsushita Electric Industrial Co. in 1990 when the Japanese firm bought MCA Inc. The arrival of Banner, who was paid $600,000 a year, signalled that Edgar Jr. was eager to grow through acquisition in sectors of the economy other than spirits and wine.

The first transaction completed by Edgar Jr. and Steve Banner in his new in-house role turned out to be Edgar Jr.'s last big deal in beverage alcohol. Sales of imported vodka brands were growing 30 percent a year, a phenomenal increase at a time when other spirits were in decline. Seagram did not have a premium vodka, so in 1991 Edgar Jr. set his sights on becoming the global marketer and distributor for Absolut. Ed McDonnell had spotted the possibility and did most of the initial legwork, but it was Edgar Jr. who led the negotiations with the Swedish government-controlled wine and spirits co-operative, V&S Vin & Sprit AB.

Distribution rights for Absolut were held by a competitor, Grand Metropolitan, the other party in the bidding war for Martell. Seagram had an advantage. Grand Met also distributed

Smirnoff, the best-selling vodka in the U.S. and Europe. Seagram had no such potential conflict. Once again Edgar Jr. showed his enthusiasm for the art of the deal. "He's brilliant at that kind of thing. We were dealing with the very top people in the financial area of the Swedish government. A great deal of the success of getting that brand for the company was directly to his credit. When he sets his mind to do something, he does it to perfection," says McDonnell. "He was totally selfless in getting it done, [working] weekends and holidays when somebody else that had his background could have been lounging out in Southampton."

The final three days of negotiations in October 1993 took place at a hotel outside Stockholm. At the last minute Edgar Jr. made a most unusual and unbusinesslike concession in order to close the deal. He agreed to pay $700 million for the distribution rights but to take no profits for three years unless and until higher sales levels of Absolut were achieved.

The Swedes often entertained their guests at dinners held in conjunction with such occasions, so the Seagram team decided they should do the same in celebration of their new union. Edgar Jr., McDonnell, Banner, and their support staff serenaded their hosts with Stephen Sondheim's "Together Wherever We Go" from the Broadway musical *Gypsy*. The words were not changed, only the title was altered. They called their version "Absolut Harmony."

◌

Despite his Absolut success, Edgar Jr. was growing increasingly disenchanted with the beverage alcohol side of the business. Coupled with the ever-present shame of a bootlegging past were modern-day problems. Society has a schizophrenic view about alcohol. There's the sunny side, where the pop of a champagne cork denotes a celebration, a martini says sophistication, and a bottle of wine with friends at dinner leads to a convivial evening. Then there's the darker side: alcoholism, barroom brawls, drunk drivers, illness, and death. Yes, the product is profitable, legal, and high in quality. No, booze steals pay packets, causes family problems, and attracts low-lifes.

Those who make and sell booze are equally conflicted. Edgar Jr. loved it and hated it. For him, Seagram's Spirits and Wine Group—the acronym SSWG was known internally as SWIG—was something that he would rather forget. But beverage alcohol did provide him with a public profile, create the family fortune, deliver entrees at the highest level—in all, the kind of attention he desperately wanted for himself but worried deep down whether he really deserved. Edgar Jr.'s diminishing interest in booze as a business was obvious within the organization. "He was a gentle, sensitive, thoughtful, and artistic person who was making himself listen to reports about gin sales in Germany," says Valerie Hendy. "I once saw him put his head down on the table. It just wasn't his environment. He could discuss it with insight, but whether it nourished his soul, I think not."

Edgar Jr. reminded Sophia Collier, founder of Soho Natural Beverages, of Al Gore. Both were young men whose families had programmed them to take a certain career path, without giving consideration to their interest or suitability. "There was just a touch of melancholy," says Collier. "Here is somebody who, by circumstance of birth, is doing this work that he may or may not have chosen otherwise. I had the feeling that this was a guy that would not necessarily be doing this had he not been born into it. He might have been off on some other—possibly more fun—activity."

The Absolut deal was just a tune-up. With the help of Steve Banner, Edgar Jr. was about to make his own mark in another field. "Having Steve on his team really did boost his confidence.

Steve supported his strategic thinking and was extremely bright," says Jeananne Hauswald. "I think [Steve] boosted everybody's confidence, not necessarily in themselves because occasionally he could be very hard on you, but you really felt like at least there was somebody there that was going to keep you from making the final mistake."

Edgar Jr. and Banner looked at fashion and fragrance with a view to following the strategy of France's Moët Hennessy Louis Vuitton, but nothing they liked was for sale. Next they studied entertainment because of Edgar Jr.'s interest in pop culture and the widespread expectation that the industry would grow 15 to 20 percent a year. For advice they turned to Michael Ovitz, chairman of Hollywood's Creative Artists Agency. He knew the Bronfmans; his father had worked for a Seagram distributor. In 1992, Ovitz made a presentation about media and entertainment to Edgar Sr., Edgar Jr., and Sam at Edgar Sr.'s place in Sun Valley, Idaho. Ovitz then made a similar presentation to the Seagram board.

He in turn introduced Edgar Jr. to Herbert Allen Jr., of Allen & Co., a New York–based investment banking firm. Allen had helped broker two of the biggest entertainment deals: the acquisition by Sony Corp. of Columbia Pictures and the purchase by Matsushita of MCA Inc. Since the early 1980s, Allen had hosted an annual July media conference in Sun Valley that drew the likes of Microsoft's Bill Gates and investor Warren Buffet to hobnob with entertainment industry CEOs, hear their corporate presentations, and discuss possible deals.

Edgar Jr. told Allen he had $2 billion available. For Allen, the target was obvious: Time Warner, the world's largest media and entertainment company. The choice suited Edgar Sr. too. In 1969, when he'd been chairman of MGM, Time Inc. had also been a shareholder of the movie studio, so this deal offered a reunification of sorts. In 1993, Warner Brothers was the number one studio at the box office; Warner Music had top recording stars such as Eric Clapton and Phil Collins. The company was number two in cable and had powerhouse magazines: *Time, People,* and *Sports Illustrated.* There were no large shareholders, the company was widely held, so accumulating shares was relatively easy.

In May 1993, when Edgar Jr. announced that he'd spent $700 million for 21.1 million shares or a 5.7 percent stake in Time Warner, journalists were scornful of his interest. "In an earlier interview held in his impeccably furnished office tastefully accented by an original Miró painting, he was formal and controlled, reserved to the point of appearing aloof. The neatly bearded heir literally refused to open his mouth in response to most questions about Time Warner; with lips pursed and fingers braced in a taut steeple he would silently shake his head no," wrote Eben Shapiro in *The Wall Street Journal.* "He is working mightily to put to rest the reputation that has dogged him throughout his career as a rich-kid dilettante who got his job through nepotism."

Others in the media were contemptuous of the family's financial success, saying that this investment would also fare badly. Seagram's holding in DuPont, worth $8.5 billion, had barely done better than an index fund, noted *Newsday* columnist Allan Sloan. Since 1981, when Seagram acquired DuPont, the return—including dividends—had been 17 percent a year, compared with 15 percent for the Standard & Poor's 500 during the same period. "While 2 percentage points comes out to a lot of money, it hardly makes up for Seagram's risk in owning one very cyclical industrial company rather than a diversified portfolio of 500 stocks," wrote Sloan. "I can't conceive of Seagram trying to take over Time Warner, which is still burdened with

$15 billion of debt. But I can see the Bronfmans buying themselves a seat at the entertainment table with Seagram's money. After all, that's what a family company is for, isn't it?"

Time Warner's Gerald Levin had no interest in making a seat available to the new shareholder. Levin, who had just recently become chairman and CEO of Time Warner following the December 1992 death of Steven J. Ross, did not welcome either Edgar Jr. or his money. Levin feared that Edgar Jr. had a long-term takeover plan, a concern that was reinforced by the announcement from Power Corp.'s Paul Desmarais, a Seagram director, that Power had bought three million Time Warner shares.

Levin and Edgar Jr. met for lunch numerous times, but relations between the two men remained frosty. In January 1994, by which time Seagram had acquired a total of 44.2 million shares or 11.7 percent of Time Warner, Levin put in place a shareholder rights plan, more commonly called a poison pill. Poison pills had been around since the 1980s, when hostile takeovers first came into vogue. Under the Time Warner poison pill, if Edgar Jr.'s holding reached 15 percent, the plan would be triggered, thereby flooding the market with additional shares for all shareholders except Seagram. As a result, Seagram's stake would be diluted from 15 percent down to, say, 1 or 2 percent— not much of a holding for the hundreds of millions of dollars he'd already spent. Edgar Jr. could, of course, make an offer for the entire company any time he wanted, but such a bid would be very costly—as much as $35 billion. What the poison pill prevented Edgar Jr. from doing was inching his way up from 15 percent to 17 percent then to 22 percent, where he might stop on his own at a similar level of ownership in Time Warner as he had with DuPont.

Boards and managements under siege, as Time Warner's felt themselves to be, claim that they have the best interests of their own shareholders at heart, but there is another purpose to a poison pill: the measure preserves the status quo by drawing a line at which an acquisitor must either stop buying or make a bid for all shares. The poison pill worked. By April 1995, Edgar Jr. had spent a total of $2.17 billion and owned 14.9 percent of Time Warner, a hair's breadth below the threshold that would launch the poison pill. At that point, he stopped acquiring shares.

The fact that the poison pill even existed may well have been Edgar Jr.'s own fault. Levin was still securing his new executive position in May 1993 when Seagram announced its first purchase of Time Warner shares. (U.S. securities laws require disclosure when any shareholder acquires more than 5 percent of a public company.) Several newspaper articles said that if Edgar Jr. won control, he would hire Mike Ovitz to be chairman of Time Warner. Rumours became so specific that financial partners were named and a price of $55 a share was mentioned.

Levin used the Ovitz rumours to solidify his position. He asked Terry Semel and Bob Daly, co-CEOs of Warner Brothers, "Would you rather he be chairman or I be chairman?" Their reply was unambiguous: "We'd rather you be chairman." That unity against a common foe rallied internal forces behind Levin and kept Edgar Jr. at bay. Several years later, when Semel told Edgar Jr. that story, Edgar Jr. protested that he had never said he would hire Ovitz. "I know," said Semel, "but you never said that you wouldn't. So the question of how the company was going to be managed down the road worked against you."

Edgar Jr. may also have hurt his chances by not following the advice of Steve Banner, who urged him to proceed cautiously. Banner believed that Time Warner would eventually allow Edgar Jr. to buy up to 20 percent in the company, at which point the two sides could put a standstill agreement into place, the same kind of pact as existed with DuPont. "I tried to talk to the kid. He's got no patience," Banner later told a colleague. "I tried to tell him Time Warner was the one, and to go easy on it, not to go to the 15 percent quickly. Take it easy and get there." But Edgar Jr. charged ahead. "When he wants to move, he wants to move," said Banner.

Edgar Jr. had just turned thirty-eight when he announced his ownership position in Time Warner. It was his first run at a company of such size. His two previous acquisitions, Martell and Tropicana, involved buying 100 percent of much smaller companies with more focused operations. "You have to remember that he was young at the time, unseasoned in corporate warfare. He was coming up against a lot of older, cagey, battle-scarred warriors," says Harold Vogel, an analyst for thirty years with Paine Webber and Merrill Lynch, and the author of *Entertainment Industry Economics,* one of the definitive books on the business. "He was untested, maybe naive, I don't know, but he was certainly out of his element. He was like Galahad storming the castles. Nonetheless, he could have gone to the financial institutions [and got support] for a tender offer. They were ripe for management change. Let's give him credit for seeing that was the right company to go after."

Some of Edgar Jr.'s advisers urged him to forget about the poison pill and go for 100 percent control. "When he bought, it seemed to me it was a time when he could have owned the whole thing," says Herbert Allen Jr. "He should have pursued it and could have won it. That would have been the right path to follow, but he didn't want to do that. He had other advisers who told him it wasn't the right thing to do [for] whatever reason they had. We thought it was very doable. He and the others didn't, so that was that."

Allen blames Edgar Sr. for the fact that his son lacked up-from-the-bottom business experience to draw upon in dealing with such situations. "If you're going to run a business, you have to go through the mailroom. You don't have to spend a lot of time there, but you have to go through stages. You don't start as a producer. It's just too high up. He didn't really have the building blocks that are required to run a business," says Allen. "A lot of kids raised that way end up at the bar at the racquet club, or drugged, or on the Riviera. They don't go to work in the morning. To his credit, he was in the mainstream. I regard Edgar with some degree of sympathy, and I don't mean that in any condescending way. It wasn't easy for him."

Despite Edgar Jr.'s shaky foundation in business, his father continued to push him ever higher. At the annual meeting held in Montreal on June 1, 1994, Edgar Jr. was named chief executive officer at thirty-nine. "Edgar was mesmerized by his son. There is no other way to describe it," wrote Leo Kolber in his memoir, *Leo: A Life.* "Edgar Jr. is a very nice man, very diffident, a good listener, and not a show-off in any sense of the word. He is anything but stupid. But he had no business running Seagram, and if he hadn't been named Bronfman, he wouldn't have been."

Charles did not stop Edgar Jr.'s appointment, but he did point out to shareholders at the annual meeting how well he and Edgar Sr. had done on their watch. Anyone who had invested $1,000 in Seagram in 1971, when Mr. Sam died and Charles and Edgar Sr. took over, would now have holdings worth $23,000. That annual compound growth put Seagram in the same league as long-term-investment successes like the Templeton Fund. The clear implication was that Edgar Jr. would have to perform well in the future to match past accomplishments.

Edgar Sr.'s plan was moving along just as he had intended. "My relationship with my son, Edgar, is very different from the one I had with my father," said Edgar Sr. "We are very close, very affectionate. I have complete confidence in Edgar and his professional instincts. I know that for some CEOs, handing over the reins of a company is very traumatic. But for me it was infinitely easier—first because I trusted Edgar, and second, because I had something meaningful to retire *to*." At sixty-four, he remained chairman of Seagram, which meant he presided over all board meetings and controlled the agenda. There were also his many volunteer pursuits: the World Jewish Congress, the World Jewish Restitution Organization, and Hillel: The Foundation for Jewish Campus Life.

Edgar Sr. and Edgar Jr. rarely disagreed when other Seagram executives were around. If the two had something to discuss, they'd first iron out their differences in private and then present a united front. Maintaining that public consensus wasn't easy. Edgar Jr. has admitted that he had to work hard to deal with what was clearly a very difficult and complex relationship with his father. "Psychotherapy alone was not responsible for Edgar's and my relationship improving, but it would be inaccurate to say it's had nothing to do with it. A relationship takes two people, and both Edgar and I have grown," said Edgar Jr. in an article published in the July 1995 issue of *Vanity Fair*. For Edgar Jr., some of that adjustment must have had to do with dealing with a father who had been absent during his childhood and then, when he was an adult, had become focused on the success of his son. Phyllis has said that to Mr. Sam the second generation was a projection of him; Edgar Sr. had a similar view of his son. The two had gone from having a distant relationship to one that bordered on codependency.

For his part, Edgar Jr. had grown so much that he was beginning to sound like his father: arrogant about the abundance of his talent and convinced of his invincibility. After the 1994 annual meeting when he was named CEO, Edgar Jr. met in Toronto with analysts from Canadian brokerage firms who were skeptical about his Time Warner investment. Asked one analyst: "Is it true you just wanted to have dinner with movie stars and you spent $2 billion to do it?" Replied Edgar Jr.: "I'm not going down in history as the one Bronfman who pissed away the family fortune." That declaration, and the overweening pride it represented, would prove to be his downfall.

FIVE

GOING HOLLYWOOD

EDGAR JR. SEEMED UNUSUALLY nervous on the Friday evening before his wedding in Caracas, Venezuela. He ate sparingly, his eyes darted around at the fifty friends and family members gathered for dinner in the garden of his soon-to-be in-laws. Edgar Jr. sat between his mother, Ann Loeb Bronfman, and his surrogate mother, Patsy Puttnam. Finally, the reason for his distracted behaviour became apparent when he stood and recited from memory a long love poem he had written for his fiancée, Clarissa Alcock. As he concluded and the guests applauded, Frank Alcock, Clarissa's father, hugged Edgar Jr. The poem and the embrace marked the successful conclusion of Edgar Jr.'s three-year courtship of Clarissa, a wooing process that lasted longer than some of his father's marriages.

The wedding was held the next evening, February 19, 1994, on the hillside estate of Clarissa's grandmother outside Caracas. The 1,200 guests were ferried by buses to the torch-light ceremony conducted by a priest, a rabbi, and a local bishop. At one point there was a discussion about the couple kneeling at the altar, but Edgar Jr. ruled that out. He said he did not want to look up and see the crucifix. "We have our limits," he told a colleague.

There were fewer than two hundred chairs, so most of the guests stood, clustered as close as possible to the couple to create some sense of intimacy. After the ceremony the newlyweds greeted guests; a candlelit buffet dinner at tables for ten followed. For Edgar Jr. and Clarissa's first dance, Bruce Roberts sang "If I Didn't Love You," a song he and Edgar Jr. had written for Clarissa that was later recorded by Barbra Streisand. The celebration lasted for hours. Three orchestras provided music for a guest list that was dominated by Venezuelan friends and family of the bride. Among Edgar Jr.'s friends who attended were members of the Hollywood elite such as Michael Ovitz, Barry Diller, and Michael Douglas. New York friends included John and Violaine Bernbach and John and Susan Hess. From London came David and Patsy Puttnam as well as Arrelle von Hurter. Von Hurter, who was originally from California and about five years older than Edgar Jr., first had a relationship with the teenaged Edgar Jr. when they were both living in New York. Although she married, the two remained close over the years, with Von Hurter regularly acting as a sounding board and confidante.

Edgar Jr. had first met Clarissa in 1990. While on a business trip to Venezuela, Edgar Jr. said to the wife of a local Seagram official, "If there's anyone as pretty as you, I'd love to meet her." That evening she introduced him to Clarissa. The two got off to a rocky start; she was bored by his talk of business. Two weeks later, in New York, he took her to see *Phantom of the Opera,* and the relationship blossomed. "She's very strong-willed and intelligent. I don't think that she was overly impressed that he was a Bronfman, which I think was one of the things that was great about her," said John Bernbach, who batched with Edgar Jr. in his townhouse on East Seventy-third Street for ten months after Bernbach's own first marriage had come apart.

Clarissa's mother came from a wealthy Venezuelan family with extensive land holdings. Her father was a retired chief operating officer of Petróleos de Venezuela, the national oil company. When Clarissa informed her Roman Catholic parents about Edgar Jr., she said, "There are a few things I have to tell you about him. One, he's Jewish. Two, he's been married before. And three, he's got three children."

Clarissa was no pushover. Edgar Jr. sent flowers daily and flew to Venezuela on weekends. Educated in Caracas, New York, and Paris, Clarissa eventually gave up her job as a strategist at Sivensa, a steel producer, and moved to New York to take her MBA at New York University. Her education became part of Edgar Jr.'s campaign to win her as his wife. Barry Diller, who left Fox in 1992, had told Edgar Jr. how helpful he found the Macintosh PowerBook in his new life. Always eager to follow Diller's lead, Edgar Jr. and Clarissa both signed up for computer training at a company run by Bruce Stark, Edgar Jr.'s Broadway partner from high school days. She also received help in her post-graduate studies from Seagram executives. Controller Ed Falkenberg, for example, tutored her in accounting.

Edgar Jr. proposed marriage to Clarissa several times, but she always put him off. One evening in 1993, at the Carlyle Hotel, it was Clarissa who popped the question; he accepted. This time Edgar Jr. had his father's blessing. "Once again, the backgrounds are different, but there's hope," said Edgar Sr. "Isn't that what the wag said about a second marriage—the triumph of hope over experience?"

The couple honeymooned on Little St. James, a private island off St. Thomas in the U.S. Virgin Islands. A post-nuptial reception at the Roseland Ballroom on West Fifty-second Street in New York, a huge facility used for prizefights, fundraising dinners, and rock concerts, was attended by a thousand of their closest friends who either weren't invited to Caracas or had been unable to travel to the wedding.

Clarissa moved into Edgar Jr.'s house on East Seventy-third Street, with its tasteful antiques and chintz furniture. Over the next six years they had four children, two boys and two girls, including twins. Clarissa wanted different space, so Edgar Jr. paid $4.375 million for what had been a five-storey nine-unit apartment building on East Sixty-fourth Street near Fifth Avenue, in the same block as Donatella Versace and Ivana Trump. They hired Canadian architect Peter Rose, who was recommended by Phyllis because he had designed her Canadian Centre for Architecture in Montreal. "I told Peter two things," said Edgar Jr. "It had to be anti-artifice, no faux anything. And it had to be noble, not grand, but something that speaks for itself eloquently and quietly." Rose confessed that he never understood what the "anti-artifice" part of his patron's instructions meant, then added, "but I know I've responded to it."

Creation of a single-family dwelling took two years of planning and two years of construction. (Edgar Jr. sold Seventy-third Street for $4.5 million.) Edgar Jr., who had always sought personal privacy, opened the 31-foot-wide house in September 1999 to the prying eyes of a writer and photographer from *The New York Times*. The core had been gutted. The main floor was turned into an entertainment area with a soaring two-and-a-half-storey atrium dominated by a skylight and life-size Nigerian fertility statue. "Light means happiness," said Clarissa. "Give me a court in the middle, in honour of my Latin upbringing." The sparsely furnished living room off the atrium featured a Le Corbusier chaise and a painting by Roberto Matta, the Chilean surrealist. The other two rooms used for entertaining were a dining room and a library with an interior window and a balcony. The top two and a half storeys were for private family use, with access through a secret door to steep stairs, three landings, the bedrooms, a children's playroom, and a second interior courtyard. After all that effort, Edgar Jr. put the house on the market in 2002 with an asking price of $40 million. It didn't sell.

Clarissa became an integral part of the New York social scene as a member of the Carnegie Hall board of trustees. She also co-chaired fundraising events such as the Costume Institute gala for the Metropolitan Museum. In 2001, Clarissa and some female partners launched entre-nos.com, a Spanish-language website for women. Visitors could e-mail details of their dreams and receive explanations from psychologists.

Clarissa made Edgar Jr. more contented than he'd been for years. In an interview after he remarried, Edgar Jr. hinted at his previous marital problems. "Being happy is better than not being happy. And I am very happy. Certainly the happier one is, the greater the opportunity for contribution to the corporate effort. And I'm no different from anybody else in that regard."

No different except for his ready access to ever-flowing funds. When Edgar Jr. admired a dress created by Hervé Léger, rather than order a few gowns for Clarissa, he bought an interest in the Parisian couturier famous for "bandage dresses" with their body-hugging style, plunging necklines, and see-through lace. Over lunch at Le Divellec, one of his favourite restaurants in Paris, Edgar Jr. revealed his purchase to Hubert Millet, head of global brands for Seagram, and asked him to oversee the acquisition. "It didn't fit the rest of the business. His rationale [was] that it would be interesting to have a foot in that kind of industry to see how it worked," says Millet. "We lost money every year." Edgar Jr. finally got rid of Hervé Léger by selling it to Los Angeles–based designer BCBG Max Azria in 1998.

Clarissa also tried to move Edgar Jr. beyond his preoccupation with Mr. Sam's warning about the third generation. In an interview for a 1996 television documentary, fully thirty years after his grandfather had first revealed his fears, Edgar Jr. was still fixated on those words and the photograph of Mr. Sam that he'd hung in his office. "It's the one that we all love, him playing solitaire. And then I put his saying underneath that picture, which says: 'Shirtsleeves to shirtsleeves in three generations. I'm worried about the third generation.' I have that here and I look at it every day. I don't want to let anybody down, least of all myself." Then Edgar Jr. paused and added, with a confident smile, "Shirtsleeves to shirtsleeves in three generations ain't happening here."

On Clarissa's instructions, Edgar Jr. removed the photo as part of an office refurbishment in 1998. The English antique furniture was replaced with a contemporary look. For all the decorative change, however, the important influence of Edgar Sr. remained close by. Father and son both had offices on the fifth floor, originally designated by Mr. Sam for the family and senior executives because he had a phobia about heights. After Mr. Sam's death, Edgar Sr. had taken over his father's office; Edgar Jr.'s office as CEO was just down the hall. Both men had views of Park Avenue and they shared a conference room in between. Other perks on the executive floor included a steam facility, whirlpool bath, sun machine, and sauna.

Edgar Jr.'s feelings of family obligation were plainly evident. "It was clear that it was something that was omnipresent. He was always aware of it and it was a tremendous burden," says John Bernbach. Over time, Clarissa's presence was beneficial. "I don't mean this to sound frivolous at all, but she was very, very good, and she continues to be good and say all this is very important, but guess what? You've got some things in life now that are really important. You've got a good marriage, wonderful children. They lost a child, they had to go through that together. It was a terrible experience. She is very well grounded and he is very well grounded right now. He is as happy from that standpoint as I've ever known him. She has to be credited with playing a large part of that."

With Edgar Jr.'s marriage to Clarissa coming in the same year as he was named CEO, all the pieces—personal and professional—that he needed to transform Seagram had fallen into place. He had modernized upper management by bringing in experienced outsiders. For executive vice-president of human resources he'd hired John Borgia from Bristol-Myers, where he'd held a similar position. Edgar Jr. had also recruited as vice-chairman and chief financial officer Bob Matschullat, former head of investment banking at Morgan Stanley.

Clarissa made him feel capable and courageous; Edgar Sr. gave him the permission and power. Edgar Sr.'s sincere desire not to shackle his son was laudable; Mr. Sam had certainly held him back. But the freedoms Edgar Sr. granted his son bordered on careless disregard. If Edgar Jr. didn't want to go to college, that was fine with his father. If he chose to produce feature films and Broadway shows, money was available. Bigger projects in his adult years were no different. Buy Time Warner? Get rid of DuPont? Go ahead.

Seagram's stake in DuPont—E.I. du Pont de Nemours & Co., to give the company its full name—had come about in a manner that was both circuitous and serendipitous. Mr. Sam had taken Seagram into energy in 1953 by starting Frankfort Oil Co. in Oklahoma. In 1963, Seagram paid $277 million for Texas Pacific Coal and Oil Co., then merged the acquisition with Frankfort to create Texas Pacific Oil Co. In 1980, Edgar Sr. sold Texas Pacific for $2.3 billion, then set out to reinvest the proceeds.

The first target was St. Joe Minerals Corp. In March 1981, Seagram bid $2.1 billion for St. Joe, but the company fought the acquisition, so Seagram switched targets and offered $2.6 billion for 41 percent of Conoco Inc. At that point DuPont also became interested in Conoco, and ended up paying $7.5 billion in cash and stock for all of Conoco. Seagram took the 27.8 million Conoco shares it had accumulated during the bidding war and converted them into a 20.2 percent stake in DuPont as a kind of consolation prize. "DuPont was the deal of the century. It gave them a stability in the marketplace that few other companies had. They were not exclusively at the mercy of the liquor business any more," says Seagram director Jean de Grandpré, who had also been a director on the DuPont Canada board.

The outcome owed more to blind luck than brilliant planning. Fluor Corp., the successful bidder for St. Joe, struggled for years to make that acquisition work in the face of falling mineral prices. Seagram was far better off with DuPont. Founded in 1802, DuPont was not only the largest chemical company in the U.S., it was also an industrial icon. While DuPont family members still owned shares, professional executives carried out management duties. There was no need for Seagram or the Bronfmans to do anything but wallow in the $120 million in annual dividends that immediately began flowing from DuPont. Seagram used the money to buy more DuPont shares. By 1994, Seagram owned 24 percent of DuPont and had six seats on the DuPont board. The annual dividend had grown to $299 million, an amount that was almost three-quarters of Seagram's annual income.

Despite Edgar Sr.'s historic ties to Seagram's beverage alcohol business or any personal achievement that he might have felt about owning DuPont, he had no difficulty in backing Edgar Jr.'s desire to get into entertainment, thereby moving Seagram away from both beverage alcohol and the DuPont cash cow. "The whiskey business is not a growth business, and you can't ask a forty-year-old chief executive to run a stagnant company," said Edgar Sr. "We could have taken over DuPont, but what fun would it have been to go to Wilmington, Delaware, and run that business?"

In November 1994, as Edgar Jr. was preparing to sell Seagram's DuPont stake, Steve Banner, his confidant and right-hand man, was diagnosed with lung cancer. By January, Banner was no longer coming into the office, but word did reach him that Matsushita Electric Industrial Co. Ltd., Japanese owners since 1990 of MCA Inc., was interested in selling the Hollywood studio. Banner passed the information along but had no further involvement. The cancer progressed quickly; he died in May 1995. Edgar Jr. would employ other chief financial officers, but none with whom he was as close as he had been with Banner.

As Edgar Jr. travelled the world on Seagram business, he couldn't help but notice America's most successful export: culture. Beverage alcohol was one of the first global-brands businesses. Now, everywhere he went, American movies and music were playing, people were wearing logo-bedecked clothing and baseball caps. Entertainment was a world he knew, a world he loved; why not make MCA his? Said Dionne Warwick, who knew entertainment's appeal to Edgar Jr. as well as anyone, "It's something he obviously has always wanted to be a part of."

Lew Wasserman ran MCA, founded in 1924 by ophthalmologist Jules Stein as the Music Corporation of America. He joined in 1936, became president in 1946, and succeeded Stein as chairman in 1973. By then MCA had acquired Universal Studios, begun in 1915 when motion picture pioneer Carl Laemmle created

Universal City with sound stages and several hundred acres of out-door scenery for filming in the San Fernando Valley.

The news about MCA's availability suited Edgar Sr. In 1990, when Edgar Jr. had first started to think about investing in entertainment, MCA had been Edgar Sr.'s first choice for acqui-sition by Seagram. Any possibility of that ended when Matsushita bought MCA. The Japanese had hoped to combine their hardware (TVs, tape decks and VCRs) with MCA's soft-ware (films and music), but the hoped-for synergies never hap-pened. Wasserman had expected the Japanese owners would invest in an expanding MCA, but the Japanese economy crashed. Matsushita had no interest in spending more money, so they foiled all of Wasserman's expansion plans. Relations hit bot-tom in October 1994 when Wasserman flew to Japan to recom-mend MCA buy CBS. He was kept waiting for hours, only to have his idea rejected. "We had gone from a publicly traded, free-standing corporation that was pretty significant in the American stock market to suddenly being listed in the annual report under the category of 'other.' Washing machines was probably a bigger product line for them than the film business," says Blair Westlake, who had joined MCA in 1982 and headed the Pay-TV division during Matsushita's ownership.

Matsushita president Akio Tanii had been replaced by Yoichi Morishita, who could sell MCA without losing face because he had not been a part of the original studio purchase. In order to raise the necessary funds for the deal, Edgar Jr. approached DuPont CEO Edgar S. Woolard Jr. to inquire if Woolard would be interested in buying Seagram's shares. As CEO since 1989, Woolard had drastically altered the DuPont corporate culture from bureaucratic to more entrepreneurial. Job security had been replaced by pay for performance; employment had been reduced by almost one-third. He'd trimmed head office space by half, split the company into twenty separate business units, and set profit targets for individual managers. The payoff was just beginning to become apparent. DuPont's sales in 1994 were up only 6 percent, but net income rose 65 percent to a record $2.7 billion. Woolard was delighted to hear of Edgar Jr.'s interest. Woolard believed share prices would soon respond to growing profits and go higher. For him, now was the time to buy, not sell.

Edgar Jr. pondered the possibilities for much of February, then flew to Palm Beach where Charles had a winter home to tell Charles and Leo Kolber that he intended to acquire MCA with funds from the sale of DuPont. In his memoir, Kolber recounts the meeting, replete with his own internal dialogue. "Junior said that the sale of DuPont wasn't related to the MCA play, which was the silliest damn thing I ever heard. 'We're selling DuPont because it is the right thing to do,' he said, 'not because we are buying something else.' He actually seemed to believe what he was saying. DuPont, he added, was just 'a commodity play.' Some commodities. Nylon, Dacron. Teflon. Textron. As it turned out, the stupidity of it was breathtaking." Charles may have agreed with Kolber, but he did not say no to Edgar Jr.'s plan.

All chief executives were coming under increased pressure to perform. After the high-flying 1980s and the recession that followed in the early 1990s, the economy was growing stronger again. Shareholders, both individual and institutional, wanted to make up for lost time and see share prices rise. Increased sales and higher profits is a slow process; it's always quicker to add productive assets through acquisition. Investment bankers were part of the hype; every time they persuaded a CEO to do a deal, they received hefty fees for their advice. Personal ego also played a role: CEOs enjoy the thrill of the hunt and the accolades that flow when they bag a trophy. In addition to all of those demands, Edgar Jr. had his own personal motives. He wanted to preside over a different business, one where he could be more hands-on rather than clip coupons coming from DuPont. MCA offered him the chance to make that leap, to buy into an exciting sector for which he felt some enthusiasm. He'd take movies over manufacturing any time.

Ancestral echoes also played a role. Ed Falkenberg, a thirty-year veteran who joined Seagram in 1967, in the days of Mr. Sam, saw a parallel between Edgar Jr.'s interest in selling DuPont and the move by Edgar Sr. to sell the Seagram Building in 1979 to the Teachers Insurance & Annuity Association of America for $85.5 million then lease back space. "I always thought that psychologically Edgar Sr. wanted to undo what the father did, and when they sold DuPont I thought the same thing, maybe Junior was undoing what his father had done," said Falkenberg. "His actions were those of an arrogant man. Everything Seagram had, he disposed of it, and then he jumped into Hollywood and he didn't have much experience."

On March 6, Edgar Jr. flew by helicopter from Manhattan to the Westchester airport, where the Seagram fleet was kept. There he boarded his Gulfstream IV for Japan's Kansai International Airport. The Gulfstream IV was the ultimate executive toy, and Seagram owned three of them. Such luxury meant no bother with airline schedules, airport security, or milling about with the great unwashed. Built in Savannah, Georgia, the G-IV started at $35 million and typically came with a dozen club chairs, a three-seat divan that served as a bed, and a shower. The three-member crew included a flight attendant who served meals. Two Rolls-Royce engines permitted non-stop flights of 6,500 nautical miles at 51,000 feet, altitudes usually reserved for military aircraft where there is little turbulence to jostle the occupants. (When the $40-million G-V replaced the G-IV, Seagram bought the first one off the assembly line.)

After the sixteen-hour flight, Edgar Jr. changed from jeans to more appropriate dinner attire. President Yoichi Morishita was pleased Edgar Jr. had brought no entourage of lawyers and advisers, not even a note taker. During the conversation Edgar Jr. drew parallels between Mr. Sam and Konosuke Matsushita, who had founded the company in 1918 and had just died the previous year at ninety-four. Edgar Jr. also spoke passionately about MCA's assets and his personal interest in movies and music.

When the two men met again the next morning, Edgar Jr. said he did not want to participate in an auction for MCA. Morishita agreed to negotiate exclusively with Seagram—with two provisos. First, Morishita wanted to retain a 20 percent interest, so only 80 percent was for sale. Second, Edgar Jr. had to make an offer within two weeks, because Morishita hoped a speedy deal would keep negotiations secret from Lew Wasserman.

The Seagram board met on March 15, 1995, to hear Edgar Jr.'s reasons to sell DuPont and buy MCA. A report from Boston Consulting supported his presentation with details about DuPont's slow-growth future. Goldman Sachs described how the DuPont deal could be structured to reduce taxes. Charles would miss his liaison role with DuPont and the regular dividends of $300 million a year, but for him the biggest loss was DuPont's management. He worried about Edgar Jr.'s capacity to preserve the family fortune without the help from strong management provided by DuPont.

Edgar Sr. backed his son without reservation. Charles agreed to allow discussions to continue as long as Edgar Jr. returned to the board to receive final approval. "The one problem I have with *show* business," Charles was fond of saying, "is that there is *no* business." Charles had put up with Edgar Sr.'s past involvement with MGM; Charles had even made a little money on that deal himself. But his other connection to the entertainment industry was more conservative. The Bronfmans and MCA were both shareholders in Cineplex Odeon Corp., run by Toronto impresario Garth Drabinksy until 1989. The interest continued until Cineplex, by then merged with Loews, was sold in 2001. But Cineplex was not showbiz; it was the exhibition side of the movie business, which is all about real estate, advantageous leases, and squeezing pennies on popcorn costs.

Edgar Jr. flew to Japan again and opened talks by saying MCA was worth $6.5 billion. Yoichi Morishita countered at $7.2 billion. Their respective investment bankers were told to reach a deal. On April 4, *The New York Times* and the *Los Angeles Times* ran stories saying Seagram was in negotiations to buy MCA. Both sides agreed to rush the process, with April 9 as the new deadline. Edgar Jr. flew to Montreal to make sure Charles would approve the deal. "I'm sixty-four years old," said Charles. "I have a billion and a half dollars. What do I need this for?" Replied Edgar Jr.: "You don't need it. The problem is I don't have a lot of other shareholders who have the same profile."

The conversation demonstrated the family's attitude about Seagram and their investment. As far as they were concerned, the family came first, other shareholders came second. The Bronfmans weighed any transaction or possible change in strategy by asking: "What's in it for us?" In a public company such as Seagram, with six thousand shareholders, such an approach was narrow-minded at best and inappropriate at worst. If professional management, rather than a member of the family, had been running Seagram, the priorities would surely have been different. A non-family chief executive who felt he worked for all the shareholders would look at a potential acquisition through a different prism than a family member whose kin controlled the company. As it was, the debate over the MCA acquisition was narrowly focused on what Edgar Jr. wanted to do and whether Charles would let him, rather than on what was right for the company and the best interests of all shareholders. No one asked the question: Does Edgar Jr. have the skills to be an activist operator, or would he be better off remaining a passive manager? For Edgar Jr., his identity was so closely wrapped up in Seagram that, as far as he was concerned, there was no difference between his personal interests and what was best for the corporation.

Edgar Jr. left the meeting without knowing whether Charles would exercise his veto and kill the deal, so Edgar Jr. called in the big guns. On April 5, Edgar Sr. made the same pilgrimage north. After he and Charles had visited their bedridden mother, the two brothers ate lunch in the breakfast room of their boyhood home. (Saidye died three months later at ninety-eight. Charles's son Stephen bought 15 Belvedere from the estate.) Edgar Sr., who had always been a far more adventuresome investor than his conservative brother, pointed out that there was money to be made in movie studios, citing the 1989 sale of Columbia Pictures by Coca-Cola to Sony.

Charles capitulated, not because he'd changed his mind about Hollywood but because he did not want to cause a family feud. "You don't always win every argument," Charles told *The Jerusalem Post* in an interview conducted in 1999. "The only reason I finally said yes, was, one, I wanted the family unified, and two, I knew we weren't endangering the security of Seagram's core assets. Even if things don't go well, we're not imperilling the fundamental value of Seagram, because you can always sell those entertainment companies. Maybe you take something of a hit, but not a serious one."

The Seagram board met in New York on April 6 to formally approve the sale of DuPont. According to the official DuPont corporate history, "Woolard accepted the offer, partly because reducing the number of shares increased their value, but also

because there was little point in holding on to an investor whose
heart was elsewhere." Seagram received $7.7 billion after paying
taxes of $615 million, far less than the $2.1 billion the company
would have paid in capital gains taxes if the deal had been
treated as a simple sale. Seagram went to great lengths to carry
out a convoluted transaction, involving warrants and the reten-
tion of a small portion of stock, so it could describe the payment
from DuPont as a taxable dividend. Congress later changed the
law. (The deal remains contentious. On August 21, 2003, long
after Seagram had been swallowed up by Vivendi, the IRS
announced Vivendi had to pay additional taxes of $1.5 billion,
plus interest, a total of $2.7 billion. Resolution could take sev-
eral more years.)

Edgar Jr. then made his pitch to the board about MCA. "We
can take this company, we can grow it, we can find the right
management, we can make the right decisions," he said. "We're
not going to get screwed by Hollywood." Any Seagram director
who had concerns about selling DuPont or buying MCA kept
quiet. "I just can't figure out why the hell we let the golden goose
go and took on this other stuff," says Ed McDonnell, former
president of the spirits and wine group, and a Seagram director
at the time. "I think the trouble with the Seagram board, and
I'm a classic example of it, is insider board members. That's
something that you should never have. I voted the party line,
and [so did] everybody else that was inside and a lot of the outside board members that were close to the family. There was
never any public discussions that were provocative and stimu-
lating in terms of really assessing the strategy that was being proposed and carried through. Clearly, Edgar Jr.'s first love has
always been the entertainment business, and he sincerely
believed that it was the thing of the future for the family and he
obviously convinced them that that's what he should do."

Being an insider, as McDonnell defined it, was seen as a privilege, whether as a Seagram director, executive officer, or lowly employee. It's not that the people who work at family-run companies are any less competent than those who work elsewhere, but they are different, and they accept the fact that they toil in a different culture. Working for Seagram meant working for the Bronfman family and feeling honoured to be in their service. You weren't just doing any job in society; it was like working at Buckingham Palace. You might only be a backstairs butler, but there was a certain cachet involved.

As the elder statesman, one of Edgar Sr.'s self-appointed roles was making managers feel special and ensuring the continuum of that culture. Shortly after Donard Gaynor joined the spirits and wine division in 1992, he attended a dinner for Seagram executives and their spouses at Edgar Sr.'s Fifth Avenue apartment, with its unimpeded views of Central Park. "You're joining a family here," Edgar Sr. said to Gaynor, and then swung into a mock wedding ceremony. "Do you accept the family? Say 'I do.'" He then turned to Gaynor's wife, Janet, and said, "Do you accept the family? Say 'I do.'" After the oaths were taken, he announced, "OK, you're members of the family." Some might see Edgar Sr.'s little ceremony as silly. Gaynor saw a point to the exercise. "There was a recognition by all the people at that [event] that I was joining at a senior enough level to be taken seriously."

Being accepted into service also meant never coming to either Edgar Sr. or Edgar Jr. with a problem for them to solve. "Ultimately you can come to me, but just know that the first time you come to me to solve a problem will probably be the last time," Gaynor was told. "You were very much reminded that they stood apart, and only in the most exceptional of circumstances would you ever even consider going there. I saw many people at Seagram over the years make the mistake of thinking that they were not only part of the family—because it had a very family-like atmosphere—but they could *behave* like a member of the family. That would stretch to how they regarded themselves in the company of the Bronfmans, or in some cases I'm sure it would be professing title to certain privileges in life. The Bronfmans would get very upset about that."

That kind of culture meant less rigorous scrutiny of ideas and too few rough-and-tumble debates where all sides were heard and all outcomes considered. When Seagram officers or investment bankers made presentations to board committees or the full board, directors would ask questions, but approval on any matter was always a foregone conclusion. The Seagram board was like the good fairy; the family's wishes were always granted. Regular board meetings were scheduled for six or eight times a year, usually in the second-floor boardroom of the Peel Street headquarters in Montreal. Meetings would start at 10 A.M. and last until 1 P.M., when lunch was served. Since the early 1970s, by order of Edgar Sr., the menu always included smoked-meat sandwiches like those he'd grown up eating at Ben's Delicatessen in Montreal. "Edgar Sr., and at some stages Charles, did a lot of lobbying pre-board-meeting to make arguments about accepting this or accepting that. I don't remember any really controversial things happening at board meetings," says Mel Griffin, who retired in 1988 after ten years as a director.

At a family-controlled company like Seagram, directors accept certain constraints from the moment they agree to join. Here's how one director, who spoke on the condition of anonymity, described the dilemma. "When you agree to become a director, you willingly become one of those people who's going to help this person. He comes to the board and says, 'We have this opportunity.' You're not totally sold, but you don't know how to put him off. If you say, 'I'm not going to approve that deal,' what you're doing is pulling the rug out from under the one person that you've gone on the board to help." A year might pass before another difficult issue arises. "You say, 'One more and I blow the whistle.' But the third occasion takes another year, at which point you say, 'Why did I take three years to get rid of this guy?' These guys like to look decisive, like they're leaders. They all say [during acquisition negotiations] this is all subject to the approval of my board. Then the board says to themselves, 'If we don't let him do this, he's going to look like an ass.'"

Edgar Jr. had both a compliant board and the unconditional support of his father. "It was absolutely unbelievable, the respect and admiration they had for each other. Neither Junior nor his father would ever say anything against the other. It was a mutual admiration society," says McDonnell. That agreeable mood extended to Charles. William Davis, a former premier of Ontario who was on the Seagram board from 1985 to 1999, states: "My recollections at the board meetings was that while one might sense reservations by whoever, I don't recall ever hearing Charles say, 'I don't think we should be doing this.' Whether he may have felt this, I don't know. Never in my recollection was the board put in the position where a significant part of the family was not in support of what was being presented." In the face of such family unity, directors took the hint. If Charles did not feel strongly enough to exercise his veto and stop Edgar Jr.—let alone even bring up the topic for discussion—why would they kick up a fuss?

The final round of negotiations with MCA took place in the New York offices of Seagram's lawyers, Simpson Thacher. On Friday, April 7, the one remaining element, price, was settled during a two-hour telephone call between Edgar Jr. in New York and Morishita in Osaka. Edgar Jr. agreed to pay $5.7 billion for 80 percent of MCA, an amount that valued MCA at $7.125 billion, much closer to Morishita's initial estimate of $7.2 billion than Edgar Jr.'s $6.5 billion. Matsushita kept the stipulated 20 percent. Comedian Dennis Miller later joked it was the first time Seagram had ever left a fifth on the table.

Despite his inability to persuade Morishita to move very far from his price, Edgar Jr. was praised by industry players such as Barry Diller and Herb Allen, whose advice Edgar Jr. had sought. "He really went and seduced the Japanese to make what was really a solid, good deal for Seagram," says Barry Diller. "The results appeared effortless, which is what you want in any kind of an acquisition. The reason it was so flawlessly executed is that it was secretly done, with great stealth." Says Allen: "Obviously, the inflamed issue of the day was should he have sold DuPont in order to buy MCA? I think it was an issue of principle. Did he want to become an operating company or did he want to continue to be effectively a one-stock mutual fund? He wanted to be more aggressive in an operating business and didn't believe that the liquor business had as much of a future as the other did. He set out to do that, he accomplished his objectives." Allen offered the ultimate accolade by inviting Edgar Jr. to make the opening presentation at his annual Sun Valley gathering of entertainment bigwigs that summer.

The "inflamed issue" would last longer than just the day. According to analyst and author Harold Vogel, "This will dog Edgar forever in terms of 'Why did you sell the DuPont? You could have made much more on the DuPont than you ever made with MCA.' He didn't understand the media and entertainment business. He was taken in by the hype of Wall Street and by the hype of the people in the business."

With the deal set to be signed on April 9 in Los Angeles, all three of Seagram's Gulfstream IVs were pressed into service to transport the two Edgars and their entourage of senior executives, investment bankers, attorneys, and other advisers. In the air, Edgar Jr. fretted about the documents. He turned to one of the lawyers who drew up the papers and asked if he was certain there were no errors. He assured Edgar Jr. that they had been checked and double-checked. "Do me a favour," said Edgar Jr. "Go to the back of the plane and read through the deal again." The lawyer did so and reported that every page was letter-perfect.

After landing at Santa Monica Airport, Edgar Jr. and Edgar Sr. registered at the Biltmore Hotel under phony names in one last ploy to maintain secrecy. In New York, the Seagram board met at 5 p.m. Eastern time to approve the purchase. Everyone, including Charles, voted yes. John L. Weinberg abstained, saying that he had a conflict because his firm, Goldman Sachs, had advised the Japanese.

When the signing ceremony with the Japanese at the Biltmore was completed, there were toasts with Perrier-Jouët champagne, a Seagram brand with its distinctive green "flower bottle" decorated with handcrafted anemones.

According to Edgar Sr., he and a grumpy Charles had a conversation sometime later about the acquisition that went like this:

"Now the rules are that if you say 'no,' we don't do it. Did you ever say no?"

"Well, no, but . . ."

"Charles, did you ever say no?"

"No. I didn't want to start a family feud."

"There probably would have been one, but if you had said no, we wouldn't have made the deal. Now stop it. We've already made the deal. Let's get on with it."

The words and the tone demonstrate how easily the brothers reverted to their traditional family roles. Edgar Jr. had also remained right in character, letting his father help smooth his way forward. As CEO, Edgar Jr. received no more direction from Edgar Sr. than he had as an indulged teenager. For different reasons, Charles also let Edgar Jr. have his way, but the outcome was the same. As for the Seagram board, the directors were little more than a Hallelujah chorus. No one took a stand or tried to rally support for another view. It was as if Seagram were running on remote control, dependent on good luck rather than good management.

SIX

MOVING IN

THOM MOUNT WAS VISITING his parents in North Carolina when Edgar Jr. called him and asked: "Guess where I am?"

"Mars."

"No, but close. I'm standing in your living room."

"My living room?"

"Yes, I just bought your old beach house, Number One Malibu Colony. It was always my favourite house in all of Los Angeles, and this is where I'm going to live."

"God bless you. I'm delighted. May I ask a stupid question? How much did you pay for it?"

"Five million."

"Remind me not to sell it the next time."

In the art world, the provenance of a painting is established when an auction house is able to trace previous ownership to ensure authenticity. Number One Malibu Colony certainly had the proper provenance. Edgar Jr. bought the house from Bob Newhart who'd bought it from Robert Redford who'd bought it from Mount in 1983. The house was originally built by Bing Crosby with the royalties he received from "White Christmas."

Architecturally, the house is more New England than California; Mount calls it a Connecticut cottage on steroids. The main floor of the four-bedroom dwelling is dominated by a massive stone fireplace in a vaulted great room with kitchen and dining areas. There are panoramic views past a white flagpole on a patch of grass, over a white picket fence, and across a stretch of beach to the Pacific Ocean beyond. There's also a guest house, servants' quarters, a gazebo, a garage, and an outdoor lap pool, the latter installed by Edgar Jr.

No longer was he the struggling young producer living in rented digs on Escondido Beach, scrambling for deals. He now dwelt in Malibu Colony, home to the stars since 1928, including such contemporary household names as Tom Hanks, Dyan Cannon, and Larry Hagman. Bootlegging be gone. Edgar Bronfman Jr. had better things to do than taste the Glenlivet. He now bestrode Hollywood as one of half a dozen moguls presiding over the world's biggest dream factory. Movies, music, television, and theme parks were all about moxie and money and marketing—and wasn't he an expert in all of those? Andrew Birkin, his friend from *Melody*, wrote to Edgar Jr. exhorting him to enjoy his prize, saying, "I hope you'll take courage in both hands and now go out and direct a movie. What an amazing opportunity. You own a studio—Citizen Kane."

Edgar Jr. had just turned forty when he bought MCA, the same age as his father had been when he enjoyed his brief stay atop another movie studio, MGM. If ever a boy had beaten his father at his own game, while at the same time restoring the family reputation in Hollywood, surely this was such an occasion. Edgar Jr. began his new life as the very model of a modern major studio owner, using a technique known as management by wandering around. Jay Boberg, who with partner Miles Copeland had started IRS Records and run it for fourteen years, had sold the independent label and joined MCA in October 1994 as head of the music publishing division. A few weeks after the announcement that MCA had been sold, Boberg's assistant buzzed him to say, "There's a guy named Edgar Bronfman here to see you." "Yeah, right," replied Boberg, only to have the new owner appear in his doorway. "He came across as the nicest, most unassuming, smart music guy. He knew music, records, songs. He knew the business," says Boberg. "He had taken the time to get my background. He talked about how important music publishing was and asked me what my thoughts were. That was the start of a very good relationship. He was very supportive." Ron Bension, CEO of the theme park division, met Edgar Jr. briefly during one of his early visits. When Bension next saw Edgar Jr. three months later, "He remembered my name. I was impressed. That's a learned skill, but he was brilliant at that. You wanted to work for him."

In April, Edgar toured the Universal lot, met senior executives, and spoke at the opening dinner of a three-day retreat held by the motion picture group. Among the one hundred who met in Palm Springs were creative executives, marketing and distribution staff, as well as the attorneys and accountants who worked with them. Edgar Jr. recounted how he'd gone over budget on *The Border*. The haphazard work ethic of Jack Nicholson was blamed, so Ned Tanen, the senior studio executive who had approved the movie, visited the set to admonish Nicholson. Before returning to Los Angeles, Tanen told Edgar Jr. and director Tony Richardson that Nicholson had promised to be more accommodating. Edgar Jr. visited Nicholson in his trailer and asked, "So, it's all solved?" As he recounted the story, Edgar Jr. paused for effect and then said, "Jack just winked at me."

Edgar Jr. also related how he'd run afoul of the Universal bureaucracy. He wanted to repaint the interior of his bungalow

and get rid of the institutional green that was the only hue permitted during the days of Jules Stein and his wife, Doris. The
request was referred higher and higher, until he finally got the
go-ahead from Tanen himself.

People laughed at such tales, but they also wondered if
Edgar Jr. wasn't trapped in a time warp, believing that the place
hadn't changed in the fifteen years since he'd been on the lot. As
for Tanen, he grew tired of hearing reports of Edgar Jr.'s paint
story. "The asshole only had one encounter with me," says
Tanen. "He never had a problem *with* me, maybe he had a problem getting *to* me." Tanen said his response at the time was simple: "If he wanted to paint his office, he should paint it."

Edgar Jr. now owned a piece of Hollywood history and the studio his father had encouraged him to buy in 1990. With its
library of 3,500 movies and 16,000 hours of television programming, MCA was part of the family kingdom. The music division
was profitable, with rock groups Aerosmith and Guns N' Roses,
country stars Reba McIntyre and Vince Gill, as well as pop
singers Mary J. Blige and Patti LaBelle. The television division,
however, had lost $40 million in 1994, and movies were yielding
a return on investment somewhere between 1 percent and 5 percent, depending on the year, but that was an industry-wide phe-
nomenon. In the theme park business, Disney was the leader.
Universal was a profitable but distant second, with Universal
Studios Hollywood, built thirty years earlier, and Universal
Studios Florida, opened in 1990, as well as Islands of Adventure,
planned for Orlando. The latter two were jointly owned with
The Rank Organisation.

Other family dynasties had bought into the Hollywood
mystique. In the 1920s, Joseph Kennedy, father of the president,

was chairman of Pathe Pictures during that free-booting era when Jules Stein was booking singers into the same speakeasies that were being supplied with booze from Seagram.

The studio's next blockbuster was supposed to be Kevin Costner's *Waterworld,* at $175 million the most expensive movie ever made. As part of the negotiations with the Japanese, Edgar Jr. had limited his participation in any loss to a maximum of $50 million, which was just as well since the picture went on to do poorly. Edgar Jr. believed that his 1982 box office flop had taught him how to succeed. "*The Border* was a good picture, but it wasn't a great picture. It had a sufficiently downbeat kind of quality. Those are the kind of pictures that have got to be great pictures. If you don't turn in a great picture, that kind of movie doesn't work. It gives me a better ability to understand and manage the business than if the picture I had made had been a great success."

Journalists were divided about Edgar Jr.'s prospects. According to a *Forbes* calculation, MCA was worth $9 billion at the time of the acquisition, so by that arithmetic Edgar Jr.'s 80 percent, for which he paid $5.7 billion, was actually worth $7.2 billion. Within five years, the magazine said, the value of Edgar Jr.'s Universal holdings could be worth more than $13 billion. Other commentators questioned his management prowess. "As far as I know [he] has never done a successful deal at Seagram," said Allan Sloan of *Newsweek.* "All he's managed to do in Hollywood is write a big check." *The Wall Street Journal* dubbed Edgar Jr. "the star-struck whiskey king."

The media's dismissive view of Edgar Jr. in Hollywood became common wisdom. There was no honeymoon, no wait-and-see period during which observers offered him a chance to settle in. Seagram shareholders also seemed to lack confidence. "You're taking us on a voyage, a very turbulent voyage," warned a shareholder at the standing-room-only Seagram annual meeting held in Montreal on May 31, 1995. "The world is looking at you very, very carefully." A money manager urged that Seagram be broken into separate units, movies and booze, so investors could choose between the two rather than have to invest in one behemoth with twenty-four thousand employees, double the number a year earlier. Nothing captured the change in corporate direction more vividly than the video shown that day. Westmount ladies with blue-rinsed hair winced as they watched dinosaurs chasing Jeff Goldblum, B.B. King singing the blues, and Jean-Claude Van Damme beating up on the bad guys.

In the months that followed, Seagram directors enjoyed discussing the new topics that appeared on the board agenda. Entertainment was intrinsically more interesting than manufacturing schedules and distillery reports. "When you were told the dividend from DuPont this quarter was this, and Crown Royal went up another half a percent in share, or we were looking at Absolut and men having to visit Sweden, that didn't compare with second-guessing what movies were being produced," says former director William Davis. "We were all experts, television, movies, music. I tell you, it was a far more interesting board meeting. Some of us were constructively helpful in how the theme park should evolve. When you have twelve grandchildren, you know far more about that than whether or not any of them are going to end up drinking Crown Royal."

Edgar Jr.'s immediate problem was the recent departure from Universal of Steven Spielberg, maker of the studio's biggest hits, including: *E.T. The Extra-Terrestrial* in 1982 and *Jurassic Park* in 1993. In conjunction with Jeffrey Katzenberg and David Geffen, Spielberg had started a new studio, DreamWorks. Edgar Jr. wanted at least a distribution deal with DreamWorks. Dispatched to negotiate on behalf of DreamWorks was Geffen, who had made his fortune by founding record companies then selling out to MCA. As a major shareholder in MCA, Geffen cashed out holdings of $700 million when the Japanese bought the studio. Edgar Jr. decided to appeal to Geffen's sense of fairness. "I don't want this to be a protracted, difficult, unfriendly negotiation," said Edgar Jr. "Let me tell you exactly what's going to happen. You're going to tell me what the deal is, and I'm going to say yes." And so they agreed in June 1995 to a ten-year arrangement by which Universal was granted international distribution rights to DreamWorks films, as well as domestic rights to home videos and music.

Although Edgar Jr.'s approach may have appeared to be naive and one-sided, his one-time investment of $54 million did end up generating $50 million in annual revenue for Universal. Moreover, Edgar Jr. ensured a continuing relationship between Universal and Spielberg that included *The Lost World,* the sequel to *Jurassic Park,* as well as the right to use DreamWorks movies in Universal's theme parks. Even doing well, however, didn't make Edgar Jr. feel he was on solid footing. As he and Geffen prepared to announce their deal at a news conference to be held at Universal Studios in June, Edgar Jr. politely asked a studio employee if he would make a minor change to the physical set-up. Geffen was taken aback by his modest demeanour. Most Hollywood bosses would announce instructions, knowing exactly what they wanted, assuming that they would be carried out immediately.

Edgar Jr. contributed to the growing perception that he was poorly equipped for the ruthlessness of Hollywood by repeatedly telling a particular story about himself. Both he and his brother Sam had attended Collegiate until Sam was sent in the tenth grade to Deerfield Academy, a boarding school in Massachusetts. Edgar Sr. thought Edgar Jr. might benefit from a similar move. Unable to accompany his son on the interviews, he sent Edgar Jr. alone on the corporate plane. Asked one New England headmaster, "Are you here with your father?" "No," replied Edgar Jr., "I'm here with my pilot." Edgar Jr. liked the anecdote because he saw it as an example of his youthful self-reliance. Most denizens of Hollywood, who came from more humble backgrounds and had fought their way to the top by whatever means necessary, wondered if a coddled Edgar Jr. would ever survive their cutthroat world.

Patsy Puttnam, who had lived in Hollywood in the 1980s when her husband ran Columbia, suspected that Edgar Jr. was motivated to return to the entertainment business both by his sense of filial duty and by a need to settle his own old scores. "He is trying to be the son that will make his father proud. I can only imagine it's 'two fingers up to Hollywood' when they probably treated him very badly when he was a young kid, and he wanted to get back at them." But she also worried whether he really understood that world or was tough enough to fend off their wiles. "Here he was going in with his own studio and his own money. Those people, my God, they smell out money so quickly. It's a world that shafts you."

As had been the case with Tropicana, Edgar Jr. had bought a company in a sector of the economy where none of his Seagram colleagues had any personal experience or professional expertise. He needed help fast, so he set out to hire Michael Ovitz, chairman of Creative Artists Agency (CAA), as his CEO. Ovitz had built an agency that represented stars such as Tom Hanks, Demi Moore, and Kevin Costner. Edgar Jr. had retained Ovitz when he acquired Time Warner shares as well as on the MCA transaction. Now he wanted Ovitz full-time. The plan was for Ovitz to bring with him a team that would include two other CAA founders, Ron Meyer and Bill Haber. Reports at the time said Ovitz demanded a compensation package, including an equity stake in MCA, worth $250 million. According to Bernard Dick's *City of Dreams,* the history of Universal, the equity portion was as much as $285 million plus a salary for Ovitz of $50 million, $25 million worth of Seagram stock, and bonuses, for a total of at least $360 million.

Whatever the precise numbers, Charles told Edgar Jr. that Ovitz's demands were out of line. For once, Edgar Sr. agreed with his brother. Edgar Jr. reduced the value of the deal, asked Ovitz to invest some of his own money in MCA, and told him he'd have to take a greater portion of his compensation in stock options. Ovitz recoiled at the notion that other Bronfmans might have a say in the matter; he thought it made Edgar Jr. look weak. Also getting in the way of an agreement was the fact that while Ovitz might be able to bargain well on behalf of his clients, he could not close a deal for himself. At one point he and Edgar Jr. seemed to have reached an understanding, but Ovitz could not stop raising new issues. Edgar Jr. interrupted, asking: "Can't we just enjoy the moment?"

In fact, the man and the moment were gone. Edgar Jr. later claimed he never made a formal offer to Ovitz. "Part of the negotiation with each other was learning about each other," said Edgar Jr. "The more we talked, the more it became clear to me that this would be a difficult dynamic." On Monday, June 5, Ovitz announced to his staff at CAA's weekly meeting that he was staying put. (Ovitz soon found another suitor. In October he was named president of Walt Disney Co. He lasted little more than a year, leaving in December 1996 with a severance package worth $100 million.)

For Edgar Jr., the timing of Ovitz's pullout from the talks couldn't have been worse. He was having lunch that same day with the top twenty MCA executives in the private dining room at the back of the Universal commissary. Edgar Jr. sat in the middle of one of the long sides of the antique dining-room table. He faced a wallpapered hunting scene, his back to a mirrored wall. With Lew Wasserman on his right and MCA president Sid Sheinberg on his left, Edgar Jr. glumly told the group that Ovitz would not be joining MCA, then added, "There is no Plan B." Wasserman was relieved. Not normally a man to share his views spontaneously with such a large group, Wasserman said that while he had not consulted anyone else in the room, as far as he was concerned this was the most positive news he'd heard in a long time.

With Ovitz out of the picture, Edgar Jr. next turned his sights on Ovitz's partner at CAA, Ron Meyer. Meyer had grown up in a tough Los Angeles neighbourhood. He joined the Marines at seventeen before graduating from high school, then in 1963 started his Hollywood career in the mailroom of a small talent agency. "He saw [MCA] as a sleeping giant that had enormous untapped potential," says Meyer. "It had been a company that had not moved into the next century. Edgar saw an opportunity, given the times and the technology and what was available. He felt that it had all the potential to be built into one of the leading entertainment companies in the industry. I think he felt it had not attracted necessarily the right personnel and the right talent to do that."

Meyer was named president and chief operating officer on July 10 with a five-year contract worth $50 million plus performance bonuses. The fact that Meyer's title was one notch below the CEO role Edgar Jr. had offered Ovitz caused some at Universal to think that Edgar Jr. might assume a more hands-on role for himself.

Meyer arrived on a Monday. Sid Sheinberg had left the previous Friday. Edgar Jr. gave Sheinberg and his two sons, Jonathan and Bill, a lucrative movie deal, but they delivered duds such as *Flipper* and *McHale's Navy* that cost Universal more than $100 million before Edgar Jr. cancelled the deal in 1997. Edgar Jr. appointed Wasserman chairman emeritus, gave him a $1-million annual consulting fee, put him on the Seagram board, and named Universal's head office, known as the Black Tower, after him. Wasserman continued to come to work daily at 9 A.M., would call some cronies, then at 12:30 go for lunch in the commissary. At 1:45 P.M., Wasserman's driver would escort him out a side door to his Mercedes-Benz and drive home the last of the Hollywood moguls.

When it came to former management, Edgar Sr. did not show the same magnanimous behaviour. In December 1995, Edgar Jr. organized a testimonial dinner for Lew and Edie Wasserman on a Universal sound stage attended by studio personnel and stars such as Angela Lansbury, Jamie Lee Curtis, and Charlton Heston. Edgar Jr. announced a $1-million donation to the Motion Picture & Television Fund in honour of the couple. During the event Edgar Sr. looked around and loudly asked, "Efer, what are all these people doing in *our* room?"

With the *ancien régime* safely bought off, Edgar Jr. changed the corporate name from MCA Inc. to Universal Studios Inc., a brand that he planned to apply to every division: movies, TV, music, and theme parks. While that move suggested he had arrived with a grand new vision in mind, much of his energy was wasted on cosmetics. He renovated the commissary and hired a gourmet chef. He renamed the streets on the Universal lot in honour of singers such as Ella Fitzgerald, Jimi Hendrix, and Buddy Holly. He commandeered Jules Stein's former offices on the top floor and replaced the George III furniture with a more contemporary look. Clarissa became involved and brought in their New York decorator. When other executives saw what was happening, they hired their own designers and also acquired fine art. After the work was complete, Edgar Jr. decided that he was unhappy. The elevator didn't go to sixteen; everyone had to walk up from the floor below. He moved to a smaller office on the fourteenth floor and converted part of his former suite to a personal gym, keeping his boardroom for executive meetings.

To Edgar Jr., image was everything. He wanted a West Coast symbol that would be equivalent to the architectural statement Mr. Sam had made in the East. Where the Seagram Building on Park Avenue was all grace and grandeur, to Edgar Jr. the Black Tower looked dreary and decrepit. He hired Dutch architect Rem Koolhaas to design a new headquarters complex on the 420-acre Universal lot. Edgar Jr. gave Koolhaas a free hand; his only instruction was to get rid of the Black Tower. Koolhaas produced a $400-million design that included a second theme park and a group of office towers with oversized windows that could be opened to let in the breezes.

Within six months of the June 1995 acquisition, most of Wasserman's top dozen executives were gone. Among the few old hands who did stay, no one lasted long. CFO Dick Baker remained for a while to help on a short-term project; Tom Pollock, the former chairman of the motion picture group, was named a vice-chairman by Edgar Jr. but left in March 1996. Ron Bension, head of theme park division when Edgar Jr. took over, set the record for longevity by remaining until the end of 1996. "There were certain people we spoke about in some cases, but I don't think for Edgar or for me that was an easy decision to make. We both had to be here awhile to see from the inside out who fit with what our plans were and who didn't," says Meyer. "Some left of their own accord, some left because we felt it wasn't going to work, and some contracts ran out. Changing the culture required changing people."

Meyer hired as executive vice-presidents two of his friends who he knew would be loyal to him. Sandy Climan, a CAA colleague skilled in strategy and business development, oversaw consumer products, pay TV, home video, and new media. Howard Weitzman, a high-profile litigator who had successfully defended John DeLorean on cocaine charges and was O.J. Simpson's first lawyer on his murder charge, ran human resources, studio operations, and real estate.

In November, Edgar Jr. promoted Casey Silver, who had joined Universal Pictures in 1987, to chairman of Universal Pictures. He hired Greg Meidel, formerly of Fox and Paramount, as chairman of the television group.

Edgar Jr. also added to the mix Doug Morris, whom he'd hired earlier. In June 1995, when Morris was fired after seventeen years with Warner Music, Edgar Jr. had called him and told him to go see *The Shawshank Redemption,* the prison movie in which Andy, played by Tim Robbins, spends years tunnelling his way to freedom. Andy leaves money hidden outside so Red, played by Morgan Freeman, can join Andy in Mexico. "I've seen the movie, why?" asked Morris. "Because I'm the guy waiting on the beach for you," replied Edgar Jr.

The two shared more than a taste for the same movies. Like Edgar Jr., Morris had also written songs. His biggest hit, co-written with Eliot Greenberg, was "Sweet Talkin' Guy," recorded by the Chiffons in 1966. "Since I was a young boy, I was always interested in putting together melodies and words and hearing how they came out. It was thrilling to me," says Morris. "It was the same thing with him. He was fascinated by anything he would write. He'd play it over and over again, the same as any songwriter. The last thing you write is the one you like the most, for that moment."

Edgar Jr. hired Morris to start a new label, Rising Tide Records, a word play on his beach analogy, and agreed to invest up to $100 million. "You know how you have a feeling about someone when you meet them, you either have a good vibe or a bad vibe. I liked him enormously. He's a very seductive, charming man," says Morris. "He is a person who gives off a feeling of understanding what a person is about. He feels like a musician when you meet him. All my life I've dealt with musicians and that's what he felt like. He is not a musician, but he has a tremendous love for music. It's a passion."

When Al Teller, head of the music division, left, Edgar Jr. named Morris to run all of Universal Music. Morris quickly expanded the division. In March 1996, Universal paid $200 million for half of Interscope Records, founded in 1990 by Jimmy Iovine, thereby increasing Universal's market share in music from 8 percent to 14 percent. "That really changed the culture of this group of companies forever," says Morris. "When you're in front of the parade with cutting-edge music, all of the other artists look at it and admire it. All of a sudden, wow, Universal [was] hot on the East Coast, Interscope on the West Coast. Suddenly, we were a force to be reckoned with."

The purchase of Interscope, known for its urban music, also meant distributing songs with lyrics that celebrated sex and violence, sung by artists such as Dr. Dre, Tupac, and Nine Inch Nails. Interscope was already under political pressure from Washington. Edgar Jr. promised legislators that Interscope would not release songs with lyrics that were too controversial. "The fact that he had personal relationships with members of the Senate and they understood him to be a decent guy and a moral guy helped when we were under the gun on lyrics. In particular, some artists from his company—Marilyn Manson and Eminem— were getting lots of negative attention," says Hilary Rosen, president and CEO of the Recording Industry Association of America. "Edgar's personal credibility significantly helped that issue because people didn't believe he was the kind of guy who would do that. That made a big difference."

In addition to hiring experienced Hollywood types, Edgar Jr. named Seagram executive Bruce Hack to be Universal's chief financial officer. "As the owner, he was not afraid to say you were doing well or not. He would ask for explanations about why we should do things that we recommended," says Hack, who had joined Seagram's treasury department in 1982 and had previously been CFO of Tropicana. "The intensity of his involvement was rather extreme. If you sent him an e-mail, you heard back immediately. [Universal Music president] Zach Horowitz and I used to say that Edgar was the fastest e-mail response we had."

Edgar Jr.'s executive appointments met with cautious approval from those who had known the rigours of the Wasserman regime. "Edgar wanted a fresh look when he came out, and I think made a serious effort to give it a different feel and a different look," says Ron Olson, an attorney with Munger, Tolles and Olson of Los Angeles who had represented Universal for twenty years. The previous corporate culture had been ultra-conservative. "They emphasized stability. They were hard-nosed business people. They were able to see around the corner of deals in Hollywood probably faster than anybody. For anybody to step into those shoes there would be differences, and particularly differences for somebody who hadn't grown up in the industry."

Of all Edgar Jr.'s moves, the hiring of Ron Meyer and Doug Morris drew the widest praise. "I think Doug Morris is the single best operator in the music business and Ron Meyer is the single best operator in the film business. Disney attracts good people, they just can't keep them," says Laura Martin, who was at the time a California-based entertainment analyst with Credit Suisse First Boston. With the arrival of Edgar Jr. she saw a drastic change from the Wasserman–Sheinberg era. "Universal became more business-oriented, more Wall Street friendly. Edgar Jr. cared a lot more about cash flow. There was more emphasis on less waste, lower expenses, and fewer parties. From a Wall Street point of view, as someone who allocates capital, you're more willing to allocate capital to a firm that's becoming more efficient in its use of that capital."

Edgar Jr.'s initial plan to spend up to four days a week at Universal didn't last. According to Blair Westlake, then executive vice-president of the home entertainment group, "What Edgar set out to do, and what he eventually did, didn't line up. He thought he'd spend more time in Los Angeles. If there are 250 or 260 business days in a year, I don't think Edgar was on the property more than 30, maybe 40. He was still running the company based at 375 Park Avenue."

The best CEOs don't try to manage all aspects of their company; they hire the right people, give them responsibility, then check in from time to time. But Edgar Jr. had initially seemed so eager to be more closely involved in running Universal that his pullback was unusual. Ron Meyer initiated a Monday meeting of Universal's dozen senior managers. Edgar Jr. attended in person perhaps once a month, participating in other meetings by video conference. "He was out here enough to know what was going on," says Meyer, who spoke by phone to Edgar Jr. daily. "He was very hands-on as far as understanding the finances of the company and the P&L [profit and loss] of the company."

Edgar Jr.'s management style may have worked for some of his senior executives, but others got side-swiped. Says Ron Bension, who joined Universal in 1971 as a sweeper and worked his way up to head the theme park division: "There were a lot of decision makers in the decision making. You never knew what was real and what was Memorex, what was Howard [Weitzman] and Sandy [Climan] trying to create their own agendas and what was really coming down from Edgar. There was this cloak of secrecy and whispering. It was just craziness, in my opinion. There's always politics in a big company, but the thing about Lew and Sid was that you could argue with them. You could push back with them." Part of the problem was that Edgar Jr.'s views weren't consistent, he could send mixed signals. "He would be very open and friendly in meetings, but then the bad news would come down, through others, the next day or two or three days later. I found him to be very pleasant and gentlemanly, but it was difficult to have a substantive face-to-face with him," says Bension.

But whenever ownership of any organization changes, some people fall by the wayside as the new owner heads in a different direction and hires new blood. "The team that he put together at the record company is a really strong team. He has an affinity for that business and did a good job of assembling a team, motivating, and creating an esprit de corps," says Gordon Crawford, an influential institutional investor at Capital Research and Management in Los Angeles. "It took a while, but he put together a good team at Universal. There aren't a lot of good people. Getting people who have both good business sense and the creative flair to deal with the creative process—there is probably less than one handful of people that you'd really trust with the keys to a big record company or a big movie company."

DuPont was gone, replaced by the more unpredictable Universal. Seagram was no longer the solid performer of old, and some securities analysts were dubious about Edgar Jr.'s new vision for the family firm. Michael Palmer, an analyst with First Associates Investments of Toronto, says: "On the street it became a far more promotional company. The emphasis on EBITDA (earnings before interest, taxes, depreciation, and amortization), the whole accounting, the whole presentation to the street changed. Instead of just being stodgy old Seagram there was a deliberate attempt to structure the numbers in such a way that the market would like. The whole thing went from being a company that was interested in generating cash to being a quasi stock promotion company. It was a huge change."

Change had only just begun.

SEVEN

RE-ENGINEERING THE CORPORATION

IN JANUARY 1996, EDGAR JR. invited Universal's top eighty executives to a downtown Los Angeles hotel. Their only instruction was to wear jeans; this was going to be an informal, working session. Now that his new team was in place, Edgar Jr. wanted to alter the corporate culture by getting rid of what he saw as the "silo" mentality of the Wasserman era, where employees in each division kept to themselves and did not talk to anyone in the other areas.

In his speech to the gathering, Edgar Jr. set out his goals. He wanted hit movies, of course, but he also wanted to expand TV production through USA Network and Sci-Fi Channel. He declared he was going to take on Disney's preeminence by opening new theme parks, both in Florida and outside North America. He sought to globalize the music division as well. Sales were largely in the U.S.; he intended to increase artists' international exposure. Edgar Jr. assured the group that he was there for the long haul, he was someone who believed in buying, improving, and keeping companies. He pointed out that he and others at Seagram had experience in marketing that would benefit Universal in the years ahead.

So far, so good. Employees had waited more than six months to get a sense of his leadership beyond the changes he'd made to senior management. Then Edgar Jr. dropped a bombshell. Universal would undergo re-engineering. In his mind, re-engineering would lead to new ways of approving scripts, producing TV shows, or distributing home videos. He promised financial rewards for directors who delivered pictures on time, a shocking concept for the creative mind. Everyone was given a stack of reading material to take with them. Among the handouts was *Control Your Destiny or Someone Else Will,* a book about how re-engineering revolutionized General Electric.

Re-engineering, which had become popular during the recession of the early 1990s, was a rigorous method for totally rethinking the way work was done and then redesigning entire processes. On its simplest level, a company might ask: Do so many people need to receive monthly sales figures? Let's save time and money by reducing the circulation of such reports. Or the study could go deeper and devise a new way to produce widgets using different material and fewer steps, so widgets cost less and are more durable. For many companies, however, re-engineering was all about improving productivity and reducing costs by firing employees. While the hoped-for outcome of re-engineering is arguably beneficial—more productivity and higher profits—the path can be chaotic and clogged with consultants trying to push through changes that are not always embraced by employees worried about job security.

Edgar Jr. had first revealed his enthusiasm for re-engineering at Seagram's 1994 annual meeting. The initial company-wide gathering to establish re-engineering teams occurred early in 1995 at the Doral Arrowwood, a resort hotel and conference centre in Rye Brook, New York, near the Connecticut border. The night before, attendees held a farewell party for Ed McDonnell, who was retiring as president of the spirits and wine group but remaining on the Seagram board. The lavish festivities, featuring entertainment by singer Tommy Makem, were in stark contrast to the cost-cutting to come. In a follow-on meeting, Edgar Jr. said that there would be no sacred cows, then corrected himself, saying that the corporate jets were exempt.

Edgar Jr. hired Boston Consulting Group (BCG) to advise him on re-engineering at both Tropicana and the spirits and wine group. "This was as broad a definition of re-engineering as I have seen," says Steven Gunby, BCG's lead consultant on the project. "Under the rubric of re-engineering we looked at the strategies of various businesses, we looked at different ways to drive brands, entry strategies, supply chain issues, manufacturing issues. It was both ways to change the business to drive revenue as well as drive costs out. It was pretty holistic. There weren't that many things that were out of scope. There are companies that go through a tweaking change effort; this was a major change effort." Seagram had previously tried various ways to improve performance, with limited success. "Edgar thought that there needed to be a more fundamental look at the businesses to get them going. He knew he had a set of businesses that weren't performing. The spirits and wine group probably had more problems than anybody really knew. There wasn't a good culture of communication within the ranks, so people hid problems."

Consultants swarmed throughout the Seagram empire and ended up working with the spirits and wine division for six years. Once Edgar Jr. bought the movie studio, he retained two more consulting firms, Booz Allen Hamilton and Price Waterhouse, to guide Universal through a similar process. Steve Kalagher and John Preston presided over twenty-three re-engineering teams at spirits and wine and Tropicana; former

Universal CFO Dick Baker oversaw the first year at Universal using thirty-five teams. Fees charged by the consultants were mind-boggling. Seagram paid Boston Consulting Group $100 million for its work with Tropicana and the spirits and wine group. Booz Allen and Price Waterhouse split another $100 million for their advice at Universal.

Leading the Booz Allen squad was Michael J. Wolf, chief media and entertainment consultant. He became such an integral member of the Seagram family that in 1999, when he published his book *The Entertainment Economy,* Edgar Jr.'s brother Matthew and Strauss Zelnick, who ran BMG Entertainment, threw a launch party. (Zelnick was not only a family friend, he and Matthew had married sisters, Wendy and Lisa Belzberg.) "Entertainment companies occupy a place in the cultural landscape far out of proportion to their relative place in the scheme of big companies," wrote Wolf. "They are the conquistadors of modern business."

Executives and employees forced to deal with re-engineering did not have the same high opinion towards consultants. "Re-engineering was very costly, very time-consuming, and very disruptive. Some people's careers ended over it. They were taken out of the mix, and by the time they were prepared to go back into the mix, it was like they'd been off on a mission somewhere with the church. [Leading a team] was the best thing that never happened to me. I could very well have lost my job," says Blair Westlake, who in December 1997 was promoted instead to chairman of Universal's television and network group.

Participants blamed Edgar Jr. for forcing them to put up with inexperienced consultants who promoted arcane procedures such as Six Sigma, a means of improving quality by reducing defects that was more suited to manufacturing than movies. Tom Pollock, former chairman of the motion picture group who was named vice-chairman of MCA by Edgar Jr., recalls: "A lot of kids in their twenties come and talk to you about Six Sigma as if it is a mantra that somehow you can wring pennies out of your supply chain of economics. At the end of the day you probably got two, three, four million dollars of savings. I begged him, as did Ron Meyer to his credit, to delay re-engineering for a year, until the new people could get a handle on the company. He didn't want to wait. He wanted to show himself as a strong, tough, money-minded manager to Wall Street."

While Edgar Jr. was all too willing to hire consultants to tell him what to do, he would rarely listen to advice from his own colleagues. This Bronfman belief in their own infallibility was genetic. Mr. Sam was tough to convince; Edgar Sr. could be an equally hard sell. While those two may not always have paid attention to the views of others, their instincts were often right about the direction that Seagram should take. Edgar Jr. did not have the same intuitive judgment as his forebears. His "gut feel" wasn't as good, but he heeded it anyway. As a result, the organization under him became a breeding ground for "yes men." Because he did not listen to recommendations from underlings or appear to be open to criticism, people followed the "go along to get along" philosophy. "You could read him pretty quickly. People would do somersaults to line up with him. There was very little push back in the whole organization. It wasn't healthy. Usually there's an interchange and then a decision. I never saw any interchange," says Ed Falkenberg, controller at Seagram. "Edgar Sr. had more vision. Re-engineering, I don't think Junior thought about that for more than an hour. Senior was more restrained, more measured before he committed to something."

Re-engineering had a positive impact at Tropicana because the organization was relatively small and the product line limited. Moreover, Ellen Marram had replaced most of the senior people with outsiders who had experience in other industries and were more willing to try new methods to solve obvious problems. At Universal, there was more foot-dragging. Senior executives insisted that re-engineering would constrain creativity. Edgar Jr. was unwilling to order managers to get in line for fear they'd refuse, and he'd have to fire them and pay out their lucrative multi-year contracts. For different reasons, there was resistance at the spirits and wine group too. Members of that more stodgy culture spent unnecessary hours worrying about how things would look to the Bronfman family rather than getting on with the program. According to Marram, "They were like royalty to people, and I think that that in some ways probably worked against them. People hated to give them bad news or hated to argue with them. It's terrible as a CEO, or as a manager, in my opinion, if your people don't feel comfortable telling you why they disagree with you."

As for the marketing help Edgar Jr. promised Seagram might deliver to Universal, there was very little crossover. There was no concerted effort to use Seagram products in movies. The only proviso was that competitors' products should not appear. For example, the opening scene of *Jurassic Park II* called for champagne, so Perrier-Jouët is visible.

In 1997, Edgar Jr. hired Hellene Runtagh, a twenty-five-year GE veteran, to implement the recommendations at Universal that flowed from twelve months of re-engineering team meetings. A retreat at a golf resort in Santa Barbara was the unlikely location in March 1997 to put in motion the steps that were supposed to achieve savings. Those who implemented that next phase claim Universal saved $100 million in the first year, then $50 million in each of 1998 and 1999, savings that continued every year thereafter for a total of $600 million during the years 1997–2003. "I thought it was a worthwhile process," says Ron Meyer. "I think it probably grew to be something more than was necessary, but I'm not sure if there's anybody to blame for that. I think probably the consultants are more to blame for that than anything. I think that it could be done probably more efficiently and quicker. You don't have to have the circus come to town."

Meyer's estimate is probably high. Specific examples of dollar amounts saved at Universal are hard to come by, but they include $20 million from closing regional marketing offices and $15 million saved on overhead in TV production. Purchasing was consolidated; so were printing and advertising contracts. The human resources and legal departments were combined. Employment was reduced by 20 percent but most of those fired were low-wage earners, so the total payroll fell by only 5 percent. Universal switched to one cellphone provider and got better rates, but everyone's phone number changed and service was spotty.

A manufacturing operation like Tropicana was more responsive. For example, the value of inventory maintained in Europe was reduced by $50 million. "Tropicana went from a no-growth business in terms of earnings to a growth business. The culture improved. They felt part of a winning team," claims Boston Consulting's Gunby. "Edgar attracts a lot of bad PR. On re-engineering he drove a major change effort, he was hands-on involved, and he actually got a lot of significant results. Tropicana went from [a value of] $1 billion to $3.3 billion. There was a management team that was excited and motivated."

If Tropicana was the lone re-engineering success, Edgar Jr. had only himself to blame. His low-key style meant there were occasions when he did not step in to mediate re-engineering arguments when he should have. Nor was he particularly interested in the ongoing details, and re-engineering programs are all about the details. Re-engineering can only succeed if the organization is committed to tearing everything apart with a view to improving basic procedures. If the CEO doesn't seem totally committed, fervour for the project soon dissipates in the ranks.

Update meetings at Universal accomplished less than they should have because Edgar Jr. didn't want to hear about better performance so much as he simply wanted to preside, like an enthroned ruler to whom courtiers bowed and scraped. "People had to fly in from New York. Everybody had to be in the room with Edgar, which is totally contrary to the usual way," says someone who was close to the process. "I'm not sure he ever really focused on it. He didn't make the tough decisions that needed to be made. They didn't get the leadership they needed. They were discouraged by profligate spending."

Indeed, some of the money saved by re-engineering at Universal was spent on new projects approved by Edgar Jr. Renovations to the Black Tower and commissary cost $30 million, a new music royalty tracking system cost $30 million, billings for the Koolhaas design were $20 million, new computer systems gobbled up another $25 million. Worried about the loss of Spielberg, Edgar Jr. spent untold millions on production deals as well as contracts with movie stars such as Sylvester Stallone, who got $60 million for three movies. Add severance pay and contract buyouts for a panoply of departing senior executives and more than $200 million of the savings achieved through re-engineering was spent elsewhere.

According to Cathy Nichols, a former McKinsey consultant hired by Edgar Jr. in 1997 to run the theme park division, the rule of thumb for such projects is that savings achieved should be five to ten times the fees. On that basis, savings at Universal should have been $500 million to $1 billion over five years. In her view, the $100 million in fees paid to the consulting firms

Saidye and Mr. Sam in armchairs on the occasion of his eightieth birthday in 1971. From left, Charles and Barbara with their two children, Stephen and Ellen; back row, Alain and Minda de Gunzburg, Phyllis Lambert, Ann and Edgar Sr.; nearby, Alain and Minda's two sons, Jean and Charles. Perched on a sofa over Mr. Sam's left shoulder are Ann and Edgar Sr.'s five: Sam, Holly, Edgar Jr., Adam, and Matthew.

Mr. Sam and Saidye's
Montreal home,
15 Belvedere Rd.

Edgar Jr. was born in New York while his parents lived on Montreal's Aberdeen Avenue.

(Right) The famous photo of Mr. Sam that Edgar Jr. hung in his office.

(Below) 1966 family portrait, front row, Ann, Matthew, Holly, Edgar Sr., and Adam; rear, Sam and Edgar Jr., aged eleven.

Edgar Jr.'s 1973 graduation photo from Collegiate.

Cover of *Fortune*, March 17, 1986, when Edgar Sr. announced his chosen successor.

Edgar Jr. and his first wife, Sherry, in 1986.

Seagram's baronial head
office in Montreal and
executive offices on New
York's Park Avenue.

Edgar Jr. and Hannah, youngest child from his first marriage.

STAR BLACK

With second wife, Clarissa, and singer Smokey Robinson.

STAR BLACK

With brothers Matthew (left) and Adam.

All photos 2001.

STAR BLACK

Edgar Jr. and Barry Diller announce their controversial TV deal in October 1997.

From left, Charles, Stephen, Sam, Edgar Jr., and Edgar Sr. at 1999 annual meeting.

Edgar Jr. reaches the pinnacle with the Vivendi-Seagram merger.

Edgar Jr. and Jean-Marie Messier toast the merger in Paris, June 20, 2000.

Edgar Jr. and Clarissa
at the opening of
Never Gonna Dance
in December 2003.

Edgar Jr.'s Malibu Colony beach house built by Bing Crosby.

for re-engineering at Universal was far too high and should have been in the $10 million to $25 million range.

At one point someone had the temerity to suggest getting rid of some, not even all, of Seagram's corporate jets. Ron Meyer had doubts that employee morale would be improved by such a half-hearted gesture on the part of Edgar Jr., so he sarcastically said: "Should the kings eat less caviar?" As far as Meyer was concerned, the only meaningful step would be to get rid of the entire fleet. Nothing of the kind occurred. Air Seagram continued to fly.

After Edgar Jr. bought Universal, his free time for songwriting decreased, but he did write one song that ended up on the soundtrack of a Universal movie. Under the pseudonym Sam Roman, Edgar Jr. co-wrote with Bruce Roberts "Whenever There Is Love," a ballad sung by Donna Summer for *Daylight,* starring Sylvester Stallone. The 1996 movie fit nicely into Edgar Jr.'s underground genre that began with *The Blockhouse.* A traffic accident and resulting explosion traps commuters in a tunnel underneath the Hudson River between Manhattan and New Jersey. Stallone plays the disgraced former chief of Emergency Medical Services who redeems himself by coming to their rescue.

Ron Meyer, president of Universal Studios, claims there was no pressure to use the boss's song, in fact there was an attempt to dissuade the director, Rob Cohen, from using it. "Rob Cohen had every right not to use it. We would have been relieved for Rob Cohen not to want it, but he wanted it. We said you don't get any points for this, there's no bonus in this for you. We don't get more jobs because of it, we don't get treated better because of it. He wanted the song," says Meyer. Once the decision was made to use the song, one of forty co-written with Bruce Roberts, there was then an effort to downplay Edgar Jr.'s involvement. "Everybody took great pains for it not to be visible. We kept it so quiet until, of course, like everything it leaks out. Then it became the biggest aspect of [the movie]," says Meyer. "It was not like he was just a fop trying to come up with a song. He's had Celine Dion record his music, he's had Barbra Streisand record his music. He's had success."

Of all the possible love-song themes, Edgar Jr. usually writes about the same ephemeral topics: love's elusive nature and how love can be a balm for pain. To journalists who wrote profiles about Edgar Jr., his lyrics were sappy. To them his songwriting was another example of his amateurism. According to Patsy Puttnam, Edgar's relationship with Roberts was helpful, almost therapeutic. "There's nothing like being able to write out your pain, is there? We've seen it all through history. I don't think he ever set himself up to be any great lyricist. He did it because that's what he needed to do. Aren't people cruel? Not to see that beneath that is something that he feels he needs to do. Why does everything have to be judged against the best?"

Songwriting is a deep-seated need for Edgar Jr. "He's very private, almost shy about it. It comes from a very personal place and a very creative place," says Hilary Rosen, CEO of the Recording Industry Association of America from 1998 to 2003. "He has described to me how he's always been part of something bigger than just him in his professional life and his career. He's valued that, I don't think he's resented it, he's embraced it. He appreciated the notion of being the scion of a family business, but I think his music was just his own, his own creation. It was something that initially he did for himself."

Edgar Jr.'s new status as a Hollywood celebrity was recognized in July 1996 when he was honoured along with singer Neil

Diamond and Jill Barad, president of Mattel Inc., at an AIDS benefit held at the Universal Amphitheatre. Edgar Jr. was introduced by Michael Douglas, who first met him in the early 1980s. As the son of movie star Kirk Douglas, Michael Douglas was able to appreciate Edgar Jr.'s efforts to differentiate himself from his father. "We shared a unique connection and understanding of each other. We were both raised by well-known families of achievement, and both of us struggled to define ourselves and establish our own identities," said Douglas. "I believe I know what it takes to develop a sense of *self* in that environment—to find your creative centre and take the risks that define us as individuals. And I know Edgar's struggle was not an easy one." Douglas reminded the assembled that Edgar Jr. was no Hollywood neophyte, that his first job, at fifteen, was in movies. "Edgar always felt a need to express himself creatively and intellectually as a songwriter, as a filmmaker, and now as head of a studio. I think Edgar's left brain and right brain have found a way to blissfully coexist."

Whatever side of Edgar Jr.'s brain was at work, corporate turn-arounds proved to be tough for him and his appointees. Tropicana, acquired in 1988, went sideways for five years even after plant modernization and increased advertising. But entrenched problems at a Florida juice company attracted scant national attention. By contrast, Universal was closely watched by Hollywood gossips and stargazers everywhere. Seagram had previously been covered by a handful of securities analysts familiar with the beverage alcohol industry. Eighteen months after Seagram acquired Universal, the number of analysts had increased to two dozen who were assessing financial results, appraising management, and publishing their views about

Seagram as an investment and Edgar Jr. as a business leader in media and entertainment.

For many of them, Edgar Jr. lacked the background and the thick skin needed for the role. "Edgar came into the business through acquisition, from another industry. He didn't have the same kind of experience that the other executives of companies that I follow have. The mistakes that he made were incredibly public," says Jessica Reif Cohen, an analyst with Merrill Lynch in New York who followed thirty media and entertainment companies. "I really like Edgar a lot. He's an incredible gentleman. There are times when he may not have had the best advice. For someone coming into the industry who's relatively fresh, that's critical. There are a lot of sharks out there."

The perspective on the West Coast was the same. "In Hollywood there never was the belief that Edgar Bronfman had the experience of the other CEOs. He had a fan interest, like a kid-in-a-candy-shop situation, where you had somebody who likes to write songs and isn't necessarily somebody who had thirty years' experience in the industry," says David Davis, senior vice-president of Houlihan, Lokey, Howard & Zukin, a Los Angeles investment bank that advises media and entertainment companies. "Some of the other companies that he was doing deals with were taking advantage of the fact that he wasn't as experienced as other sharks or CEOs who ran companies."

The fact that he was a third-generation inheritor contributed to their negative view. "Nobody wants to believe that somebody could be as blessed as he was," says one analyst from those days who requested anonymity. "A man who is born into the kind of position that he was born into, you want to believe that he's stupid. If he was a woman, it would be sort of like Christina Onassis, and Joan Rivers making jokes about how ugly she is. We can all feel better about the fact that she's richer than God because she's ugly. It's OK for him to be rich and tall and handsome and gracious and have a beautiful wife and have basically, from the outside at least, the world as his oyster, but it's OK, we don't have to hate him because, actually, he's stupid."

Box office results at Universal fed the perception that Edgar Jr. didn't have the royal jelly needed to run a studio. When Edgar Jr. bought Universal in 1995, the studio had 10 percent of ticket sales in North America; by 1998, that figure had fallen to 4 percent. Media commentators, who picked up on criticism by analysts and industry officials, concluded he was in over his head. In April 1998, editor Peter Bart published an open letter to Edgar Jr. in *Variety* that began: "Have you noticed a whirring sound lately, Edgar? It may be unfamiliar to you, but those of us who have worked in Hollywood for a time know it all too well. That whir is the sound of Hollywood collectively turning on someone." Bart, whose career also included seventeen years as a studio production executive, quoted an unnamed Hollywood agent who said: "We all understand where Rupert Murdoch wants to take his company. We understand Michael Eisner. We don't get Edgar." Bart offered Edgar Jr. some tough-love advice:

> The combination of your gracious low-key nature and your behind-the-scenes management style inevitably will set you up to take a lot of guff. Here's the reality: Today's vast entertainment megacompanies are more akin to nation states. They need to have extroverted, communicative spokesmen at the helm. Investors and creative partners alike want to know their aims and objectives. Universal has accomplished some admirable things over the past three years. It's also becoming something like a stealth missile, trying to fly beneath the radar. That can't be done, Edgar. Bigness is both

a blessing and a curse. That's why, like it or not, it's your turn
in the barrel.

Being relegated to such a place was not uncommon. "In the
film business, you are in the barrel frequently. You're at least in
it once," says Barry Diller, who had suffered a similar experience
during his first two years at Paramount. "I've only been in it
once, but it was very tough, probably the most difficult period
of my life, but, yes, we came out of it. I think one of Edgar's
great strengths is that he really doesn't complain very much. I
don't think about Edgar as whining about his condition at any
time, and he's had some very hideously tough conditions."

In this instance, Edgar Jr. screwed up his courage and
phoned Bart to complain that his column had missed the point.
"I have a plan," he said. "I realize it may not seem like I do, but
I do." His opening fusillade soon fizzled out. Edgar Jr. switched
gears into his more usual conversational tone, the one he
employed when he wanted people to like him. He schmoozed
Bart about his early years in Hollywood when he was a hopeful
producer and Bart was a studio executive. "I was schlepping
around projects no one wanted to make," said Edgar Jr. "I
remember bringing some of them to you. At least you were
polite in turning me down, which was better than most. That's
why I can't get too pissed at you for the column. Look, if the
town has turned against me, it will turn again. We've both seen
that happen often enough."

Bart's advice to get out and tell the corporate story was wise,
but Edgar Jr.'s communications staff reinforced his natural shy-
ness by keeping him away from the media. In the early 1990s,
Rosemary Moore managed Edgar Jr.'s public persona. She joined
Seagram in 1988, was named vice-president of corporate communications in 1990, assistant to the president in 1993, and senior

vice-president in 1995. During Moore's regime her department grew from a small operation to a staff of fifteen, but more media contact with Edgar Jr. was not part of the mandate. "Rosemary wouldn't let him talk to the press," says Valerie Hendy, who worked in corporate communications at the time. Edgar Jr. agreed with Moore's plan for him to stay out of the limelight. His attitude, as he told Hendy, was, "As a rich kid, why not avoid rude questions?" With neither a game plan nor a co-operative boss, staff felt their hands were tied. "It was tough doing PR for Edgar Jr. He's very thin-skinned. I realized at some point that only time and performance would win over the naysayers," says Chris Tofalli, director of communications from 1991 to 1996.

On those rare occasions when Edgar Jr. did sit down with a journalist, he failed to impress. It took months to fulfill an interview request from Eric Reguly, then of *The Financial Post.* When the session finally took place in 1993, Reguly found Edgar Jr. painfully introverted and not particularly informative. "It was one of the most boring interviews I've ever done in my life," says Reguly. "He didn't seem to me like a businessman with a killer instinct."

According to Barry Diller, Edgar Jr.'s problem with the media was almost visceral. "Some people, and it's no comment on them, aren't good with the media for a whole host of reasons. Usually it's a deep mistrust and a real uncomfortability. I think he's definitely in that group. He's never had a comfortable relationship with the print media." In Edgar Jr.'s situation, the media focused on "history and mythology," defined by Diller as a combination of leaving school early, joining the family firm, taking the family into the entertainment business, plus writing songs, something the media will never let him live down. "What's the media going to do? Of course they're going to discount it until proven otherwise. He's not a sympathetic character," says Diller.

In addition to his media problems, Edgar Jr. could be equally uncomfortable at the receptions that are such an integral part of corporate life. He could be relaxed when touring Seagram facilities such as the distillery in Relay, Maryland, because he was in total control, but put him in the doorway of a room filled with strangers and Edgar Jr. acted very differently from his brother Sam. "The way he explained the difference between him and Sam was that if Sam walked into a room, Sam would walk over to the people and shake their hands. If Edgar walked into a room—this is Edgar describing himself—he would stand there and let other people come to him and shake his hand," says Ellen Marram. "I don't know if shy is too strong a word, but I don't think he is somebody who wants to walk into a room and command it. I don't want to say he's not sociable because he's very sociable, but I think some of his aloofness comes from a comfort level as opposed to an arrogance level. When people come up to him to talk to him I don't think that he's imperious at all."

Seagram's keep-out-of-the-news approach affected the most minor aspects of its operations. There was a conference room on the fourth floor of the Seagram Building that could quickly be converted into a screening room by rolling in rows of hidden chairs and raising a wall panel to expose a projection screen. A journalist heard about this dual-purpose room and called to confirm its existence. Chris Tofalli was told not only to deny there was such a screening room but also to show the reporter the space in its conference-room format as proof.

After Moore left Seagram in 1996, Ray Boyce, her replacement as vice-president of communications, achieved little through his efforts to improve Edgar Jr.'s image. "Knowing him personally was different than how he would appear to the media. He seemed withdrawn, unless he knew someone, so they got a negative outlook. He tried to be too honest. He couldn't 'phony' it up, he couldn't gloss over something," says Boyce. "I always found him to be arrogant, dismissive, and superior. You can tolerate a dressing-down from a Diller, but I always felt there was an absence of logic to things Edgar would say or do," says Richard Siklos, who wrote about media and entertainment for *Business Week*. "Edgar Jr. was always creating the idea that journalists could get bought off by a G-IV ride. He seemed like a guy with a lot of blind spots. He was somehow incomplete. He never should have been CEO."

Edgar Jr.'s colleagues believed the media treated him unfairly. "His baggage was checked in before he arrived. He was looked at as a rich man's son and wasn't given the credit. He'd been a producer, been a songwriter—and wasn't college educated—but I will tell you that he's smarter than anybody who went to college that I've known. He's brilliantly self-educated and understands all of the businesses that he's involved in as well as any CEO of any company could understand them. He deserved more credit than he was given," says Ron Meyer.

Some industry leaders were supportive. "I find a lot of the press reports about Edgar to be strangely contradictory to the Edgar I know. It is warrantless abuse," says Jack Valenti, president and CEO of the Motion Picture Association of America for nearly forty years. "He was respectful of people, but he wasn't a pussycat. They knew who was in charge, but he allowed that creative horizon to move outwards. I never found anybody in private conversation at Universal that didn't think he was a first-class leader. He was very knowledgeable. His zest for the business always impressed me."

Valenti's public support was not the norm. More typical was a derisive three-page article in the April 27, 1998, issue of *Barron's*. The influential investment journal categorically declared Edgar Jr.'s career an abysmal failure, saying: "Almost every one of his corporate moves at Seagram has been the target of derision." He "wildly overpaid" for Tropicana; the MCA acquisition was "seemingly ill-timed." Among twenty-four analysts who followed Seagram, the story noted that only five had a "buy" or a "hold" on the stock; the other nineteen were urging clients to sell. Even the Gulfstream IV on which journalist Jonathan R. Laing from *Barron's* interviewed Edgar Jr. for the story was sadly deficient. "This is my least favourite of the company planes," grumbled Edgar Jr. "It doesn't have e-mail capability, which makes it tough to conduct business."

Edgar Jr. had thrown so much money at problems—sums that were massive even by Hollywood standards—that he had come to be seen by everyone as an easy mark. When the previously impregnable DreamWorks looked like it might need financial help, Edgar Jr. was described by Connie Bruck in an article for *The New Yorker* as the most likely source of funds. An unnamed entertainment executive was quoted as comparing him to a party piñata: "Hit him and money comes out."

While the quote took on a life of its own and was used against Edgar Jr. on countless occasions, some of his own comments in that same article caused just as much trouble. The problem with being born rich and being raised to be able to say anything you want to your teachers or to producers who bring their movies to your home is that sometimes you talk without thinking. In private, for a Bronfman, that could mean being rough-tongued with people, as Edgar Sr. had been when he was younger. For Edgar Jr., it could mean comments that were at best ill-considered. Edgar Jr. could not seem to give an interview without making some remark that would cause a communications adviser to cringe in disbelief. The worst example in the Bruck interview occurred when Edgar Jr. complained to her that while Wall Street admired a particular deal he'd done, "Hollywood thinks it was dumb." Why was that? Bruck asked. "It's a dumb town," replied Edgar Jr. The respect he sought among his peers was unlikely to be forthcoming in the face of such sweeping derogatory remarks.

Even Edgar Jr.'s big-picture ideas, proposals he presumably had thought through carefully, seemed impractical and open to ridicule. During a March 31, 1998, speech in New York, Edgar Jr. recommended that the movie business abandon the one-price admission system and move to a tiered arrangement that reflected actual costs of production. Why, he wondered, should customers pay the same amount to see a movie that cost $2 million to make and market as a movie that cost $200 million? "This is a pricing model which makes no sense, and I believe the entire industry should and must revisit it," he said. He described the industry's reliance on increased attendance for revenue growth as a "death paradigm" and announced that Universal would proceed with its own tiered pricing plan, but the studio never did. The proposal was declared unworkable by a panel of film executives that very afternoon and widely derided in the months that followed.

Through all the criticism, Edgar Jr. at least managed to keep his sense of humour. Analysts from the U.S. and Canada were invited to a daylong briefing and tour of the Islands of Adventure theme park in Orlando when the construction site was mostly mud. Wearing jeans and a cashmere jacket, Edgar Jr. climbed aboard the bus carrying the analysts and told them that he had an announcement. "Today is a very important day in the history of the Bronfman family," he said. There was a hush as his captive audience waited on his every word, then Edgar Jr. smiled and said: "We got good press in *The New York Times*."

That was about as close as he ever came to registering a public complaint. "Edgar's always above the fray. It's one of his strongest and most admirable qualities," says Thom Mount. "It's also tough on him. Rather than engage in Diller-esque warfare or practise the black art of exclusion and revenge, Edgar—probably derived from the security of being born a prince—takes the high road. That does him good personally, but it doesn't do him any good professionally."

Tod Hullin, who was hired as senior vice-president of communications, replaced Ray Boyce in the fall of 1998. Hullin, who had worked for ten CEOs, most recently Time Warner's Gerald Levin, saw another side. "I heard him tell a reporter when we were on an airplane flying somewhere that he was such a gentle person and such a soft speaker that some have taken his demeanour as a sign of weakness." Hullin quoted Edgar Jr. as saying, "No one should ever take my soft-spoken nature as a sign of weakness. Look at the number of executives who are no longer with us."

But the batch of high-level departures from Universal during a ten-day period in April 1998 also demonstrated internal disarray. Gone were executive vice-president Howard Weitzman, president of production Marc Platt, and heads of marketing Kathy Jones and Buffy Shutt. Sandy Climan had left a few months earlier. Rumours circulated that Edgar Jr. was about to sell Universal to Barry Diller or Steven Spielberg. The Toronto Stock Exchange halted trading in Seagram shares on April 17 so the company could issue reassuring comments. Through it all, the Seagram board of directors was not concerned about so much management churn. "At least he was wise enough to understand that whoever was there was not the right person, and he didn't hesitate to make a change," says Seagram director William Davis. "You might be critical that he didn't make a change as early as he might have, but he ultimately made, in a lot of cases, the right change."

Political forces were also gathering. In March 1998, Edgar Jr. won the first annual Silver Sewer award, a manhole cover with a dollar sign on it, bestowed by Senator Joe Lieberman, Democrat from Connecticut, and Republican Bill Bennett, secretary of education in the Reagan administration. According to Bennett, Edgar Jr. had called to ask for a meeting shortly after he bought MCA. By the time the meeting took place, Edgar Jr. had acquired Interscope Records, with its shock rock singer Marilyn Manson. Edgar Jr. told Bennett that Seagram would not profit by disseminating objectionable music. "Watch us and judge us," he told Bennett. Bennett did so, and found him wanting. In an appearance before the Senate Committee on Commerce in 1999, Bennett read aloud some of Manson's more offensive lyrics. "I have asked Bronfman to publicly debate these issues, in Los Angeles, in New York, anywhere. But so far all we have heard from one of the world's largest communications companies and its board is the Sound of Silence," said Bennett.

All the negativity had an impact on share price. An investment of $100 in Seagram on June 30, 1993, grew to $172 by June 30, 1998. The same $100 invested in the Toronto Stock Exchange 300 composite index would have reached $206. If placed in a basket of companies from Seagram's peer group (beverage alcohol, juice, and entertainment firms), the $100 became $222, or an even more robust $282 if invested in the S&P 500 index. A shareholder who expressed concern about that lagging performance during the annual meeting in Montreal on November 4, 1998, received no sympathy. Edgar Sr. quoted Mr. Sam, who, when asked a similar question years earlier, had replied, "I have more to lose than you do, and that is my answer to you."

That fall's movie offerings by Universal were the worst yet. Edgar Jr. had been counting on *Meet Joe Black,* starring Brad Pitt and Anthony Hopkins, and *Babe: Pig in the City,* a sequel to the popular movie about a talking pig. Costs for each exceeded $100 million. But as had so often been the case before, Edgar Jr. could not tell boffo from flop. Edgar Jr. loved *Meet Joe Black* so much that he told director Martin Brest that the film, already three hours long, could be longer. When it was released, *Meet Joe Black* was panned by critics. *Babe: Pig in the City* did a meagre $8.5 million in business on the five-day Thanksgiving weekend and then sank out of sight. Casey Silver, chairman of Universal Pictures for three years, took the blame and was axed.

With $377 million in box office receipts, Universal ranked ninth that year among all the major studios, barely ahead of perennial weakling MGM/UA. Edgar Jr. ordered Universal to sell international rights on some movies as a way of reducing the studio's production costs. Stacey Snider, who joined Universal from Sony in 1996 as co-president of production, urged him to reconsider his decision, but he was adamant, saying, "The magnitude of the hemorrhage warrants a one-time-only crisis management move." *Erin Brockovich* and *American Pie* were among the movies whose foreign rights were sold. In return for a relatively small injection of funds, Universal ended up having to share sizable profits when both films proved to be popular. Another victim of the cutbacks was the Koolhaas design for a new headquarters. Officials at Universal had spent three years applying for the necessary permits. In 1998, Edgar Jr. concluded that he couldn't afford the ambitious project and the Koolhaas design was quietly shelved.

Edgar Jr. asked Brian Mulligan, Universal's executive vice-president of operations and finance, to devise a cost-cutting plan. Mulligan, who grew up in the entertainment business, had joined Universal as controller in 1990 when he was thirty. He knew what to do from his time in the Wasserman era, when teams would spend twelve-hour days penny-pinching all projects in every division before anything went ahead. In January 1999, Mulligan and Ron Meyer presented the new dollar-wise diet to the Seagram directors. The board approved a 50 percent cut in the $1.5-billion annual investment on new movies, limited the number of new movies to fifteen, gave each a specific budget ceiling, and brought in co-financing partners. "I was always concerned about the unpredictability and the absolute level of returns in the live action motion picture business," says Bob Matschullat, Seagram's vice-chairman and chief financial officer. "You have a cost of capital which is more or less 10 percent, so the returns need to be above 10 percent. If they're not, you're not doing what you're supposed to be doing for your shareholders. Or, even if they are above 10 percent, if they're very unpredictable, it's not very helpful to the stock price because Wall Street loves predictability. I was concerned about the level of capital we were putting into the motion picture business. I always pushed for capital limitations in that business. Accordingly, we brought it down and we put a cap on it. As it turned out, tougher capital allocation decisions led to much better results."

By June 1999, the division was rebounding—but the upswing predated both the firing of Silver and all the cost-cutting. Movies take two years from first concept to final release, so the improvement had been underway for some time. Beginning with *Patch Adams,* the Robin Williams film released on Christmas Day 1998, Universal had a series of hits that included *The Mummy* and *Notting Hill.* On October 2, 1999, Universal's box office receipts for that calendar year reached $710 million, breaking the studio's previous record for a full twelve months set in 1982, the year of *E. T.: The Extra-Terrestrial.*

The bottom line was recovering at last, but the excessive management turnover that occurred along the way had been disruptive. "Edgar was impressed with a number of executives in

Los Angeles to his own detriment," says Thom Mount. "Edgar believed, in the beginning, the myth of power in Hollywood. Here, there's always the presumption that somebody knows something, but [screenwriter] Bill Goldman is ultimately right, nobody knows anything. In that sense, it took Edgar three years of bad choices and getting rid of those bad choices and paying the price for it. There's always a learning curve. Everybody screws up in the beginning."

Ron Meyer shoulders some of the blame. "There were a lot of comings and goings. Early on I made some not great personnel choices, some not great business choices in the kind of films we were making and the way we operated our business. It took me a while to learn what I needed to learn to make this, from my purposes, a better company. He stuck with me and he was very supportive at a time when I was learning a different business, at least stuck with us long enough to make it successful. What I thought could be done in six months probably took three years."

During that time the company looked like Office Overload, with high-priced temps coming and going. But of all the hires by Edgar Jr., the most bizarre by far was Frank Biondi Jr., recruited for the key role of chief executive officer. The tale of how Edgar Jr. battled to hire Biondi is entangled with a long-standing partnership between Viacom and Universal. The dispute over that joint venture, coupled with the hiring and subsequent firing of Frank Biondi, reveals much about the character of Edgar Jr., a man with the harmful habit of falling in— and then just as quickly out of—love.

EIGHT

SHARK ATTACKS

When Edgar Jr. acquired MCA from the Japanese, he inherited a television partnership with Viacom that had been in place since 1981. The two competitors were joint owners of USA Network, the highest-rated prime-time cable network, with 67 million subscribers watching everything from wrestling matches, through sitcom reruns, to special events such as the Westminster Kennel Club Dog Show.

USA Network, along with the much smaller Sci-Fi Channel, were Edgar Jr.'s only entrees into the fast-growing world of cable TV. Initially, the partnership with Viacom seemed secure. In the summer of 1995, Barry Diller, then chairman and CEO of Home Shopping Network, failed in an attempt to buy CBS. Diller urged Edgar Jr. to take a run at CBS himself through USA Network. Edgar Jr. agreed it was a good idea and said he'd confer with his partner, Sumner Redstone, chairman and CEO of Viacom.

Redstone's background in the media business far outweighed Edgar Jr.'s limited experience. Redstone served in military intelligence during the Second World War and graduated from Harvard Law School. He joined his father's drive-in movie business in 1954 and over the next four decades built that small chain of theatres into Viacom, a media giant with 1,100 screens as well as pay-TV channels Showtime and The Movie Channel. Along with the 50 percent interest in USA Network and Sci-Fi, shared with Edgar Jr., Viacom also had a 50 percent interest in the Comedy Channel and was sole owner of music channels MTV and VH1, Nick-at-Nite for sitcoms, and Nickelodeon, the children's channel.

Edgar Jr. and Redstone met several times to discuss their mutual interest in the CBS bid. During a meeting on September 12, Edgar Jr. asked Redstone about another of Viacom's broadcasting partnerships, this one with Chris-Craft Industries Inc., of New York. Viacom had the opportunity, before the end of the year, to buy a 50 percent interest in UPN, a new network that Chris-Craft was trying to launch. Redstone said he didn't feel the UPN deal prohibited him from making a bid for CBS with Edgar Jr. According to Edgar Jr., Redstone told him, "The partnership agreement with Chris-Craft is pretty loose, and I think we can get around that." Commented Edgar Jr.: "In other words, we are the partner you are not going to screw." Redstone later denied saying he could get around the Chris-Craft partnership. He did, however, recall Edgar's retort. Their discussion about buying CBS together was rendered irrelevant when Westinghouse Corporation bought the network that fall.

In October 1995, Viacom announced plans for a new channel, called TV Land, aiming for an on-air date early in 1996. Viacom claimed all it was doing was shuffling some programming. Nickelodeon was a children's channel during the day; in the evening it became Nick-at-Nite and broadcast reruns such as *The Mary Tyler Moore Show*. Viacom intended to expand children's programming on Nickelodeon into the evening and move the sitcoms onto TV Land, where there would be more time available to add other syndicated shows such as *Gunsmoke* and *Cannon.* In Edgar Jr.'s view, TV Land was nothing less than a new channel in disguise. He argued that unless Universal was given a share of TV Land's profits, Viacom would be in contravention of their agreement that said neither partner could unilaterally launch a new channel. Redstone claimed TV Land was just an extension of something that already existed, a "Nick-at-Nite All Day Long," although TV Land would occupy its own channel and eventually, Viacom hoped, be on the air twenty-four hours a day.

When Edgar Jr. hired Bob Matschullat to replace the late Steven Banner as Seagram CFO on October 1, 1995, Matschullat's first assignment was to sort out the partnership problems. The more he looked at the situation, the more irritants he found. Edgar Jr. suggested Matschullat might get a better hearing from Frank Biondi, the CEO of Viacom. Biondi, a Harvard MBA, had been a Wall Street investment banker and had previously run Coca-Cola's entertainment division as well as Home Box Office. Meetings involving Edgar Jr. and Matschullat with Biondi and Viacom deputy chair Phillipe Dauman made no progress.

Then, without warning, Redstone fired Biondi on January 17, 1996. Redstone called Edgar Jr. to explain he'd dumped Biondi because he wasn't sufficiently hands-on. Undeterred, Edgar Jr. called Biondi to say he'd like to talk to him about becoming CEO of Universal. Biondi expressed interest but noted that Redstone's consent was needed: Biondi's severance agreement included a clause that prohibited him from working for a competitor for a year.

Edgar Jr., who was still looking for the senior entertainment presence he had hoped Michael Ovitz would be, wanted Biondi. Edgar Jr. met with Redstone in his New York office on Friday,

February 9, and asked him to release Biondi from the no-compete clause. Redstone said he was willing to reduce the one-year period to ninety days. Edgar Jr. asked for thirty days. Redstone agreed to consider sixty days, but said he was worried about Biondi, who had been involved in planning TV Land, joining Universal if Edgar Jr. planned to press his complaint about TV Land. Redstone offered a trade-off: Edgar Jr. could have Biondi if he agreed Viacom could launch TV Land with no complaint from Edgar Jr. Both men agreed to consider their respective positions over the weekend.

On Monday, when Edgar Jr. arrived alone for the meeting with Redstone, Viacom deputy chairman Dauman was also present. An agreement that would allow Edgar Jr. to hire Biondi appeared possible. They discussed which law firms they'd use for the paperwork. As Edgar Jr. rose to leave, Dauman said, "So, we have an agreement. You don't litigate on MTV, and we release Frank in thirty days." Edgar Jr. did not correct Dauman when he said "MTV" rather than "TV Land." He assumed Dauman had simply misspoken, so Edgar Jr. replied, "Yeah." Everyone shook hands and Edgar Jr. left.

To Dauman and Redstone, MTV was no slip of the tongue. The way Dauman used the designation, MTV was the umbrella name for all of Viacom's cable holdings, including MTV, VH1, Nickelodeon, Nick-at-Nite, Comedy Central— and TV Land. Redstone and Dauman believed that Edgar Jr. had abandoned all of his concerns. Edgar Jr. thought the settlement was much narrower. When the draft document, drawn up by Viacom's lawyers, arrived in early March, Edgar Jr. was aghast. He called Dauman to say that the wording did not reflect his recollection of their understanding. "This is ridiculous," said Edgar Jr. "If you guys think that we want Frank Biondi so badly that we are just going to waive all of our legal rights in a substantive dispute, you are crazy. And I really resent this kind of behavior."

Dauman reminded Edgar Jr. that he had agreed not to litigate on MTV. "Didn't you understand that meant everything?"

"No," Edgar Jr. replied, "I didn't understand that meant everything."

Dauman said he'd review the wording, but the next draft was little different. On March 8, Edgar Jr. called Redstone to protest, saying he didn't like being "leveraged" in this way.

"Edgar, I don't like that word," said Redstone.

"Sumner, it's the nicest word I can think of. But this agreement has nothing whatsoever to do with our discussions, what I agreed to or what you asked me for."

Redstone reminded him that they had discussed the MTV networks, so he should have known precisely what Dauman meant. "I haven't lost my marbles," said Redstone, who recalled Edgar Jr. saying, "I did agree to a waiver of the MTV Networks, but I didn't understand the implications of what I was agreeing to." According to Edgar Jr., his response was: "Sumner, even if I agreed to what you say I agreed to, which I didn't, what you sent me twice now doesn't reflect what your view is."

Edgar Jr. read to Sumner some of the clauses from the draft agreement. According to Edgar Jr., Redstone admitted that the draft went beyond what they'd talked about and said he'd send a revised version. The new wording didn't help, however, nor did various propositions for each side to buy out the other or split the assets. In early April, Edgar Jr. had lunch with Lew Wasserman. Among the items Edgar Jr. raised was his deteriorating relationship with Redstone. He told Wasserman he might end up suing Redstone. "Well, Edgar," said Wasserman, "that's the only language Sumner understands."

Edgar Jr. concluded that Wasserman was right, and phoned Redstone to say he was going to sue. "I know how to wage war, but I don't want war," said Redstone. "It's a mistake. You're my partner."

Edgar Jr. said he didn't want war either. "I have been trying to do everything I know how to avoid having a war. But the problem is pretty intractable," he said. Edgar Jr. cited as an example a Paramount product, the popular TV series *Hill Street Blues,* which was about to go into syndication. If the series appeared on USA Network, Universal would share in the ad revenues. Under Viacom's plan to air the show on TV Land, Viacom would get all the ad revenue and Edgar Jr.'s Universal would get nothing.

Redstone countered by saying he had tried to be responsive but found Edgar Jr. impossible to deal with: "You propose things. We accept them. Then you reject your own proposals."

Suddenly, on April 22, Redstone told Edgar Jr. he had decided to release Frank Biondi with no strings attached and no explanation offered. Perhaps Redstone concluded the three months that had passed since Biondi was fired was a sufficient cooling-off period. Whatever the reason, Edgar Jr. wasted no time. He hired Biondi the next day at an annual salary of $1 million and an annual bonus of $4.5 million that could double, depending upon performance, to $9 million, for a total of as much as $10 million a year. Biondi also received 2.5 million stock options and was reimbursed $380,454 for his move from New York to Los Angeles. His new house in Brentwood was given two upgrades: Edgar Jr. agreed to install a clay tennis court complete with an underground watering system to keep the surface in top playing condition; he also paid $2.1 million to build a screening room so Biondi could show the latest Universal films to his friends. Add Biondi's severance pay from

Viacom of $4 million a year until 1999, and his total annual income from employers past and present could hit $14 million. Edgar Jr. had, however, at last filled the role of CEO that had been vacant for a year.

Frank Biondi appeared to be the perfect appointment. At fifty-one, he was ten years older than Edgar Jr. and much more seasoned in the entertainment business. Wall Street admired him for his knowledge of television and technology. "The job was a natural segue for me. Edgar thought [MCA] was under-managed and possibly under-invested—particularly under the Japanese—and I think most people in the industry would agree with that," says Biondi. "He needed somebody, as he said, to run the place, to do what CEOs do—execute the plan." Reporting to Biondi were Ron Meyer and Bruce Hack as well as Universal's general counsel and the head of human resources. The operating divisions—music, movies, and theme parks—continued to be Meyer's responsibility.

Sumner Redstone's release of Biondi, however, did not end the wrangle that flowed from the differing interpretations of the February 12 meeting. On April 29, TV Land went on the air. Edgar Jr. promptly sued. "He made the bold judgment to challenge a big player in the industry. I don't know very many business people who would step up to bat like that," says Ron Olson, the Los Angeles attorney who acted for Edgar Jr. as co-counsel with Michael Schwartz, of New York law firm Wachtell, Lipton, Rosen & Katz.

Redstone counter-sued, claiming that Seagram was trying to coerce Viacom into selling its half of USA Network.

Edgar Jr. needed USA Network, not just for its $500 million in annual revenue, but also as a way to make Universal's TV library (with such shows as *McHale's Navy* and *Leave It to Beaver*) available to USA subscribers. TV reruns are money-spinners in syndication because production costs are long since spent; advertising revenue goes straight to the bottom line. But there was also another agenda: Edgar Jr.'s personal stature and public standing. "To Bronfman and Redstone, USA [Network] owner-ship was never the real issue," said Bernard F. Dick in *Engulfed*, his book about Paramount. "The issue was who could flex more muscle, who had the higher testosterone level, and, ultimately, who would be crowned victor."

The trial began October 15, 1996, in Chancery Court in Wilmington, Delaware. Room 107 was a nondescript place barely big enough for that day's witnesses and the dozen attor-neys involved. Delaware had been the preferred legal home for U.S. corporations since the late nineteenth century, when the state made registration simple by requiring only a few forms and a modest filing fee. Delaware maintained its pre-eminence because Chancery Court gained a reputation as the best venue to settle corporate disputes. Judges (called vice-chancellors) are knowledgeable, matters move onto the docket quickly, there are no juries to award damages, and rulings are relatively speedy.

During his two days of testimony at the end of October before vice-chancellor Myron Steele, Edgar Jr. reiterated his dependence on the partnership.

> MCA's sole opportunity in the cable industry since 1981 has been USA Network. We have no other networks. We have developed no other networks. And therefore, for us to sell our interest in USA Network to Viacom would leave us with no cable networks whatsoever. And that is important to a com-pany which is in the business of producing large amounts of programming, be it film or television.

Edgar Jr. admitted that he'd blundered at the February 12 meeting by not correcting Phillipe Dauman when he said "MTV," not "TV Land": "I certainly now wish I had, but I did not. I remember registering it as a misstatement. But it did not occur to me that it could be more than that."

Redstone testified that he was angry with Edgar Jr. after the deal fell apart, telling him, "This is not like you have to be a genius, [like] you have to go to law school. This is very simple. You wanted Frank. We didn't want Frank to be in an inconsistent position on any issue. You agreed to give us a waiver of TV Land and the MTV Networks. I don't know what you mean when you say I don't know—you didn't understand what the implication was." Then, in a voice tinged with incredulity, Redstone addressed the court and said, "This man actually ran Seagram's."

When Viacom portrayed him as some naïf who did not understand the implications of the February agreement, Edgar Jr. was his usual restrained self. "There has been a consistent pattern of bad faith. I don't know how else to characterize it. I don't wish to sling mud. I don't want to call names. We have consistently had very different points of view about events. Consistently we have been unable to reach a meeting of the minds." Yet Edgar Jr.'s courtroom strategy did seem intended to make him appear out of his depth. His lawyers all but held up his lack of specific business knowledge and formal education as a reason why the court should protect him from others who were smarter and better schooled. During his testimony his lawyer, Michael Schwartz, led Edgar Jr. through the following exchange:

Q: Are you an expert on securities regulation?
A: No, sir.
Q: You are not a lawyer. Is that correct?
A: No, I am not a lawyer.

Q: What is your educational background?

A: I completed high school. I did not attend college.

Q: And you went to work?

A: I did. I started work. I started work at fifteen. I completed high school but I continued to work.

After fourteen witnesses over twenty-three days, the trial spluttered to a close on December 6 with a final foul-up after Seagram's expert witness was found to have exaggerated his qualifications.

In May 1997, Delaware vice-chancellor Myron Steele ruled that Viacom had breached the partnership agreement. Edgar Jr. had won; Sumner Redstone had lost. In his fifty-four-page opinion Steele described Viacom as a "disloyal partner," calling Viacom's arguments "illogical" and "entirely specious." Steele also rejected Redstone's claim that he and Edgar Jr. had an oral agreement at the contentious February meeting, saying "it is simply unreasonable to conclude that either Bronfman or Redstone (or Dauman for that matter) intended then and there to bind their respective companies to a multi-billion-dollar agreement."

Steele ordered the two sides to dissolve the partnership and gave them thirty days to come up with a mutually agreed plan. If they were unable to do so, they were to submit separate plans within forty-five days. If they failed to do that, Steele said he would impose a solution.

Even under such court-ordered duress, acrimony persisted; the court extended the deadline into September. On September 22, the two sides finally announced an agreement. Edgar Jr. and Universal would pay $1.7 billion to buy Viacom's half of USA Network and Sci-Fi Channel.

☙

Remarkably, even after such a lengthy and bitter battle, Edgar Jr. had no interest in sole ownership of USA Network. In May, as soon as the court ruled in his favour but well before the purchase was settled, Edgar Jr. put out a feeler to Barry Diller. Edgar Jr. had been looking for a way to work with Diller ever since the two first met more than twenty years earlier; this represented his best chance yet. Diller started his career in the mailroom of the William Morris Agency at nineteen, and spent the next three years soaking up the history of the business by reading the entire contents of the file room, all the deals the agency had ever done. Diller joined ABC in 1966, where he invented the Movie of the Week, then went to Paramount Pictures in 1974 at thirty-one. After two bad years he enjoyed seven good years, overseeing such blockbuster movies as *Grease* and *Raiders of the Lost Ark,* as well as the television hit *Cheers.* Diller next worked for Rupert Murdoch at Fox, where he did what no one thought was possible: he launched a new television network. By 1997, Diller had reinvented himself once again and was building a shopping-channel empire.

At long last, Edgar Jr. had something that he knew Diller would salivate over: access to millions of cable subscribers. But Edgar Jr. also knew that when Diller left Fox in 1992, he had said he would never work under anyone again. Edgar Jr. knew better than to try to hire Diller; he needed a plan to involve Diller in a way that made it look like he had kept his vow to be his own boss.

Edgar Jr. had two other reasons for turning to Diller. First, he had decided that Frank Biondi wasn't the man he wanted to run his TV assets. Second, Edgar Jr. had concluded that he wasn't even all that interested in TV. The change in direction was drastic on both counts. He had fought hard to get Biondi's knowledge under the roof and had battled Redstone to win all of USA Network. As soon as he'd achieved what he wanted, he tossed both aside, arguing that it would cost too much for Universal to become a major force in cable television.

It was true that buying such assets had become expensive. In 1996, Time Warner paid $7.5 billion in stock for Turner Broadcasting System. Edgar Jr. had watched that deal closely because the outcome made Turner the largest shareholder, with 10 percent of Time Warner. Seagram's holding had been diluted by the deal from 15 percent to 9 percent. Edgar Jr. did not have the same freedom to issue Seagram shares to pay for acquisitions. If he did, he would dilute his own family's holdings. If he were going to spend additional billions of dollars, Edgar Jr. did not want to do it in TV, but instead in music—his first love.

Edgar Jr. and his advisers had come to believe that USA Network was too small to worry about. "You're competing against Time Warner, which has all the Time Warner networks plus all of the Turner networks they had acquired. You're competing against Fox, Viacom, and Disney. They each have several networks that are important. We had one network, and a little one," says Seagram CFO Bob Matschullat. "Under the Warren Buffett theory of business, if you can't be a leader, why be in it? You're talking about [investing] another eight to ten billion dollars to be closer to the leaders in that business, not to be *the* leader. We knew we wanted to be a leader in the music business. We knew there was going to be an opportunity not too far down the road, and we couldn't do both."

Edgar Jr. was beginning to make a habit of changing horses in midstream, a leadership style that could mystify his own management, not to mention the financial community whose support he needed. Unperturbed about the possible repercussions, over dinner in May 1997 Edgar Jr. first floated the idea to Diller of finding a joint venture arrangement that would mean

Diller ran the television networks while Edgar Jr. retained a say in strategy.

In the fall, once Edgar Jr. owned 100 percent of USA Network, he and Diller hammered out an agreement. "We came up with the financial concept jointly, which was the lend lease concept," says Diller. "They would sell us [USA Network] for cash and for stock in our own company, and we would give them an eventual path to control. I would have the voting rights to their stock—I already had the voting rights to the stock that was owned at the time by Liberty—and I would have voting control until I ceased to be CEO. At that point there was a mechanism for Seagram's to buy out Liberty's interest, and they would control the company—the lend-lease nature of it—which was a really clever idea."

In October, Edgar Jr. announced that he had sold to Diller USA Network and Sci-Fi as well as Universal's domestic television production business. When the deal closed in February 1998, Seagram received $4.1 billion in the form of $1.3 billion in cash and a 46 percent interest in a new company called USA Networks Inc. (USAi). USAi included Edgar Jr.'s former TV and cable assets as well as those companies previously controlled by Diller: Home Shopping Network, Ticketmaster, plus television stations in twelve markets.

The complicated agreement also meant that Edgar Jr. had what was called the "path to control." In 2002 he could raise his ownership level in USAi from 46 percent to a 50.1 percent majority position, then could add annual increments until he reached 57.5 percent. Diller had operational control of Edgar Jr.'s shares—meaning that Diller ran the company on a day-to-day basis—but Edgar Jr. retained the final say over strategy, including a veto on any acquisition larger than 10 percent of the value of the company. If Diller quit or retired or died, Edgar Jr.

had the right to buy his shares as well as those of Liberty Media, 20 percent owners of USAi.

At last, Edgar Jr. had the kind of close relationship with Diller that he had sought since they first met. With such a savvy ally, Edgar Jr. was sure that his critics would see the deal as affirmation of his sound business judgment. The photographs of their news conference portray Edgar Jr. sitting to Diller's left, looking at his new partner with a contentment known only to those truly in love. Indeed, when Edgar Jr. and Diller showed up at the office of USA Network founder Kay Koplovitz immediately following the announcement, she thought they looked "for all the world like a pair of newlyweds . . . glowing with the thrill of their new partnership." As a wedding gift, Diller told Koplovitz that he would be taking her title as chairman of USA Network. Six months later, Koplovitz was gone.

For Diller, the deal was sweet, but not because Edgar Jr. was at his side. Diller had lost out in 1994 to Redstone and Viacom in the bidding for Paramount; now Diller had snared Redstone's television assets for himself in what he regarded as a personal coup. After Diller left Fox in 1992, Gail Sheehy interviewed him several times over the next few years while researching her book *Understanding Men's Passages,* published in 1998. In those sessions Diller revealed how he'd been physically tortured by his older brother from the time he was three until he was seven. Diller vowed he'd never again place himself in such a vulnerable position by being a mere employee working for someone else, like Rupert Murdoch at Fox; it was too reminiscent of his boyhood humiliation.

By 1995, Diller's Home Shopping Network had $600 million in sales, but the company didn't provide the prestige he needed. "In men who lost prowess in their career, you see the hunger in their eyes, or the sadness. They haven't translated the power into influence," Diller told Sheehy. Sheehy viewed the deal with Edgar Jr. as Diller's comeback; he had become a player again after missing out on bids for Paramount and CBS. "It had taken him six years, but it had been worth every step and stumble of the passage. Diller was more than his old 'self.' And he had accomplished that redefinition on his own terms," wrote Sheehy.

Diller got what he wanted out of the deal; Edgar Jr. got nothing but scorn. Peter Bart, editor of *Variety,* wrote:

> To the Hollywood establishment, the deal was fuzzy-minded. By separating TV from movies, it violated the fundamental laws of synergy. Even the math failed to make sense. Aside from the numbers, Hollywood was also critical of the manner in which Edgar Jr. had kept his senior managers out of the loop. Neither Ron Meyer nor Frank Biondi, his respected CEO, were aware of the Diller deal until it was a *fait accompli.* A former president of Viacom, Biondi's expertise lay in cable and TV, so the disposal of Universal's assets in this area seemed to strip him of his constituency.

Analysts saw the deal as unnecessarily complicated. "I didn't like the deal. It was hard to explain. I was the guy who had to write things up and explain deals to other people," says Harold Vogel. Edgar Jr. had called Vogel on the morning of the announcement, but even after listening carefully to Edgar Jr.'s explanation, matters remained muddy in Vogel's mind. "As time went on, Edgar tried to justify the deal by saying that the value of USA Network had doubled to $4 billion from $2 billion. But the problem was, you couldn't realize the value. You couldn't sell it or spin it off. But most of all, what I didn't like was that it was counter-trend to the concentration of power of intellectual property."

There was just as much puzzlement inside Universal, but there was also hurt and anger. Edgar Jr. had kept in the dark Frank Biondi, the man he'd fought so hard to hire as CEO and the colleague who knew USA Network best. When Edgar Jr. belatedly told Biondi what he'd done, Biondi said, "You're selling the best asset we have, and you're selling it cheap." Biondi was not surprised when Edgar Jr. told him that it was Diller's idea to keep Biondi in the dark. (Diller says he did not specifically tell Edgar Jr. to keep Biondi out of the loop, he just told him to keep their talks confidential.) "Barry knew I would have killed it. Barry certainly got the better of the transaction. I just don't think it ever dawned on Edgar that he could get more [money] than that or that, if he'd held on to it, his cash flow would have gone up dramatically from the USA assets, which would have increased his borrowing power," says Biondi.

Biondi remained in the job for another year, but his usefulness had expired. On November 16, 1998, Edgar Jr., accompanied by his head of human resources, John Borgia, met with Biondi to tell him he was fired. Edgar Jr.'s explanation was that he wanted to be more involved in the business, so he didn't need Biondi as CEO. Biondi had received advance warning; word had leaked to the *Los Angeles Times* the previous week. "I guess you don't need me around here much," he said, "so I might as well go play tennis today."

In retrospect, there were signs all along that Biondi would not last in the Seagram empire. He had run afoul of Edgar Jr. soon after arriving when he told him that no one liked the new Universal logo he'd had designed. "He had commissioned an agency to do a design that I can only describe as coming out looking like a Western gold belt buckle with a globe under it. Nobody was happy with it. Everybody was terrified to tell him that. So, lo and behold, my first message to the boss was

'Everybody hates this.' He was surprised because no one had said anything. He said the right thing, which was, 'OK, I don't want you to spend another $1 million, but can you get a quick retake and let me take a look at it?' But I think in the end he was always totally offended by the fact that people didn't like what he'd done. Edgar doesn't like being told what to do. It's just not one of his strengths," says Biondi.

Beyond such specific flashpoints, throughout his two and a half years as chairman and CEO of Universal, Biondi was given little opportunity to use the business knowledge for which he'd been hired. When Edgar Jr. and Biondi met with Doug Morris, for example, all Edgar Jr. wanted to do was riff about music. "Doug and Edgar can talk music in a language that you and I don't understand," says Borgia. "Frank would be in the room wanting to talk about the expenses, the P&L in the music division, and they'd be talking about, 'Do you think that's going to be a hit?' 'I don't like that song, do you?' 'How did that writer hook up with . . .' 'I don't like that arrangement, I like the other.' And Frank would be [saying] 'Could we get back to the advertising ratios?' It was a tough spot for him. It never really connected."

As was his custom, Edgar Jr. paid for his recruiting mistake by lavishing the dearly departed with plenty of the company's money. He gave Biondi a $25-million severance package, substantially more than the $15-million severance paid to Biondi by Sumner Redstone. Edgar Jr. also let Biondi keep the screening room, which was supposed to be company property. "I guess what I learned was that you're probably naive to think an owner—no matter how good a temperament or how well presented—is really capable of letting professional management run the business," says Biondi. "That's probably shame on me more than shame on him, but it just seemed like such a natural fit coming out of Viacom that I was willing to overlook that possibility."

With Biondi gone, Edgar Jr. split Seagram into three divisions: movies, music, and spirits and wine. Reporting to Edgar Jr. were studio head Ron Meyer and Doug Morris at music. In the spirits and wine division there was a triumvirate, all reporting to Edgar Jr. They included newly installed chairman John Hunter, who had worked at Coca-Cola, CEO Steve Kalagher, and Edgar Jr.'s brother Sam at Seagram Chateau & Estate Wines.

The reorganization looked more like what everyone thought he had in mind three years earlier, but after all that time he still hadn't found a CEO he could trust, someone who could be his true partner. His competitors knew they needed help. At various stages Disney's Michael Eisner had Frank Wells, Rupert Murdoch had Peter Chernin, Sumner Redstone had Mel Karmazin. "The competition were people who were really seasoned and had lots of experience. He was missing the partner who could help him run the company at the top. He needed his partner, and by the way, most people do," says Terry Semel, who as co-CEO of Warner Brothers had been approached in 1996 by Edgar Jr. to be his CEO but turned him down. "He didn't get Mike. He went that period of time without. And then he got Frank, and for better or for worse it didn't work. Here he was, up against a lot of pressure, and didn't have that internal partner who helped him day by day and who brought both experience and perspective to the issues. It's really a lot for anyone to have to do on their own."

The deal with Diller was a watershed for Edgar Jr. Now, not only did outsiders doubt his strategy, some of his own colleagues could not see the business case for the deal he'd done. Universal had enjoyed a long and profitable history in TV that started in 1952 with *GE Theatre* hosted by Ronald Reagan and was followed by such hits as *Alfred Hitchcock Presents* and *Leave It to Beaver*. Once Edgar Jr. did the Diller deal, Universal was the only major Hollywood studio with no TV arm.

"The highest-performing assets and the best positioned for growth were the cable companies. The last thing in the world you want to sell would be the high-growth assets," says Tom Pollock, who headed the motion picture business when Edgar Jr. acquired MCA. "You can exist without a record company, if you are an entertainment company, but the true synergy is between film and television, both in terms of use of talent and of content and branding. And you cannot exist today in the television business without television distribution. USA and Sci-Fi were the only distribution assets on which to build the television business, and they were growth engines in their own right. I will never understand why that deal was made. When I asked Edgar about it [he said], 'It was the only way I could get Barry Diller.' But he didn't get Barry Diller, Barry Diller got him."

Moreover, the deal ran counter to Edgar Jr.'s previously stated branding strategy of naming everything Universal and building on the strengths of the various entities. He'd done that with movies and theme parks; now he was doing just the opposite with TV. Edgar Jr. had reverted to the holding-company strategy, with Seagram as something of a passive investor, a style he'd rejected when he sold DuPont.

But Edgar Jr.'s strategy of linking with industry leaders, whether Geffen and DreamWorks or Diller and USAi, also drew praise. "Diller on the movie side was like Geffen on the record side. You couldn't find two more superior intellects, two more successful navigators through that dimly lit environment than these two guys. I'd pay a premium," says Jack Valenti of the Motion Picture Association of America. "He can get in bed with a helluva lot more inferior people than those two."

Initially, Diller was happy with the deal and defended Edgar Jr.'s decision to go against the grain by defying his detractors. "Edgar was not a popular arrival in the entertainment business for the media and certainly wasn't for people who were Seagram's life shareholders," says Diller. "Edgar had the courage to be impervious to that and to do what he thought was the right thing to do, all the steps of the way, knowing that often they were going to throw tomatoes at him. This transaction, when it was announced, what people said is: Omigod, how can you separate a movie company from a television company. How can he do this, the synergies—which by the way, none of which existed, none enough to count, ever have, ever will. He made a determination that he wanted to get the film company right and he couldn't get the television company right because he'd looked around for the people to do it and he couldn't find anybody that he had any confidence in to do the work."

The debate whether Edgar Jr. was right or wrong to make the Diller deal will never be settled. Both sides have valid arguments. What was becoming clear, however, was something far more important: there was a sycophantic pattern in Edgar Jr.'s life. He needed to be associated with powerful people—whatever the personal cost to him. Whether it was Mike Ovitz or David Geffen or Barry Diller, all his high-level links fell into the same category. He approached big names he wanted to be close to, believing they would help him, only to have those people use him to get what they wanted for themselves, often leaving less on his plate than theirs. The best deals in business are balanced, each side gains. But so eager was Edgar Jr. to be associated with powerful people who had influence that he was prepared to accept their terms rather than face a future without them. Such arrangements were as much about Edgar Jr.'s own insecurity and need for acceptance as they were about building the business. He didn't think he could be a somebody without them.

From the time in high school when he'd inveigled his way into the band, Edgar Jr. believed he had to give others everything they wanted in order to join the group in which he might not otherwise be welcome. In so doing, he was often out of his league. "Barry is always going to be a better poker player than Edgar. He's older, he's smarter, and he's totally immersed in his business. He's a very tough customer. He outmanoeuvred Edgar. He knew what he was doing every step of the way and Edgar didn't. That probably helped create a kind of illusion in Edgar's mind that he was on top of things when he really wasn't," says Porter Bibb. "I think he became reliant on Barry, I think he was infatuated with Barry. He was extremely conversant and in very close touch all the time with Barry. I'm not sure that was in Edgar's best interest."

For most Hollywood observers, Edgar Jr. had done the unthinkable with the Diller deal: he had given up turf. He might be able to overrule Diller on the long-term direction of Universal, but on a day-to-day basis Edgar Jr. had lost control of the company, he had handed over his power. In Hollywood, if you look like you're losing power, people avoid you. When you don't know which film will be a hit and which won't, when you don't know where the power comes from, you stay away from those you think are losers because you don't want to risk catching their disease.

Within a year, the value of Seagram's holding in USAi had increased by $1.5 billion. But Edgar Jr. had been wrong to think that the deal would bring him closer to Diller. It was one thing for Diller to agree to such a shared arrangement in theory, but he bristled under Edgar Jr.'s strategic control and veto power. In 1998, Diller negotiated a deal to buy NBC that eventually foundered because Diller would not accept the proposed corporate governance arrangements. Half of the board of directors of the merged company were to be chosen by him, half by NBC. A three-quarters vote of the directors would be required to oust Diller. Many executives would find those terms acceptable. If the directors chosen by the other side were unanimous in wanting Diller removed, all he needed was fifty percent plus one of his own appointees to halt his ouster. But that wasn't good enough for Diller; he refused to accept a structure that contained even the slightest risk to his authority. "I had worked for a company, a series of companies, three, until I was forty-nine. After I was forty-nine I said never again will I put myself in a position where I do not control my life. That means I would never sign an employment agreement, and I've never signed one. It means I will never engage in something that I do not control."

Edgar Jr. also had reasons not to like the NBC deal. If he put no new money into the NBC deal, his 46 percent stake in USAi might fall to, say, 20 percent in the new, larger company, thereby turning him into a bit-part player. To avoid such dilution and maintain his ownership position in the larger company, Edgar Jr. would have had to invest $6 billion to $8 billion. If Edgar Jr. was going to spend that kind of money, he wanted to do it in music. Moreover, he could not understand Diller's reluctance to accept the voting arrangement on the new board. "He didn't see why that wasn't good enough," says Diller. "He felt that my issues were immature. I said, 'You approach it from a different point of view, you approach it from a point of view I can understand, which is you approach it from the point of view of your family, where in fact everyone in your life is some sort of an employee. I approach it from a different point of view wherein I say, 'That's very well, but that's not my family.'"

In Diller's mind, Edgar Jr. was not acting in everyone's best interests. "Edgar would not give up eventual control. He had to have, quote, a path to control, which was the initial bargain. While I was angry with him, I could not say, ever, he acted in bad faith, he didn't, but I was very frustrated with him and I became increasingly frustrated. Here we were, having great success. We were building a very serious enterprise, and this path to control was frustrating because you don't want to be diluted and I want to grow the business. So we have a breach and you are actually acting against the best interests of ordinary shareholders of USA," says Diller.

A final overarching issue was that Edgar Jr. did not have the same belief in television as a business enterprise as he did in movie studios. "A large part of business is your own curiosity that then allows you to form beliefs after you've learned something. I wouldn't say he was disrespectful, I'd just say he never really was a believer that owning television stations, for instance, was an everlastingly good business," says Diller.

After the NBC transaction did not go ahead, there was anger on both sides. The two men barely spoke for more than a year.

Over dinner at his Malibu beach house with old friend John Bernbach, Edgar Jr. confided that the constant carping about the Diller deal and Universal's poor performance was beginning to get to him. "He'd gone through some flops at the box office. No matter what he did, the USA deal being emblematic of it, he got this avalanche of criticism," recalls Bernbach. "I can still see him—he wasn't bitter, angry, or weepy—he looked at me and said, 'I don't know what I have to do any more. I'm coming to the conclusion that no matter what I do, people are going to criticize me, so the best thing for me to do is to do what I think is right, put my head down, damn the torpedoes, full speed ahead.'"

In the past, Edgar Jr. always did what he wanted and expected people to fall into line. Now he'd given up asking for advice or expecting support, as if he had moved into his own private world where no one else, or their views, mattered. If songwriting could provide balm for his personal pain, maybe a music company would deliver salvation for his corporate soul.

NINE

THE MUSIC MAN

HIS CRITICS MIGHT CAUSE him distress, but Edgar Jr.'s real dilemma was of his own doing. He couldn't seem to just buy something, settle down, and run it. He had the attention span of a newt. Maybe he believed if he could buy something and build it, he'd be seen to be successful, not just an inheritor. Most of the media giants, even those who'd had fathers in the business, started small. Sumner Redstone's business career began with a few drive-in theatres, Rupert Murdoch's with a single newspaper in Australia, Ted Turner's with a billboard company teetering on bankruptcy. Edgar Jr.'s bio could never match their up-by-the-bootstraps style.

Hardly had Edgar Jr. acquired Universal Studios with its relatively small music division before he went looking for a record company with international heft. In 1996, he contacted Sir Colin Southgate, chairman of U.K.-based EMI Group, as well as Cornelis Boonstra, chairman of Philips Electronics, the Dutch owners of PolyGram. In the case of Sir Colin, Edgar Jr. presented him with a bottle of 100-year-old Martell cognac. Sir Colin accepted the bottle but kept the company. Philips was equally uninterested in selling PolyGram.

Eighteen months later, after EMI's share price had fallen by one-third, Edgar Jr. again approached Sir Colin in the hopes he might now be ready to sell. As word spread of Edgar Jr.'s continued interest in music, Boonstra called to say PolyGram might be available. Philips controlled 75 percent of PolyGram and was looking for a low-profile exit. A PolyGram deal made more sense; Edgar Jr. could negotiate with a single majority owner rather than chase EMI, a widely held public company.

In negotiations that took only three weeks in May 1998, Edgar Jr. was at his best, dealing one-on-one with the owners, just as he had with the Japanese. "Music is where his heart was, where his interest was. There's no question he was more comfortable operating in that area, but he would be the first to acknowledge that the numbers analysis has got to come from somebody else. He would assimilate the material, he had the intellectual power to assimilate and use and make judgments on the material presented to him, but he was very dependent upon others to provide that kind of information to him," says Ron Olson.

Aided by Seagram CFO Bob Matschullat and Morgan Stanley managing partner Bruce Fiedorek, Edgar's style was direct and firm. "That's how you get deals done. You know what you want to pay, you don't get caught up in deal fever that would make you pay more than you wanted to and should," says Matschullat. "Edgar respects people, he's gracious, relatively soft-spoken. He's not some bully. I think, to be honest, particularly to Philips, that was important."

As part of the $10.4-billion deal, Philips bought $2 billion worth of Seagram shares, in effect making Philips participating financiers. That infusion of new capital meant that Phillips owned 11 percent of Seagram, thereby reducing the proportion of Seagram owned by the Bronfman family to 24.6 percent, a long way down from the 36 percent they had traditionally owned, and an indication of the drastic measures that Edgar Jr. was prepared to take in order to own a music company.

The $2-billion investment helped, but Edgar Jr. also needed cash to pay for his prize. The more cash he had in the deal, the less debt he'd take on in what was the largest transaction ever done by Seagram. To raise some cash, he sold his Time Warner shares and Tropicana. Edgar Jr.'s capacity to so readily jettison two earlier acquisitions raised questions about his corporate vision over the previous five years. If he was so interested in music, why didn't he just get into that business in the first place rather than keep lunging this way and that?

Edgar Jr. sold Tropicana to PepsiCo Inc. for $3.3 billion, almost three times the $1.2 billion Seagram paid. After taking account of Seagram's capital investment in plant and equipment as well as the Dole acquisition, the return on investment was somewhere in the high single digits, hardly a home run after all that management turmoil and re-engineering effort. After paying capital gains tax on his sale of Time Warner shares, he'd netted $702 million. The return on the Time Warner shares, a passive investment, was about the same—middling.

Philips's investment and those asset sales still left $4 billion to be raised through bank debt to pay for PolyGram. The timing for Seagram to take on such an amount couldn't have been worse. In September 1998, Long-Term Capital Management, a hedge fund run by a group that included two Nobel Prize winners, almost went bankrupt. A rescue package was cobbled together, but the incident spooked capital markets. Seagram's formerly excellent credit rating of A2A fell to triple B minus, one step above junk bond status, thereby raising interest rates as Seagram's long-term debt hit $8.8 billion, almost double the company's previous debt levels of $4.7 billion.

For Edgar Jr., all the effort was worth it. The PolyGram transaction transformed Seagram to a far greater degree than the MCA acquisition. After the Hollywood studio purchase, spirits and wine continued to produce 70 percent of Seagram's profits. With the addition of PolyGram, spirits and wine now supplied only 30 percent of profits. Seagram's total employment was 34,000, a substantial increase from 24,000 before the PolyGram acquisition.

"The thing that intrigued me about Edgar was the thing that intrigued me about Ted Turner. They're driven, they're competitive, they're brilliant, but they also have a commitment, passion, and understanding for the business," says Porter Bibb, who wrote a biography about Turner called *It Ain't As Easy As It Looks,* and at one point began a biography of Edgar Jr. that he later abandoned. "When Turner rolled the dice on CNN, he had a gut instinct that there was an opportunity for news as a profit centre. He was prepared to invest $100 million, saying, 'I'm going to bet the ranch on this.' I think Edgar saw the same opportunity and had the same passion."

But passion without performance is pointless. In order to begin integrating Universal and PolyGram, Edgar Jr. gathered the management teams of both companies in Los Angeles. Edgar Jr.'s speech was about how size mattered, but his table talk was about himself. Over dinner, he told those sitting near him about the time in 1995 when songwriter David Foster phoned him in the middle of the night. Foster, who had won fourteen Grammys, was directing a show in Japan with Celine Dion and needed lyrics for music he'd written for her. Edgar Jr. pitched in under his pen name of Junior Miles and received a co-writer's credit for "To Love You More." The song was used as the theme for a popular Japanese TV show, caught on in Canada, and then reached the top ten in the U.S. After buying MCA, when Edgar

Jr. had told his war stories about the Universal back lot or the fun he'd had with Jack Nicholson, he'd done so without having any real success in movies. In the music business, he came complete with bragging rights. Big time.

During the 1990s, as Edgar Jr. turned his attention to entertainment in general and music in particular, even the limited interest he had in Mr. Sam's booze business began to fade. One of the last hurrahs came in 1989 when Edgar Jr. led a six-member delegation from the spirits and wine division on a tour of operations in Japan, Hong Kong, and South Korea. Accompanying Edgar Jr. on the trip were Ed McDonnell and Hubert Millet, as well as several middle managers. Over dinner with their South Korean partners from Doosan Seagram Co. Ltd., the group fell to toasting. Koreans take their toasts seriously. Bottles of Chivas were produced and everyone was given a stemmed glass from which the foot had been removed. As the pace quickened, participants were unable to set their glasses down. The choice was either drink or lose face; consumption became substantial.

Such a joyous state was reached that Edgar Jr. fired all the Seagram underlings in sight. Or did he? Some participants remember that he fired just Millet, the newest arrival, and maybe one of the juniors. Whatever happened, in a sweeping amnesty the next day Edgar Jr. reinstated everyone. The event became legendary in the Seagram Spirits and Wine Group, perhaps because it was the last time they really felt that he was one of theirs.

By 1990, the formerly top-ranking Seagram had fallen to third place in U.S. beverage alcohol sales with about 17 percent of the market, half of the market share it held in 1955. At those sales levels Edgar Jr. didn't need all the production facilities he owned. From 1990 to 1992, Seagram closed four of its six Canadian distilleries, including the historic one in Waterloo, Ontario, that had been purchased by Mr. Sam in 1928. At its peak in the 1970s, Waterloo had 250 employees on five bottling lines producing Seagram's 83, Five Star, and Gordon's Gin, mostly for export. Seagram also abandoned distilleries in New Westminster, British Columbia, Amherstburg, Ontario, and Beaupré, Quebec, leaving only Gimli, Manitoba, and LaSalle, Quebec, the first distillery that Mr. Sam built.

Business was also slumping outside North America. In 1998, an economic downturn in Asia caused revenue to fall in that region by 60 percent from the previous year. Profits were all but wiped out; most of the gains from the purchase of Martell were gone. In a March 1998 speech to a beverage industry group, Edgar Jr. bitterly complained that since 1990 beverage alcohol had created "no value, I repeat, no value" for Seagram.

After Edgar Jr. bought Universal, the spirits and wine folks felt like poor relations compared with the Hollywood crowd. The acquisition of PolyGram left them feeling totally forgotten. There was talk the spirits and wine division might be spun off as a separate company, presumably to prepare it for eventual sale to some other owner. Meanwhile, Seagram stood idly by while consolidation in the beverage alcohol industry picked up speed. Guinness bought Arthur Bell & Sons followed by Distillers Co. Ltd.; Allied bought Hiram Walker/Gooderham & Worts; Jim Beam bought National Distillers. "We could have bought Allied, we had the money, and we would have been maybe the number one spirits and wine company in the world. The decision was different. He went into music," says Hubert Millet, head of global brands in the spirits and wine group. "We saw him less. We saw him at budget meetings and when we presented results, but we didn't see him as much as we did before."

In Edgar Jr.'s mind the spirits and wine group had become an unwanted collection of veteran employees serving out their time in a business that no longer mattered. "This wasn't a job, this was their life. They loved it. Their wives loved it. Their kids went to school because of it," says John Borgia, head of human resources at Seagram. Salaries remained overly generous. David Culver, the Seagram director who headed the board compensation committee, tried to keep a lid on pay. When Borgia was named executive vice-president of human resources in 1995, Culver told him that there were too many spirits and wine executives making $300,000 or more a year. "Young man, that's too much money," said Culver. "No one needs that much money to raise their family." Culver's view did not prevail.

As Seagram expanded into entertainment, the beverage alcohol crowd began to grouse that their compensation was too low. At Universal, executives such as Howard Weitzman and Sandy Climan were paid in the range of $1.5 million to $2 million annually. Says Borgia: "Universal had contracts and agents, the spirits business didn't. The spirits business had traditional pension plans, long-service employees, a salary structure, salary ranges, exactly what you'd expect in a well-run business. We didn't try to bring those to Universal, nor did we try to bring contracts and fancy cars and agents to the spirits side. The spirits people were always into reading about the high salaries of the entertainment people and saying, 'Can I get a piece of that?'"

All that kept the spirits and wine division going was their undying loyalty in the face of Edgar Jr.'s growing indifference. "The spirits division was sort of out of the limelight of the company because it was not as jazzy and not as fancy. It was a base business, but the division had a very high morale. We were proud to deliver the bucks," recalls Gabor Jellinek, who joined Seagram in 1957 and was vice-president of production throughout the

1990s. Like many other long-service employees, he believed implicitly in the Bronfmans, so when Edgar Jr. made his move into the music business, Jellinek approved. "I have proudly known the members of the family, the three generations, and frankly, I really did not look outside of the box. I said to myself, if Edgar wants to do something, it's his privilege, the family owns 35 percent of the shares. I'd rather look at it from the positive side: he's going to do well and that will be better for the company, better for the shareholders."

To achieve improvement, Edgar Jr. had to efficiently merge the two record companies. As a first step he named Doug Morris chairman and CEO of the combined company. Universal Music Group, as it became called, was immediately the world's largest record company, with about 22 percent of the global market share. There was little geographic overlap: 75 percent of Universal's business was in the U.S., 75 percent of PolyGram's sales were international. Universal had no classical labels, PolyGram had three: Philips, Decca/London, and Deutsche Grammophon. Universal added artists such as Shania Twain, LL Cool J, Bono, Sheryl Crow, and Luciano Pavarotti.

More than two-thirds of all corporate mergers fail because of corporate cultural problems or because cost-cutting possibilities turn out to be minimal. Edgar Jr. retained Tom Wurster and Art Peck, from the media and entertainment practice of Boston Consulting Group (BCG), to oversee the integration. As had been the case with re-engineering, Edgar Jr. liked to hire the stars. Just as Booz Allen's re-engineering guru Michael Wolf published a book, so in 2000 did Wurster. With 200,000 copies sold, Wurster's *Blown to Bits* was a best-seller. Edgar Jr. supplied a laudatory blurb for the back cover.

Forty teams, comprised of 250 Universal and PolyGram employees and 50 BCG consultants, spent a year on integration. Music is a very different business from film. A studio might release fifteen movies a year at a cost of $75 million each. If three make money, the studio is in good shape. One blockbuster might be enough; some years, every movie is a loser. Studio bosses are akin to owners of professional sports teams: they are willing to wait to make their money when they eventually sell the franchise.

Music profits are much more predictable. A record company might issue hundreds of albums each year at an average cost of $1 million. If 15 percent of the new releases succeed, the company can be profitable. To push profits higher, Universal got rid of one-third of the three thousand individual artists and groups. Two thousand employees were also fired from back-office areas such as administration and information technology. Labels were eliminated; duplicate manufacturing and distribution facilities were closed. Savings achieved were about $300 million; fees billed by BCG were about $50 million. In all, BCG billed Seagram $150 million for projects ordered by Edgar Jr. That sum, along with the $100 million paid to Booz Allen and Price Waterhouse for re-engineering, demonstrated his unusual reliance on the crutch of outside consultants.

As the newly minted music man, Edgar Jr.'s most helpful personal contribution was his ability to encourage artists and sign new acts. "He had a certain cachet of being the big guy. He would send handwritten notes to the act saying how important it would be for them to be part of the family, [saying] 'I believe in music,'" says Jay Boberg, president of MCA Records. For example, Edgar Jr. helped sign blink-182, a punk rock group that went on to sell 20 million albums.

Edgar Jr. would also stroke the egos of artists, such as Mary J. Blige, who were already under contract. "He had conversations with [songwriter] Diane Warren about songs for Mary. He'd go to her shows and talk to her. The fact that he shows interest, shows support, and shows up, that goes so far," says Boberg. When Edgar Jr. bought MCA, Blige already had two hit records, each with two million copies sold, but few foreign sales. During Edgar Jr.'s ownership, her per-album sales soared to five million copies, including two million overseas.

Because Edgar Jr. could help produce such positive results, music for him was a totally different business from movies or booze. Music carried with it no reminders of declining liquor sales or dud movies he'd made. By contrast, music was exciting and interactive. Everyone was well aware, without having to be told, that he had power—just as his father had instructed him that his life should turn out. Here he could be king and command recording artists, like minstrels in a medieval court, to appear live onstage to serenade him.

One night, Edgar Jr. was just such an honoree at a charitable event. The after-dinner entertainment began with a singer who went on too long. By the time the act had finished, most of the six hundred attendees had fled. R&B diva Patti LaBelle was backstage, waiting to perform as the show's closer. "We look around and there's thirty of us left," recalls Doug Morris. "And Edgar says, 'Who's going to tell Patti that there's thirty people here?' So I went backstage and I said, 'Patti, we have a problem because most of the audience went home. I can't believe it, it's so mortifying. What do you want to do?' She's a great woman and she said, 'Are you crazy, I'm going out there and sing, brother.' She went out there and she had Edgar onstage, she was sitting on Edgar's lap, singing to him. It was so much fun."

❧

Edgar Jr. had belatedly arrived in the business where he always should have been. Given half a chance, he might have made a success of the music business. He had the necessary knowledge and passionate enthusiasm that was matched by few chief executives in any sector. But the economic environment was about to take an unpredictable turn. Edgar Jr. rightly believed that legitimate music sales on the Internet would eventually replace the traditional music retailer just as Amazon.com had transformed the book business. What no one knew, however, was when that particular vision of the future would arrive.

There are those who say Edgar Jr. should have realized at the time of the PolyGram purchase that file-sharing would ravage the record business. In fact, piracy was nowhere on the horizon. Music sales in the U.S. in 1998, the year he bought PolyGram, were $13.7 billion and continued to increase, reaching $14.6 billion in 1999, before beginning to slide. In Canada, sales fell only slightly during the same period: $1.4 billion in 1998 to $1.3 billion in 1999. Napster, the first major file-sharing service, was incorporated in May 1999. Global music sales peaked in 1999 at $38.5 billion. If growth had continued at the previous pace, total music sales in 2003 would have reached $50 billion. Instead, rampant piracy drove global sales down to $30 billion in 2003.

Once the hemorrhaging began, Edgar Jr. was the most active among music industry CEOs when it came to offering legitimate technology and seeking a solution in the case of Napster, the worst offender. "I always counted Edgar as one of my biggest supporters," says Hilary Rosen, CEO of the Washington-based Recording Industry Association of America. "He pushed and prodded the executives in his music company to experiment and try things. He gave them money for investment that lots of other companies didn't spend. The industry wanted to legitimize Napster, and he was clearly at the forefront of thinking that ought to happen. If people had gone along with him, the peer-to-peer environment might look very different."

In the summer of 2000, Edgar Jr. led the industry negotiations with Hummer Winblad, the San Francisco venture capital firm behind Napster. For a time, a solution looked possible: the music industry would buy Napster and turn it into a legitimate website. "The companies were prepared to jump off the cliff and try the experiment at Edgar's urging, but then Hummer Winblad got greedy and that, literally, was that," says Rosen. John Hummer, a partner in the firm, told Edgar Jr. that he had been offered $2 billion for Napster. The music industry would have to match that bid. Edgar Jr. told Hummer the industry wouldn't pay anywhere near that much. "During Napster negotiations we were talking about John Hummer and how it seemed to be inevitable that Hummer was not going to allow a deal unless he saw a significant personal payday. We were incredulous at his sense of entitlement. Edgar said, 'I know from self-entitlement and this astounds even me.' I thought that was self-deprecating and insightful," recalls Rosen. There was no industry-wide deal.

Edgar Jr. was also a key player in shaping the Digital Millennium Copyright Act of 1998. "For members of Congress, he was on the A-list. Anybody would make time for him because he was willing to be politically involved, he was extremely well informed—not just about the entertainment industry but about politics in general," says Rosen. "He could have thoughtful, interesting conversations about public policy with members. I've been in a lot of meetings with executives and corporate chieftains. The corporate guys can get pretty self-centred, even as they're going in not realizing that the hat is in their hand, as opposed to the other way around. It's not a situation they're often used to. Edgar always realized that members of Congress had a bigger job to do and that what they did to support the U.S. entertainment industry also needed to have a bigger public purpose. It was good for trade, it was good for jobs, it was good for culture, and he was extremely eloquent in putting things in that context."

The doors of the White House were also open to him. Shortly after acquiring MCA, Edgar Jr. attended a White House screening of *Apollo 13* with Bill Clinton, Al Gore, and other Washington insiders. Edgar Jr. was appointed to the president's Export Council. Seagram was among the Democrats' most generous corporate donors in 1996, giving $620,000. Edgar Jr. personally gave $321,500 that year and was on hand when President Clinton attended fundraisers at David Geffen's Malibu beach house. But Edgar Jr. was also careful to have Republican friends and contacts, such as Senator Orrin Hatch. Hatch, a fellow songwriter, gave Edgar Jr. several CDs containing religious songs he'd written. Edgar Jr. invited another Republican, House Speaker Newt Gingrich, for breakfast and a tour of Universal Studios.

Beverage alcohol is a highly regulated industry, so Edgar Jr. appreciated the need for rapport with legislators on a wide range of issues. "He understands the importance of government relations and establishing the right levels of protection, and the consequences for not doing so," says Matthew Gerson, hired by Edgar Jr. in 1995 as vice-president of public policy, to run Seagram's Washington office. In those circumstances, he could follow instructions. "I would brief him before a meeting and in the middle of the meeting I would think, 'He forgot the key point. What am I going to do? I need him to say this.' And then out of nowhere he would raise the right point. He was patient, he would wait for the right time to do what needed to be done. Some people, you brief them and the first word out of their mouth is whatever the key point is. He didn't go at it that way. He waited. He had a good sense of timing, when to deliver the message and when not."

Some analysts liked the new corporate clarity that followed $35 billion worth of acquisitions by Edgar Jr. "For the first time since the 1993 purchase of a stake in Time Warner Inc., we know what The Seagram Company looks like going forward," wrote Tim Casey of Toronto-based Nesbitt Burns, in a research report dated May 21, 1998. "It will be a focused company—with over 75% of its operations in the Entertainment business. It will be an operating company—controlling virtually all its major assets. Last and definitely not least, it will be a growth company—well capitalized and well positioned."

At last, Edgar Jr. seemed to have a big-picture vision. But colleagues continued to worry that his plan was inappropriate, given how different his strategy was compared with competitors. "Viacom, News Corp., Disney, Warner—everybody else was moving toward having TV channels and/or distribution, i.e. cable. We were about as close as doing a 180 from that as we could do," says Blair Westlake, who was in charge of what little TV was left at Universal after the Diller deal. "We moved into music when every other media concern was putting as its highest priority increasing programming ownership."

Edgar Jr. also spent an inordinate amount of time on Universal's theme parks, the smallest of the company's divisions. One of the reasons for his unusual devotion seemed to be that, as with signing a group to a record contract, he could become involved in a specific aspect of the theme park and have an immediate impact. Simply letting those he had put in charge actually run what was supposed to be their responsibility was no fun. He liked to dig in and do something, even if it put noses out of joint among those who were supposed to be responsible.

Universal Studios Florida had opened in 1990 and drew 8.4 million visitors in 1996. Universal Studios Hollywood had opened in 1964 on Universal's back lot and was visited by 5.4 million people each year. The grand total of 13.8 was a distant second to Disney, the U.S. market leader, with 50 million visitors at its parks in the same two states. Edgar Jr. hoped to close the gap. In the first three years of owning Universal, Edgar Jr. bought a 37 percent interest in Port Aventura, an existing theme park near Barcelona, Spain, acquired the Wet 'n Wild water park in Orlando, and opened a small but permanent attraction in China. Edgar Jr. also invested in new theme parks to be opened in Orlando in 1999 and Osaka, Japan, in 2001. Still, the total amount spent on theme parks was relatively small. Total cost for the two new parks was $4 billion, but Seagram's share of that was only $500 million, with the rest coming from partners. Rather than pay full attention to the jug of water that was PolyGram, here he was at the theme park worrying about the equivalent of a few spilled drops.

Edgar Jr.'s main hope for theme park attendance growth was called Islands of Adventure. Universal's second "gate" in Orlando began life as Ron Bension's baby. After Seagram bought MCA, Bension went on the road and delivered individual presentations to every Seagram director. By the end of 1996, the theme park had been approved by the board, but Bension was gone.

With construction about to begin, Bension's job remained vacant until May 1997, when Edgar Jr. hired Cathy Nichols as chairman and CEO of Universal Studios Recreation Group. During his time as CEO of Seagram, Edgar Jr. made a concerted effort to increase the number of female executives. In his father's day the only woman to hold a senior position was Mary

Cunningham. She had left Bendix Corp. in 1980 after being romantically linked to her mentor, William Agee, chairman of Bendix. Cunningham joined Seagram in March 1981 as vice-president of strategic planning. She reported to Edgar Sr., worked on a global wine strategy, and then resigned in October 1983 to rejoin Agee, whom she had by then married, at his new venture capital company. Cathy Nichols was among half a dozen women in senior positions during Edgar Jr.'s regime. Jeananne Hauswald was head of human resources at Seagram for three years, then treasurer for four. Ellen Marram ran Tropicana. At Universal Studios there were three high-ranking women: general counsel Karen Randall, executive vice-president Hellene Runtagh, and Stacey Snider, co-chair of Universal Pictures.

Nichols, a Harvard MBA, began her career in 1974 in the Los Angeles office of McKinsey. In 1986 she was named the consulting firm's first female director. She had advised clients such as Taco Bell, Bank of America, and Mattel, but she had no operating experience. The specifications for the theme park role were intimidating. Seagram sought experience not only running theme parks but also in merchandising, team building, and global branding. "I think I am uniquely qualified, but you are taking a risk because I haven't managed something," she warned Edgar Jr. "He was open-minded. He didn't get upset. God incarnate could not have filled this job." Edgar Jr. hired Nichols in May 1997 at a salary of $1.5 million a year to head the division with eight thousand employees.

Attendance at Universal Studios Florida had been falling for four years. Those figures mattered because Universal earned an 8 percent management fee over and above profits, which were shared fifty–fifty with its theme park partner, the Rank Organisation of Britain. From every dollar of revenue, Universal received eight cents off the top. Initial attendance projections said the new park would draw about eight million visitors annually, the same as the first park, bringing total annual attendance at the two Florida parks to sixteen million.

Nichols believed that hoped-for total was far too high. Universal was known in the industry as a "pirate" because much of its traffic came from stealing a day from the vacation of a family that had already visited nearby Disney World. With Islands of Adventure, Edgar Jr. was aiming to attract an older age group than Disney World, where the appeal is to youngsters three to nine years old. Parents who take their children to Disney have a good time because their children are enjoying themselves. Edgar Jr. wanted to attract kids from nine and up with rides and attractions that appealed to adults too.

If Universal was going to move beyond just stealing the odd day or two from a Disney trip, the marketing effort had to reach potential visitors long before they left home, so they arrived with a holiday package that included a hotel booking and tickets to a Universal park. A survey conducted by Nichols in major U.S. cities found that aided awareness (naming the park and asking survey participants if they'd heard of it) was a mere 22 percent. Intent to visit Universal Studios was even lower. Nichols told Edgar Jr. that even with an aggressive marketing campaign they would be lucky to draw 12 to 12.5 million annually to Universal's two parks in Orlando, not the 16 million he expected. Edgar Jr. revised the forecast down from 16 million to 14 million, but warned Nichols she'd better meet the new target. If she didn't, her compensation would be affected. Said Edgar Jr.: "I won't bonus on 12.5."

During construction, Edgar Jr. visited the Islands of Adventure site every three or four months. "He cared a lot about what it was going to look like, what the façades were, what colours were going to be used," says Nichols. "He would ride rides and make comments like, 'I don't think this is very exciting. Isn't there some way we can make it more exciting?'"

The slogan for Universal Studios was *Ride the Movies*. For the May 1999 opening of Islands of Adventure, Nichols went looking for a new approach. She hired Vincent Ward, director of the fanciful 1998 movie *What Dreams May Come,* starring Robin Williams. Universal convinced other companies to spend $150 million in advertising tied to the theme park. More than $100 million of that amount was contributed by Daimler-Chrysler; the Dodge Caravan became the official theme park vehicle. Other corporate sponsors with tied ads included Discover and Target.

Universal added $50 million of its own money, putting the total marketing campaign at $200 million. It was a huge sum compared with the usual annual marketing budget for a park of $20 million—and all $200 million would be spent in the six months prior to the opening. The money went into TV ads, newspaper spreads, and sales calls on travel agents, all under the slogan *Universal Escape: Are You Ready?*

Consumers could be excused for not knowing that Universal was actually opening a new theme park since the slogan did not even hint at that salient fact. Just as Edgar Jr. tried out rides and made paint colour suggestions, he was intimately involved in the marketing. "I was never totally happy with the campaign, and we went through iteration after iteration after iteration," says Frank Biondi, who was still CEO of Seagram at the time. "It wasn't like they were disasters, it just wasn't elegant. It was workmanlike. It's like looking at a movie in rough cut. Edgar was very involved in that, on the marketing side. This was one of those roles where he inserted himself." Ron Bension watched in baffled amazement: "I can't recall a bigger debacle—maybe the GM Pacer—of botched marketing, branding, messaging. It was a disaster by all accounts, and it was [caused by] this overwhelming need to do something different, just to be different."

So eager was Edgar Jr. to attend the official park opening in May 1999 that he declined an invitation to participate that same day in a White House conference on violence following the thirteen deaths the previous month at Columbine High School in Littleton, Colorado. Forty satellite dishes sprouted on the 385-acre theme park site as seven hundred journalists ogled the attractions. Coverage was generally positive for the two dozen rides and five themed areas: Lost Continent, Jurassic Park, Toon Lagoon, Marvel Super Hero Island, and Seuss Landing.

Attendance during the first few weeks followed an unexpected pattern. "The fear was that we'd built this new park and nobody's going to come to the old park. What happened was that we got a lot to the new but even more to the old," says Nichols. One Seagram director commented that they could have saved the money they'd spent on construction and just promoted the location they already had. Still, if attendance levels in the first two months could be maintained, Nichols was confident that Universal would reach her target of 12.5 million visitors, although perhaps not the 14 million Edgar Jr. wanted.

In July, however, Seagram CFO Bob Matschullat told Nichols that the marketing budget would have to be slashed to the bone. Edgar Jr. seemed to have abruptly lost his intense pre-opening interest. Nichols believed the only possible reason was that Edgar Jr. was gearing up to sell the division, perhaps even Seagram itself, because of the heavy debt load caused by the PolyGram purchase. "It was a big change for Edgar to have been so intimately involved. We had a *USA Today* ad, a [two-page] spread. He was so proud of it and he carried it around. He was so involved, and suddenly he wasn't there," says Nichols. Without constant spending to reach consumers and target travel agents, Nichols worried that awareness would plummet and families would revert to choosing other destinations.

Nichols was told the newly modest marketing campaign would be limited to Florida, where 50 percent of theme park visitors lived. But that plan wouldn't reach either the 25 percent who came from other states or the other 25 percent who lived in foreign countries. Nichols sent Edgar Jr. and Matschullat an eight-page memo detailing how advertising in eight major cities before the opening had increased visitors to Universal from those specific cities by as much as 265 percent, but they were unmoved. With Universal's budget slashed, money from the corporate partners also dried up.

Edgar Jr. may have given final approval on the marketing campaign, but Nichols carried the can for what was widely seen as a weak opening. She left in September 1999 and was replaced by Tom Williams, like Ron Bension a veteran of the theme park division. In fact, attendance turned out to be better than Nichols had expected. According to trade publication *Amusement Business,* in 2000—the first full year that Islands of Adventure was open—the two parks drew a total of 14.1 million visitors, 8.1 million at Universal Studios and 6 million at Islands of Adventure. Edgar Jr.'s goal was reached, if only that once. In each of the next three years, 2001 to 2003, attendance ranged between 12.7 and 13 million. As with most such attractions, attendance fell after the September 11 terrorism attacks.

Despite her retrospective success, perhaps Cathy Nichols, like Frank Biondi, was doomed from the beginning. Certainly Edgar Jr.'s recruiting technique was capricious. Before Nichols met Edgar Jr. for her first interview, she was specifically told that she was not under consideration for the theme park role. A week later Edgar Jr. hired her for that very job. Within three months Edgar Jr. was discontent. "I'm beginning to hear that you're not decisive enough," he told Nichols. She protested that her management style was to consult colleagues before coming to a conclusion, but she did find decision making under Edgar Jr. difficult to define. "One day you'd be going left, one day you'd be going right," says Nichols. "I learned that being decisive meant you were absolutely clear where you were going—at that moment in time."

Edgar Jr.'s management style was riddled with such inconsistencies. On the one hand, he tried to make the executive ranks more professional with thorough performance reviews. He brought in 360s, so named because they included regular appraisals by colleagues on all sides of the individual being reviewed. On the other hand, he did not seem to be following his own vision so much as he was mimicking whatever management craze was in vogue. According to Frank Biondi, "He'd go through the right motions. I'm not quite sure it was any more than that. I just felt like he had developed a template that worked for him. It's not unconventional: a lot of budget meetings, a lot of matrix reporting, and a few spies in the corporate ranks. I guess if you're in medieval times, it works well. It wasn't terribly helpful to divisional management. It wasn't like we were trying to sandbag him. It was just that while you were in the process of developing positions, you'd find that those positions had been communicated [to Edgar Jr.] while they were still works-in-progress. There certainly wasn't the same kind of communications coming the other way."

That politicized management style was also apparent in Edgar Jr.'s willingness to put up with people who lied. Cathy Nichols talked to him at one point about her desire to fire an employee who was an inveterate liar. "This is a person who would sell his mother for a dime. He will lie to you straight to your face. He has lied to me, not once, but many times. I can't work with a person like that," Nichols told Edgar Jr. He replied, "Cathy, I have no trouble working with people that lie to me— as long as I know that they do."

When it came to hiring executives, Edgar Jr. could be charismatic and persuasive. Once he'd decided that he wanted a particular individual in his employ, he could muster arguments, use flattery, and offer money beyond belief to entice that candidate to join his team. The surroundings used for such entreaties—a four-star restaurant or the intimacy of a meal he made himself at his elegant Upper East Side townhouse—raised the curtain on the tempting world he was willing to share if only the individual agreed. Edgar Jr. would see it as a personal defeat if he failed to land someone he wanted—even if that person had insufficient skills for the role. He was swayed as much by a candidate's inherent personality as by his or her professional skills. Edgar Jr.'s hiring processes varied from the peremptory to the painstaking. In the case of Cathy Nichols it took less than a week, even though she told him she was unqualified. At the other end of the spectrum, it took eight meetings with Bob Matschullat, some of them lasting as long as three hours, before Matschullat signed on as CFO.

Edgar Jr. was a butterfly collector, always seeking another trophy for his wall. Once a new hire was pinned in place, he'd stand back and admire the addition to his collection, then set out to capture another species even more exotic than the last. In April 1995, when Ed McDonnell resigned as president of the spirits and wine division, he was replaced by Steven Kalagher, McDonnell's former chief of staff. Kalagher was eventually buttressed by a new recruit, John Hunter, a former Coca-Cola executive. Edgar Jr. had met Hunter at one of Herb Allen's Sun Valley sessions, became enamoured, and so another butterfly was named chairman to work with Kalagher.

Every once in a while Edgar Jr. tried to play tough guy as if he needed a roadkill to show who was boss. Chris McGurk joined Universal in 1996 as president of Universal Pictures. In early 1999, McGurk was approached by MGM to become vice-chairman and chief operating officer. McGurk and Edgar Jr. had not got along. All Edgar Jr. had to do was wish him well and let him go. Instead, he decided to make matters difficult, telling Ron Meyer, "I want my pound of flesh." MGM agreed to a $100-million co-production deal for three movies and dropped a lawsuit with Universal on an unrelated matter before Edgar Jr. would release McGurk.

Another unusual incident in Edgar Jr.'s personnel management history occurred with Art Peck, who must hold the record for the briefest term of any Seagram executive. Edgar Jr. hired Peck, one of the lead consultants with Boston Consulting Group during the PolyGram–Universal integration, as executive vice-president of operations. Peck started work on March 1, 1999, reporting directly to Edgar Jr. Less than a month later, Edgar Jr. fired Peck in the lobby of Orlando's Grand Cypress hotel while their colleagues waited outside at the curb with the cars. Two explanations circulated about what went wrong. In one version, Peck was said to have gone behind Edgar Jr.'s back to talk to Charles about some issue. Another tale put Peck at odds with Doug Morris, who told Edgar Jr.: "Him or me." Peck won't say what precipitated his trap-door departure, but whatever it was, Edgar Jr. was forgiving. Peck returned to BCG and resumed his previous role as a consultant to Seagram.

After almost two decades in the world of commerce, Edgar Jr. still hadn't learned how to hire, manage, and motivate people. "Edgar's an encouraging boss. He wants to be with you. To have that conversation that he knows is going to hurt someone is tough for him. It's not his specialty," says John Borgia, named head of human resources in 1995. "What happened to a lot of Seagram people along the way [was] they didn't even know there was anything wrong. They looked up [and] got whacked."

Edgar Jr.'s management style, his dealings with the press, the way he talked to legislators—all had their roots in his upbringing. At the 1996 dinner to honour Edgar Jr. as the first recipient of the Steven J. Ross Humanitarian Award, he spoke eloquently about how his parents had taught him all of the most important lessons of life. "You have no power if you have to use it," he said. "Be quiet and not boastful. Be strong, but be gentle. Persuade, don't demand. Be firm and be fair. Be proud, but not arrogant. Be grateful. Don't take for granted what life has given you. Lead, don't follow. Care."

In addition to Edgar Jr.'s comments and speeches by others, the evening's program included dinner and entertainment. Donna Summer and Bruce Roberts performed "Whenever There Is Love," the song Roberts and Edgar Jr. wrote for *Daylight*, the Sylvester Stallone movie. Patti LaBelle, who was again the closing act, invited Edgar Jr. to join her onstage while she sang "Somebody Loves You Baby," with its lyrics of reassurance for the embattled. This time, there was a full house.

LaBelle then asked Edgar Jr. to dance. He wrapped his arms around her body and buried his face in the side of her neck away from the audience, as if he were trying to hide. She slung her left arm around his head and continued to sing into the microphone held in her right hand. More than a minute later, when the awkward clinch ended, LaBelle trilled "somebody" and told Edgar Jr. to sing the word back to her. As they repeated the process six times, each of his attempts grew progressively more tuneless. He then took the mike from Labelle, held it at arm's length, opened his mouth wide, and looked as if he were about to hold forth— but emitted no sound. Finally, after almost five humiliating minutes, the routine was mercifully over. Edgar Jr. slunk back to the sanctuary of his table.

LaBelle tried to make the best of a bad scene. "He's so nice," she breathed into the microphone. "He didn't make me beg. He said, 'OK, I'm going to sing, but I'm not a singer.' That's what he was saying with his eyes." What he was saying with the rest of his body was anyone's guess.

Edgar Bronfman Jr. may be a decent songwriter, but unlike a Bruce Roberts or a Paul Williams, he can't carry a tune. Nor was he able to gracefully pull off even such a brief unscripted appearance as that one with Patti LaBelle. For Edgar Jr., smooth spontaneity was impossible. Whether he was with journalists or management, onstage or off, life was either total control or nothing at all. And control was about to slip from his hands.

TEN

WHISKY INTO WATER

FIRE REGULATIONS PERMITTED ONLY one hundred people at a time in the meeting room at the Palace Hotel in New York for the command performance by Edgar Jr. The management turnout from spirits and wine, movies, music, and theme parks was so large that there were occasions when the doorway became a choke point as some of the attendees had to wait for others to leave the room before they could re-enter. No one wanted to miss a single word for fear that the new world that was about to be revealed would pass them by.

The session held at the end of October 1999 was not the usual corporate retreat featuring gossip and golf; this one was billed as an accelerator to the future. Those who gathered ran the gamut from crotchety lifers who disliked e-mail to hipper young hires who embraced the digital age. There was rapt attention from both groups for Edgar Jr.'s keynote speech detailing how technology had forever changed business. He warned them not to make the mistake of believing they could carry on as before by nursing the status quo. If they did, new companies using new methods would readily overtake them. "It was one of the few times that Edgar got up and expressed a vision. He said, 'Here's what we're going to do, we're going to meet every two weeks. I want progress reports.' It was probably one of the few times in the five or six years Seagram owned Universal that there were really what I would call expectations," recalls Blair Westlake, chairman of Universal's TV group.

Tradition, one of the three words on the Seagram coat of arms, along with integrity and craftsmanship, was about to be tossed aside in favour of untried ideas. The company's spending on technology was poised to jump from $30 million in 1999 to $100 million in 2000. Universal Music was already testing GetMusic, an on-line sales alliance with BMG Entertainment. Ready to be launched within days was Jimmy and Doug's Farm Club. Named after music executives Jimmy Iovine and Doug Morris, the "virtual label" would allow wannabe recording artists to vie for contracts by uploading their music to the Internet. Selected talent would be featured on a one-hour USA Network show following the World Wrestling Federation's *Raw/War Zone* with its 6.6 million viewers.

Edgar Jr. was seeking other, equally nimble Internet-related ideas. In order to stimulate the group's thinking, he had invited as speakers such experts as Robert Pittman, president of America Online, and David Pecaut, who two years earlier had founded the e-commerce practice at Boston Consulting Group.

Pecaut's message that day was about how the Internet was changing "richness," the quality of information, as well as "reach," the number of people who have access to that information. Insurgents could beat incumbents, he said. To make his point about the need to be agile, Pecaut concluded his remarks with a rousing story about British admiral Horatio Nelson's victory in 1798 over a larger French fleet at the Battle of the Nile during the Napoleonic Wars. Nelson had come upon the enemy anchored in shallow water. The French assumed there would be a conventional sea battle the next morning. Instead, as night fell, Nelson ordered a surprise attack. He was confident that each of his well-trained ship's captains would conduct individual manoeuvres in the ensuing chaos with no need to wait for orders from him. The English routed the French while sustaining few losses themselves.

Edgar Jr. took the podium to thank Pecaut for his presentation. He looked directly at Jérome Hyafil, the French-born chief manufacturing officer in the spirits and wine group, and began, "With all apologies to you, Jérome. . . ." Then Edgar Jr. addressed everyone in the room, saying: "Maybe Admiral Nelson figured out what Adolf Hitler figured out. You really want to fight the French."

There was a brief silence while everyone wondered if they had correctly heard what the boss had said. Then came hoots of laughter caused by Edgar Jr.'s wisecrack that played upon the stereotype of France as a nation of lovers, not fighters. But Edgar Jr. was no Lord Nelson. His own war record against the French was poor. He had acquired Martel, enjoyed a few good years, and then saw cognac sales collapse. Buying Hervé Léger, the fashion design firm, had also backfired. The French would deliver harsher lessons ahead.

Meanwhile, the quip about Hitler was a classic Edgar Bronfman Jr. moment: assemble everyone, tell them to alter their lives irrevocably, then undercut your own message with an inappropriate remark. He'd made a similar faux pas during the interview with Connie Bruck, calling Hollywood a "dumb" town. After rallying the troops with visionary words that demonstrated his leadership capacity, his gratuitous jibe about the fall of Paris was a lethal and self-inflicted wound. As Edgar Jr. said about himself following the reorganizational fiasco he oversaw in 1985, "Any mistakes that I've made have been executional in nature, not fundamental." That misbegotten mention of Hitler was surely a bit of both.

For months the stock market had been charging higher, powered by Internet companies no one had ever heard of before, run by twenty-year-old computer geeks. Old-fashioned concepts such as customer service and steady profits no longer mattered. The vaguest dot-com concept could create multi-millionaires within hours of becoming a public company. Everybody wanted to climb aboard the rocket to instant wealth.

Edgar Jr. was right to seek new ways of reaching his audience for music or theme park tickets, but applying the Internet holus-bolus to liquor sales or movie production was a bit far-fetched. According to Edgar Jr., the new entities he had in mind would be run separately from existing divisions. Such independent operators may have worked for Lord Nelson in one focused battle, but as a global strategy it could also mean a lot of wasted time as small groups flailed about looking for solutions. Another problem was that in-house experts, those who knew the markets best, were to be kept in the dark about what was happening.

Edgar Jr. had been looking for answers across the widest possible front. In August 1999, Blair Westlake had e-mailed him suggesting a meeting with Jean-Marie Messier, chairman and CEO of Vivendi. Universal conducted business with Vivendi's pay-TV arm, Canal +, but Westlake was concerned that the growing number of Canal + ventures in other countries might mean Universal could be shunted aside. Westlake thought a relationship between Edgar Jr. and Messier might help strengthen ties. Edgar Jr. replied to Westlake's e-mail the same day, asking him to set up a meeting with Messier when Edgar Jr. and Clarissa were on holiday in Paris during October fashion week.

On October 12, two weeks before that e-commerce gathering at the Palace Hotel, Edgar Jr. met Messier for breakfast in his office near the Arc de Triomphe. Edgar Jr. wore a short-sleeved shirt; Messier was in business attire. Sartorial differences aside, the two found much to discuss. What was supposed to be a thirty-minute courtesy call turned into an animated conversation that lasted more than two hours.

At forty-two, Messier was two years younger than Edgar Jr. He had spent the previous three years changing Vivendi from the world's largest water and sewage company into a conglomerate for the Information Age. With 250,000 employees, Vivendi supplied water to customers in countries as far away as China. Messier didn't care about plumbing; he was interested in digital bits and bytes. He told Edgar Jr. about Vizzavi, a union of content and connectivity that would allow the 14 million subscribers of Canal + to see movies on their personal computers or cellphones. Messier said he could see the day when Vizzavi, his version of Yahoo!, would link all of Europe. Edgar Jr. in turn described his own media empire and Universal Music's Internet strategy, in particular Jimmy and Doug's Farm Club.

While the possibility of a merger between the two companies was not raised, Edgar Jr. felt he'd found a kindred spirit. For Edgar Jr., who was always looking to others for answers, Messier might just be his next messiah. He had the same mystique as Barry Diller and David Geffen—a capacity to succeed with apparent ease. If he could so swiftly transform an old-fashioned water company into a digital information provider, maybe some of that magic could rub off on Seagram.

Jean-Marie Messier had impeccable credentials. He had graduated from the École Polytechnique, the top school for the French business elite, as well as the École National d'Administration, where business leaders mingled with civil servants. In 1980 he joined the Ministry of Education and Finance, helping Finance Minister Edouard Balladur privatize state-owned businesses. In 1988, Messier moved to Lazard Frères, becoming the youngest-ever managing partner in the investment banking firm. He created one of Europe's first leveraged buyout funds, and was known by a particularly American nickname, Robocop.

In 1994, Messier joined Compagnie Générale des Eaux, created in 1853 by Napoleon III to supply water in the city of Lyons. After becoming CEO in 1996, Messier went on a buying binge. He acquired a 44 percent stake in Cegetel and its cellphone subsidiary SFR, as well as a 30 percent interest in Havas, a publishing group that included *L'Express* and *Le Point*. He bought a 25 percent stake in BskyB, the satellite broadcasting system, and created Vizzavi with British telecom giant Vodafone. Messier scrapped the old corporate name, Compagnie Générale des Eaux, in favor of Vivendi because it had a sassy, global sound.

During the holidays in December, Edgar Jr. discussed the family business over lunch with his father. Despite all his attempts at creating a new Seagram, the level of success he sought had so far eluded him. CEOs measure their performance by their capacity to create shareholder value. In the nearly five years since Edgar Jr. had sold DuPont then added movies and music to spirits and wine by buying MCA and PolyGram, Seagram's share price had risen a presentable 71 percent. But other media companies had done much better: Viacom had risen 126 percent during the same period, and Time Warner was up 197 percent.

As Edgar Jr. saw it, Seagram had three choices: the company could float along and do nothing, seek someone to buy them out, or acquire another company and hope that a strategy of growth by consolidation would eventually produce more profits. For a shopaholic like Edgar Jr. with a short attention span, doing

nothing did not appeal. As for the third option, Seagram didn't
have enough available cash to buy another company of any serious size. Piling on more debt for such a purchase was out of the
question. That left only door number two: find a deep-pockets
buyer for Seagram. Said Edgar Jr.: "It's better to pick your partner from a position of strength than to have your partner picked
for you from a position of weakness." Edgar Sr. counselled a
more cautious approach, saying, "What's the hurry?"

For once, Edgar Sr.'s instincts were wrong. Two weeks later,
hurry arrived with a vengeance. On January 10, 2000, America
Online Inc. announced a $160-billion merger with Time
Warner Inc. As it happened, on that particular Monday there
were few people in their offices on the Seagram executive floor.
Among them was John Borgia, head of human resources, who
spent most of the day with Edgar Jr. as they monitored com-
mentary on the largest merger in history. "I'm sure I'm exaggerating, but I think we spent five or six hours together. It feels
like most of it was in my office because I've got the television
and the computer and I'm downloading. He can't stay out of
there. He keeps walking in [and saying] 'My God, it's unbelievable, I can't believe they're doing that.' He'd try to pretend
he was concentrating and then he'd come back in and say,
'What are the headlines? What's going on?' I think that day [he
thought] 'We're going to get eaten alive here. We're going to be
in no man's land.'"

Convergence was suddenly the new corporate mantra. This
was beyond Disney buying ABC. Consumers would receive
voice, video, data, news, and entertainment on their personal
computers or cellphones. AOL would become the portal of
choice for breaking news from CNN, celebrity chatter from
People magazine, or movies and music from Warner Brothers.
Edgar Jr.'s half-formed plan to seek a partner suddenly made

sense. When market consolidation occurs, competing companies have two routes to success: they can either grow and be among the dominant or they can be niche players. The businesses that get into trouble are the ones that end up in the mushy middle, outgunned by the bigger firms and outmanoeuvred by the smaller ones. Seagram was too big to be small and too small to be big, so even if there had been no AOL Time Warner merger, Edgar Jr. would still have needed some sort of strategic alliance to survive. The AOL Time Warner announcement just sped up the process.

Edgar Jr. felt he had to act because Seagram was a market leader only in music, where piracy was beginning to bite into profits. In every other division—movies, television, theme parks, spirits and wine—Seagram was no better than number two or number three in a series of sectors where the biggest players were consolidating more rapidly than he could hope to match. A few months earlier Viacom had announced its intention to buy CBS; there would be more such vertical integration as competitors sought to own all the links in the chain from production to distribution. Even after the PolyGram purchase, Seagram ranked a distant eighth among media and entertainment companies, measured by revenues. Seagram had become a chicken dancing among elephants; the outcome could only be bloody.

In addition to those powerful market forces, there were family considerations that for the first time in the company's history not only permitted the sale of Seagram but also acted as a propellant. Charles's interest in the business was waning. In 1999, he sold more than $400 million worth of Seagram shares. Moreover, Edgar Jr.'s relationship with Charles had not always been easy in the past, but had recently begun to improve. When Charles's son Stephen joined the Seagram board at the annual meeting in November 1999, Charles congratulated Edgar Jr. in front of the shareholders on his "courageous and professional" approach, saying, "You're doing a helluva job." In these more amicable circumstances, Charles might be open to a bold new idea. He never was much interested in managing operations, anyway. Anything that freed Charles to take his money and focus on what had become his major interest—philanthropy— might be appealing.

Edgar Sr.'s personal situation was just as compelling. At seventy, there was a pressing need for him to carry out estate planning for his seven children and twenty-two grandchildren. Putting someone else in charge of Seagram might be the best solution. The family now owned only 24 percent of the company, a long way down from the control position of 36 percent that had existed when Edgar Sr. took over and when Edgar Jr. was appointed. The third generation was unlikely to be replaced by a fourth-generation Bronfman, even if one from their number showed sufficient talent when the time came. Powerful institutional shareholders would not stand silently by and allow the family to pick the next CEO, given that much diminished stake.

Edgar Jr. also had his own reasons to let go. He had joined the company in 1982 only out of a sense of familial duty. Cashing out now, at the height of the market, would satisfy that undertaking. Such a decision would also mean a life less encumbered by what his father wanted him to do. He would finally be free to go and do something else that might be more to his liking. In 1993, when Edgar Jr. was recruiting Ellen Marram to run Tropicana, he told her that he did not want to run Seagram forever. "It was meant to be motivational, so I'm not completely naive about that," says Marram. "But I also think there was a part of it that he wasn't sure that he wanted to stay in the corporate world his whole life."

The final piece of the puzzle was supplied by the investment bankers. In such a fevered merger environment as existed at the time, financial advisers tend to prod their clients into joining whatever stampede is in progress. Goldman Sachs had been counselling Seagram ever since senior partner Sidney Weinberg met Mr. Sam shortly after he came to New York. John L. Weinberg, Goldman's senior chairman, had served on the Seagram board for years and had been a father figure to Edgar Jr. His son, John S. Weinberg, had grown up as a friend of Edgar Jr. and replaced his father as a Seagram director. And so it was that on February 9, 2000, Goldman Sachs made a presentation to the Seagram directors and senior management about convergence and the merits of consolidation in the media and entertainment industry.

Media commentators were also egging them on. "Seagram risks being marginalized in the wake of the merger of America Online Inc. and Time Warner," said Richard Siklos and Ronald Grover in the February 10 issue of *Business Week*. "The New Economy arrived in the nick of time for Seagram's boy blunder, Edgar Bronfman Jr.," Eric Reguly wrote in *The Globe and Mail* on March 7. "There he was, struggling to make sense of his entertainment and booze business, when the market shouted 'convergence!' You wonder why he doesn't open the door and get an auction going."

In fact, that's exactly what he had been doing. During the first two months of 2000, Edgar Jr. talked to several possible partners, including Comcast Corp., News Corp., and Walt Disney Co. Financially, Seagram was in excellent shape for such conversations. All divisions, including the long-suffering spirits and wine group, were doing well. Universal Studios had just had its best year ever, with a record $934 million in revenues. Seagram's stake in USAi under Barry Diller had doubled in value to $8.5 billion.

But there were stumbling blocks in discussions with media companies such as News Corp., where Rupert Murdoch's control was exercised through "super voting" shares. Murdoch would have had disproportionately more say than Edgar Jr. in any merged company because the Bronfman family's holdings in Seagram were based on the one-share-one-vote system. In 1985, Seagram had tried to put in place such special super voting shares. Most Canadian-based family-controlled public companies have a two-tiered structure that's in the family's favour but that unbalanced power is usually established when the company first goes public. Shareholders don't like to become second-class citizens after they've enjoyed equality. Rumblings from investors who were opposed to any such change had caused the Bronfman family to withdraw their proposal rather than run the risk of having it defeated in a vote. Edgar Jr. wanted some offset for those super shares held by potential merger partners, but neither Comcast nor News Corp. had any interest in such fairness.

Edgar Jr. made more progress with Disney, where both sides saw the potential for a good fit. Disney had a small film library that could have easily become part of Universal. Disney was not in the record business, so there would have been no need to go through another round of integration so soon after the PolyGram purchase. Disney needed a basic entertainment channel; USA Network would have filled that bill. If Universal's theme parks had to be sold on antitrust grounds, plenty of buyers existed for those assets.

Talks with Disney continued for three weeks, but the two sides couldn't agree on price. Disney was also nervous about both rap music and the spirits and wine division. Even if those businesses were sold quickly after the merger, Disney worried that its family image might be tarnished in the interval.

Seagram's eventual dance partner was identified through a roundabout route. Terry Semel, who had retired in October 1999 as co-CEO of Warner Brothers, was in Paris in January 2000, hoping to find backers for an entrepreneurial idea he had. Among those Semel met was Vivendi's Jean-Marie Messier. Messier was not interested in Semel's plans, but he was eager to expand in the wake of the AOL Time Warner announcement. Vivendi had Europe's biggest film library but no U.S. movie or music content, so he asked Semel to find out if Seagram was interested in talking. Semel knew Edgar Jr. was shopping Seagram, and was aware that he had met Messier the previous fall. When Semel asked Edgar Jr. if he wanted to reopen that dialogue, Edgar Jr. immediately agreed.

Semel set up a mid-February meeting between Edgar Jr. and Messier in the penthouse suite of the Four Seasons Hotel in New York. The Concorde landed from Paris at 8:30 A.M., and at 11 A.M. Messier arrived with his CFO, Guillaume Hannezo, Pierre Lescure, chairman and CEO of Canal +, and Alex Berger, an American-born strategist who'd been Lescure's number two since 1994. Semel attended, but only as matchmaker. Edgar Jr. was not accompanied by any business associates or financial advisers.

This penchant of Edgar Jr.'s to conduct important meetings alone is unusual. On such occasions most CEOs like to be accompanied by a colleague or two who can provide helpful information, hash out all aspects of the conversation later, or just balance the numbers with those representing the other side. Whether it was negotiating with the Japanese over MCA or Sumner Redstone on USA Networks, Edgar Jr. preferred to be on his own. That type of loner leadership was either a sign of his arrogance or a peculiarly furtive behaviour meant to keep others in the dark. Whatever the reason, it was a misguided way to act in this or any other business. No one can pull off the big deal solo; everyone needs support each step of the way.

With the initial pleasantries out of the way, Messier proposed a merger between Canal + and Universal. That wasn't daring enough for Edgar Jr. In the wake of AOL Time Warner, Edgar Jr. had something much grander in mind. He had come to this meeting ready to roll Seagram and all of its constituent parts into a powerful entity with a global presence, not just form an alliance between two divisions. Declared Edgar Jr.: "I'd prefer to merge Canal *and* Vivendi *and* Universal." Messier was delighted with Edgar Jr.'s high-stakes mentality. He loved doing deals. A three-way merger would not only provide the content Messier wanted, it would also solve his dilemma at Canal +, where Vivendi was a minority owner with 49 percent. He could buy Seagram, take over Canal +, and become a world player all at once. As for Seagram's spirits and wine division, they could worry about that later.

Alex Berger was not happy with the surprising turn in the talks caused by Edgar Jr.'s proposal. "I was hoping that we could put together this relationship through Canal, who were much more focused and knew the businesses very clearly. I think that when Edgar took it to the next level, all of a sudden it became a financial, megamerger deal. It became more political than capitalistic."

Berger also worried about Messier's capacity for follow-through. "The Vivendi guys weren't people who knew how to build assets. They knew how to acquire. Messier was fabulous, in his way, to make deals. He was really good at it. He was good at it when he was at Lazard." But Berger knew his cautious concern was pointless. For Messier, a merger with Seagram "was a little bit more sexy than just being in the water business," says Berger.

If Berger had known Edgar Jr. better, he would have felt a similar apprehension about *his* capacity for follow-through. When it came to losing interest once a deal was done, Edgar Jr. and Messier were two peas in a pod. But if Edgar Jr. was going to achieve the kind of legacy that he had in mind, then he needed to do this deal with Messier, even though the man was someone he hardly knew and hailed from half a world away. Edgar Jr. warned Messier that any merger proposal would be a tough sell to his family and the Seagram board. Messier shrugged off that comment, taking it to mean that negotiations were underway.

The two-hour meeting had more than accomplished its goals. Each now knew the other was interested in a merger. Equally important, there was good chemistry between them. Without that spark, negotiations can ramble along, going nowhere. They shook hands and agreed to meet again later that month in Paris.

The next set of talks began on Friday, February 25, and continued into the following day. This time Edgar Jr. was accompanied by his new chief financial officer, Brian Mulligan. After four years as CFO, Bob Matschullat had resigned at the end of 1999. At the Paris talks, neither company revealed any confidential information. They shared only what was publicly available, briefing each other on the component parts of their respective companies. Edgar Jr. had little interest in Vivendi's original business: operating municipal heating plants, collecting household waste, running intercity buses and trains. More exciting to him was the media and entertainment side and how well their two companies complemented each other. Except for publishing, Vivendi was almost entirely a distribution vehicle; except for its stake in USAi, Universal was almost entirely a content vehicle. Edgar Jr. and Messier continued to get on well. At dinner, Messier ceded to

Edgar Jr.'s knowledge of wine, particularly reds from Bordeaux. Edgar Jr. bowed to Messier's cigar connoisseurship.

In March, the Seagram–Vivendi parley gained momentum. The number of participants grew to include financial and legal advisers. Edgar Jr.'s preference was for a share swap so his family wouldn't have to pay capital gains taxes. That worked for Vivendi too. It was far easier simply to issue Vivendi shares rather than pay out billions of dollars in cash. Edgar Jr. also made it clear to Messier that he would not just do the deal and then retire. Caught up in the heady days of Internet excitement, Edgar Jr. decided that he wanted continued involvement as a hands-on senior executive in charge of music and the Internet.

Rumours about Seagram as a possible takeover target drove up the share price. After five years of trading in the range of $27 to $45, Seagram share price hit $65.25 on March 6, about the same time as the bull market topped out. In public, Edgar Jr. tried to treat any merger gossip with good humour. He opened his March 3 speech to the Jupiter Communications Consumer Online Forum in New York by saying: "I am unable to announce today our much-rumoured business combination with News Corp., AT&T, and also Viacom, Disney, Bertelsmann, Yahoo, Vivendi, USA Networks, NBC, Sony, Microsoft, or any Paul Allen–affiliated company."

Denials by CEOs engaged in merger talks are a dime a dozen. Lawyers advise their clients that prudence and securities laws constrain the capacity of executives to reveal they're in negotiations until a deal is almost complete or actually concluded. Until then, CEOs usually live by obfuscation. Inexplicably, Edgar Jr. took a different tack. On March 8, he attended the annual retreat for Universal Studios executives held at La Quinta, a resort near Palm Springs. Rather than be suitably noncommittal or simply say that such discussions were always taking place, Edgar Jr. kicked off the question-and-answer period by saying he would answer the one question that was on everyone's mind before anyone asked. "The company," he said, "is not for sale." The audience applauded, but disbelief abounded. Said one attendee: "He flew in especially to lie."

In truth, talks were far enough along that Edgar Jr. was ready to introduce his suitor to the family. On March 22, Jean-Marie Messier made a presentation at the Seagram Building to Edgar Sr., Charles, Edgar Jr., Sam, plus other family members and two of their personal investment advisers. Messier was well aware that no other merger partner had made it this far. If Seagram were to be sold, Vivendi would be the buyer. Messier's presentation did not include any dollar valuation of Seagram. Instead, he used his charm to sell himself, his track record, and his vision for the future of the combined companies. In such situations Messier could be the consummate actor. He was not above letting a tear form in the corner of his eye when he talked about how much he cared. When Messier finished his spiel, everyone was convinced that they were in the presence of greatness. Edgar Sr. spoke for all of them when he said, "Jean-Marie, if you were a U.S. citizen I would tell you to run for president."

That evening, Edgar Jr. invited Messier to his house to celebrate the milestone they'd reached. "You were extremely impressive back there, Jean-Marie," said Edgar Jr. "You touched every member of my family. I think we have the green light." They watched movie trailers and Messier drooled over what he called "the holy of holies"—Edgar Jr.'s wine cellar. "I stopped before a magnum of Ducru Beaucaillou, my favourite wine," Messier later wrote in *j6m.com*. "My host took it from the rack and said, 'That's what we'll drink to celebrate the conclusion of our agreement!' It was a bottle of 1955, the year Edgar Junior was born. For my part, I was born in 1956, but that wasn't a good year for Bordeaux wines." As for what was being laid down in 2000, the year was shaping up very nicely.

ELEVEN

DOING THE DEAL

BY TRADITION, THE MARCH MEETING of the Seagram board was always a travelling affair when directors gathered at some location other than Montreal or New York. Such events were part work and part junket, combining board business with a tour of some aspect of Seagram's operations. The previous year's confab was held in Orlando so directors could admire the new theme park. After the Absolut deal, directors journeyed to Stockholm to meet their new partners.

The March 2000 meeting was held at Meadowood Napa Valley, a Relais & Châteaux resort on 250 acres near St. Helena, California. The hostelry offered golf, spa facilities, a cooking school, and a wine tutor to entertain spouses who tagged along. As official host, Sam took everyone on a visit to Sterling Vineyards, with its spectacular hilltop setting and funicular that runs from the valley floor to a glistening white structure that looks like an Aegean village.

During the two-day meeting that began on March 28, directors learned for the first time not only that Seagram was for sale but also that all members of the family were prepared to be

minor players in a merger. If capitalists can participate in a revolution, this certainly was an upheaval in the family thinking,
one that can only be explained away by their collective greed.
Seagram share price had never been so high; now was the time
to sell their heritage for whatever this Frenchman was prepared
to pay.

Directors had been rubber-stamping family proposals for
eons. Edgar Sr., who joined the board in 1955, once asked Mr.
Sam what happened at the meetings and was told, "We declare
a dividend and have a drink." Usually, when a new CEO
assumes office, over time he remakes the board in his own
image. Edgar Jr. had instead maintained the composition of the
board much as it had been in his father's day. As Seagram directors reached the normal retirement age of seventy, Edgar Jr. had
empty chairs to fill as he wished. Yet during Edgar Jr.'s six years
as CEO, he tended to choose status quo replacements who
offered safe continuity. Of his fourteen appointments, more
than three-quarters could only be described as conservative
duplications of previous office-holders or people who might be
helpful in maintaining commercial ties. Three of Edgar Jr.'s
nominees were exactly like him, sons of directors: André
Desmarais, John S. Weinberg, and Stephen Bronfman. Three
others were the result of alliances or acquisitions: Lew
Wasserman, Barry Diller, and Cornelis Boonstra. Three were
Seagram officers who came and went: Ed McDonnell, Frank
Biondi, and Bob Matschullat. Lawyer Neil Phillips was replaced
by Sam Minzberg, another lawyer with long-standing family ties
as president and CEO of Claridge Inc., Charles's holding company. Also named was Matthew Barrett, CEO of the Bank of
Montreal, bankers to Seagram for decades. (Charles served on
the bank's board for twenty years.) Only three of Edgar Jr.'s
fourteen appointees could be called anything close to outside

directors who supplied fresh thinking: Richard Brown, chairman and CEO of Electronic Data Systems Corp.; Michele Hooper, president and CEO of Voyageur Expanded Learning; and Laurent Beaudoin, chairman and CEO of Bombardier Inc. (By coincidence, Beaudoin lived in the Montreal house occupied by Edgar Jr.'s parents at the time of his birth.)

For their loyalty to Edgar Jr., directors were handsomely rewarded. In the past, directors' fees had always been set in Canadian dollars. As a result, when those fees were converted to U.S. dollars by the non-Canadian directors, the payments bounced around with currency fluctuations. With the C$ falling against the US$ during the 1990s, some directors were taking a haircut. So, on November 1, 1996, fees were changed from C$ to US$. Annual payment for each director went from C$35,000 (approximately US$25,600) to US$35,000. The stipend for each meeting rose from C$1,500 (US$1,100) to US$1,500. In 1999, the annual fee paid to each director was raised again, this time to $42,500, a 66 percent increase in only three years. Of course, all expenses related to attendance were reimbursed. At Christmas each director received a pleasant perk—a case or two of various Seagram products.

As chairman, Edgar Sr. opened discussion at the Meadowood meeting on the key agenda item by announcing, "We want the board to look at an idea of what we might do with the entertainment assets. We realize that this might mean contributing our Seagram shares." Edgar Jr. then outlined the family's thinking, described discussions he'd held with various competitors and how the candidates had already been winnowed down to one: Vivendi.

Copious information was tabled about the state of the industry. "Presentations were always thorough and professional and had the requisite bankers and lawyers in attendance," says

Seagram treasurer John Preston. "There was a lot of confidence in the Bronfmans. The board, quite correctly, said if these guys have got some skin in the game, they're not going to do something stupid. If somebody has got a large bet on the table and they raise the bet, they ought to know what they're talking about." At the end of the two-day session, the board gave Edgar Jr. a mandate to continue the Vivendi talks.

The negotiations, often held at Edgar Jr.'s house in Manhattan, were given the unremarkable code name of Operation Secret. In early April, Seagram and Vivendi began to share more detailed information. Messier started the bidding process by offering $62 a share, an amount lower than the peak reached in March before stock prices started to slide. By Easter Monday, April 24, he had raised his offer to $72.

Edgar Jr. wanted to delay discussion about price until other matters were resolved, so he focused on share ratios. Because each company had a different total number of shares as well as different share price, a simple one-to-one share swap wouldn't work. Messier proposed that one Seagram share would equal two-thirds of a Vivendi share. Those ratios could be affected also by a change in share value, so Edgar Jr. asked what would happen if Vivendi share price fell after the deal was announced. Discussion about protection for Seagram shareholders in the form of a "collar," a device that alters the ratio if share price changes, did not go beyond generalities. The collar joined price, ratios, and a host of other items on a lengthening list about which there was no consensus. Everyone needed a breather. Discussions were suspended.

On May 5, the two CFOs, Mulligan of Seagram's and Hannezo of Vivendi, spoke by phone and agreed to restart the talks. The respite worked. When negotiations resumed in New York, both sides were more committed and discussions moved more expeditiously. In most transactions there are lengthy periods when details are handled by investment bankers or the respective chief financial officers, but Messier's background at Lazard Frères meant that he revelled in being at the table all the time, involved in every nuance. Negotiations are like war: if one general is in plain view commanding his troops, the other general feels the need to be equally visible, in order to maintain a match in the battlefield ranks. As a result, Edgar Jr. felt he had to always be at the table too. Messier raised his offer again, this time to $75 a share. Edgar Jr. countered with $80. The two sides were getting close.

As a change of pace away from the negotiating table, Edgar Jr. delivered a speech on May 26 to an Internet conference in San Jose. Although stock market values continued to slide from their March highs, a widespread belief persisted in technology and the Internet. Edgar Jr.'s speech themes—piracy and anonymity, creativity and consumption—demonstrated his commitment to a digital future. "We now live in an era in which a few clicks of your mouse will make it possible for you to summon every book ever written in any language, every movie ever made, every television show ever produced, and every piece of music ever recorded," he declared. But there were perils amid the promise. "There are those who believe that because technology can access property and appropriate it, then somehow that which is yours is no longer yours—because technology has made it simple and easy for someone to take it from you. If intellectual property is not protected—across the board, in every case, with no exceptions and no sophistry about a changing world—what will happen? Intellectual property will suffer the fate of the buffalo."

As he warmed to his topic, Edgar Jr.'s language became lyrical, his passion almost palpable. "What would the Internet be without 'content'? It would be a valueless collection of silent machines with grey screens. It would be the electronic equivalent of a marine desert—lovely elements, nice colours, no life. It would be nothing." The challenge ahead for business was not the usual concerns about regulation or government interference. "It is, rather, to manage, preserve and protect the sun around which all these planets make their stately circles. That sun is not an operating system or even the greater-than-the-sum-of-its-parts Internet itself: it is the content, without which the Internet would die in a day."

On June 4, the parties signed confidentiality agreements as talks moved into the final phase. This was a three-way merger. Vivendi was issuing shares in itself to holders of shares in Canal + and Seagram. For every share of Canal +, a Canal + shareholder would get two shares of Vivendi. For every Seagram share, a Seagram shareholder would receive seven-tenths of a Vivendi share. The collar meant that Seagram shareholders enjoyed some protection if Vivendi share price changed. If, after the deal was announced, the Vivendi share price fell by 12.5 percent, every Seagram share would be worth eight-tenths of a Vivendi share, slightly more than the previous seven-tenths. But that was the protective limit. If share price continued to fall beyond the 12.5 percent collar, no further adjustment would be made. For Messier, the collar also provided protection if the stock price went higher, as Edgar Jr. believed it would, once financial markets saw the wisdom of the deal he'd struck. That erroneous view on his part was another reason why he was willing to do an all-stock deal and not even take out some cash on the way by.

With the collar issue settled, the final push began on June 8 as Messier, Edgar Jr., and their key advisers wrangled about the remaining issues for thirty-six hours straight. Messier agreed to split the difference between his $75 bid and Edgar Jr.'s $80 demand by offering $77.50. (The eventual price of $77.35 came about because of currency fluctuation between the euro and the US$.) Seagram would have five of the twenty seats on the Vivendi board of directors. Edgar Jr. insisted on being named vice-chairman, the same title given to Ted Turner after he sold Turner Broadcasting System to Time Warner. Edgar Jr. also said he wanted the world to know that the title he was accepting had real meaning, that this was not one of those occasions when a spent force was merely window dressing. He fretted over the language in the final agreement, making sure it was clear that he reported directly to Messier and that no one else could hold the same title as he did, thereby detracting from his stature. Edgar Jr. was called the "sole vice-chairman" and Messier was described as "the only executive senior to Mr. Bronfman."

Edgar Jr.'s compensation was also assured in a four-year contract. Although his duties and responsibilities would be far less onerous than his role as CEO of Seagram, his compensation would be about the same. He would receive a salary of $1 million a year, plus an annual bonus that could go as high as $3 million and was guaranteed to be at least $2 million during each of the first two years.

With everything negotiated, now it was Edgar Jr.'s turn to feel the pressure. "Give me some more time. This is a once-in-a-lifetime decision. I'll never have to make it again. I want to sleep on it," he said.

By the next morning, Edgar Jr. had decided to proceed. Edgar Sr., who had not been at the negotiating table, pronounced himself to be greatly pleased. Their relationship had moved onto a new plateau of interdependence where Edgar Sr. sat back and waited, confident his son knew him well enough to be able to satisfy them both without having to ask how. Said Edgar Sr. when he heard the details, "My son, I don't give you my approval, I give you my congratulations."

Edgar Jr. called Montreal to speak to Charles, who was so excited to hear the price Messier had agreed to pay that he told Stephen to listen in on the line. Entertainment had worked out well for Charles and his offspring after all. Claridge had owned a stake in Netstar Communications, with its specialty cable channels The Sports Network and Discovery. Stephen was Netstar's deputy chairman from 1995 to 1999. Ellen and her husband Andrew Hauptman co-owned a film company and produced a number of movies, including *Safe Men, Gabriel & Me,* and *Thunderpants,* the story of an eleven-year-old boy who harnesses his flatulence in hopes of becoming an astronaut. (After living in London for nine years, the couple moved to Los Angeles in September 2003.)

The $77.35 price for a Seagram share worked best for those among the six thousand Seagram shareholders who immediately sold their holdings into the market. The other choice for shareholders was to follow the Bronfmans, hang on to their shares, and wait six months to receive Vivendi shares in exchange, thereby escaping capital gains taxes. But the value to be received was decreasing with every passing day. By June 20, the day of the announcement, Vivendi share price had already fallen 15 percent in a week. The full benefit of the collar came into play. Seagram shareholders would receive eight-tenths of a Vivendi share for each share they held. But that was the end of the downside protection. (The AOL Time Warner deal had no collar. By the time shareholders of the two companies approved that merger, the same month as the Vivendi–Seagram deal was announced, the value of AOL shares had fallen by 50 percent.)

Edgar Jr. had negotiated the share swap to avoid taxes. He

had further tied the family's hands by agreeing that they would not sell any of their Vivendi shares until ninety days after the deal closed in December. Whatever happened to the market price of Vivendi shares in the nine months between June 2000 and March 2001, the family could do nothing but go along for the ride. Taxes had always been anathema to the Bronfmans. Edgar Jr. had gone to great lengths to avoid taxes when he sold DuPont. Charles carried out the family's most successful tax avoidance exercise when he transferred two family trusts, one in 1985 and another in 1991, worth a total of C$2.2 billion, from Canada to the U.S. without paying capital gains tax that could have been as much as C$700 million. In 1996, the auditor general criticized the advance tax rulings that were involved, saying the rulings "may have circumvented the intent of the law." The loophole was closed in 2001.

George Harris, a Winnipeg social activist, sued Revenue Canada in 1996, claiming the transfers had received preferential treatment that was not widely available. In 1999, Federal Court Justice Francis Muldoon ruled that Harris's complaint could go forward, saying that the 1991 decision had a taint of "favouritism" and "grave maladministration." In 2001, when the matter was finally heard, Madam Justice Eleanor Dawson ruled there had been no special benefit, just "sloppy practice." Throughout all the proceedings, the specific trusts were never officially identified, but federal officials had quietly indicated along the way that the family trusts belonged to Charles.

The Seagram board of directors gathered on June 17 to study the merger agreement in a final series of meetings that stretched over three days. Vizzavi's value came under particular scrutiny from Sam Minzberg. Goldman Sachs and Morgan Stanley had both produced reports for the board that included their assessment of the valuations and share ratios agreed to at the negotiating table. Minzberg was assured that the investment bankers had used the low end of the range, valuing Vizzavi at $3 billion to $5 billion.

None of the directors knew Jean-Marie Messier, but André Desmarais's Power Corp. at least had some European alliances with Pargesa Group and its holdings in Bertelsmann, Groupe Bruxelles Lambert, and TotalFinaElf, among others. As a result, Desmarais had more exposure than most of the other directors to the strengths and weaknesses of European executives. He expressed concern about the capacity of a French company to oversee U.S. entertainment assets on Seagram's behalf. Edgar Jr. assured him that all would be well. He'd be minding music and the Internet himself.

Barry Diller, who listened in from London, had previously been excluded. Beginning with the March meeting in California, Edgar Jr. had asked Diller to stay away from board meetings because he regarded him as a potential competitor if Seagram merged with Vivendi. "I thought they were making a very speculative deal," says Diller, who remained silent through-out the board's deliberations in June. "Look, this deal was going to be approved. I had no role to play in it. I played no role in it. Understand, I'm a disaffected member of that board. I had been excluded from all the discussions. I had been thought of as a potential competitor to the transaction, so I was not a friend of the court." No one asked for Diller's view on the merger and he did not volunteer his thoughts.

Nothing could stop this juggernaut. On June 19, the Seagram board approved the merger at the proposed price and on the terms negotiated by Edgar Jr. The Vivendi and Canal + boards also approved. Vivendi would pay $34 billion for Seagram and $10.6 billion for the 51 percent of Canal + it did not already own, then merge all three. As the largest shareholder in Vivendi, with 8.6 percent of all shares, the Bronfmans were part of a new powerhouse. The movie, music, and theme park assets of Seagram would be combined with Havas, the biggest publisher in Europe, a 44 percent interest in Cegetel, the French telecom company, as well as stakes in Vodafone, a British mobile phone provider with 58 million subscribers, Canal +, the largest pay-TV broadcaster in Europe, a water and sewage empire, and, of course, Vizzavi.

For Phyllis, who had donated her last block of 750,000 Seagram shares to the Canadian Centre for Architecture in May 1999, the merger only proved that Edgar Jr. was as out of touch with the reality of everyday life as he always had been. "The wealth, the power, being able to manipulate things, never taking an airplane with other people, taking a private airplane. They're not aware of what's happening in the world, and I think it's a real problem," she said in a television interview. To her, selling Seagram was like a death in the family. "I mourned all summer. I really mourned. I mourned to see something that was built and responsible and had a great sense of culture go up in thin air."

Edgar Jr. explained his decision through a message sent to all Seagram employees on the company Intranet:

> CEOs are not allowed to be sentimental in this world, and it is ultimately a CEO's responsibility to do what he or she believes is the right thing for their shareholders. Control is valuable when it creates value. It's not valuable when it is either not creating value or in a sense, over the long term, is mitigating value. And so, we came to this very difficult con-clusion, which is that we needed to move on; that after 75 years or so of ownership in this business, that our sharehold-ers were no longer advantaged by us continuing to hold the

business in the way we were holding it. And that all of our assets—our entertainment assets clearly more urgently—but all of our assets in time, needed to be housed in broader, stronger, better financed, and better designed companies to be able to deliver against the consumer model more effectively, more efficiently, more competitively, and more profitably.

Buried in all of that biz-speak jargon, Edgar Jr. had made two startling admissions. First, he had run out of steam; second, the ship he'd built in his six years as CEO was not strong enough to sail against the winds of competition. His answer was not to build a better ship, not even to seek safe harbour and ride out the gale. Instead, he gave up, sold the company, and turned the helm over to another captain. Edgar Jr. could call this deal a merger all he liked; this was a takeover.

Even as he made that dramatic final move, he was no Lord Nelson bringing home victory. He could not even say that he had achieved this deal on his own, because his father was ever present in his thoughts, if not at his side. "The dynamic Dad has created is one where he does not impose his view, which makes me seek it. I don't consult him on daily operations regularly, but on any major strategic initiative, he's involved from the outset," Edgar Jr. told Anthony Bianco for his story on Edgar Jr. in the June 26, 2000, issue of *Business Week*.

What a complicated relationship that must have been where the father did not impose his view, thereby making the son work harder to figure out what those inner feelings were so that he could fulfill them. Bianco, who spent hours interviewing Edgar Jr., concluded that he was a puppet on a string. "His father was always very much in the picture. He was still exercising considerable influence over Edgar Jr. and the company to the point where Edgar Jr. was not really his own man. The perception they were trying to convey was different but not convincing. Edgar Jr. doesn't give the impression of someone who is forcefully himself. I came away feeling sorry for him. He was a guy in an impossible situation, held to an impossible standard that no one could meet," says Bianco.

Edgar Jr. had fallen into the same trap as his mother, who went from being a daughter to a wife to a mother without ever having her own life along the way. Except for the movie contract with Universal, Edgar Jr. had always come under the watchful eye of his father and had been coddled within the warmth of the family business. The Seagram–Vivendi merger should have allowed Edgar Jr. to escape the shadows cast by his grandfather and father, but the new corporate circumstances he had so carefully arranged did not permit any progress towards a separate identity for himself. He was Messier's man now, and he would live to rue the day that he ever put himself in that man's hands.

TWELVE

COMING UNDONE

MERGERS BETWEEN TWO CORPORATIONS in the same city or the same economic sector are tough enough to pull off at the best of times. Even setting up committees to study how departments from two different companies will be combined can be difficult. Who will be in charge? There are always too many egos to feed. As the new organization takes shape, duplication of roles means that many jobs are lost. Understandably, people fight to keep their own position before they'll even consider working for the good of some new entity for which they as yet have no loyalty. Beyond those usual challenges, a successful union between Seagram and Vivendi faced additional hurdles: two languages, a six-hour time difference between New York and Paris, slow responses by the French to phone calls or e-mails from the Americans, as well as two very different cultures: celebrity entertainment versus old-world establishment.

After the deal was announced at news conferences in Paris and New York on June 20, 2000, Edgar Jr. and Messier tried to upstage each other by showing off their respective worlds. "You know the way Europeans and Messier get seduced by

Hollywood? You sit them in a dinner with all the big stars. Messier was across the table from Julia Roberts, he's in heaven," says Alex Berger, an American who grew up in Paris and so knew both cultures. "Well, when Edgar was in Paris, we took him to Alain Ducasse Restaurant with guys who had clout. Both were seducing each other. Both of those guys were just as blasé as they could be—and it was never enough."

Messier had promised Edgar Jr. a meaningful role, but it quickly became clear that he was only going through the motions. "From day one, the only obsession with Messier was getting him out, not sharing power with anybody," says Berger. That turf war at the top set the tone. "Everybody was concentrating on the politics instead of the business. More time was spent on who was going to be the boss of whom and who was going to be doing what and how everybody was going to cater to the king and the princes instead of how we're going to grow these businesses." Fed up with the petty rivalries, Berger left Canal + in September 2000.

At least one prescient commentator foresaw problems with the merger's basic premise. In June 2000, Andrew Odlyzko, head of the Mathematics and Cryptography Research Departments at AT&T Labs, posted on his website home page the preliminary version of a paper he later published called *Content is Not King*. "Content certainly has all the glamour. What content does not have is money. Spending on connectivity is much more important for communication services than spending on content can ever be," wrote Odlyzko, who pointed out that consumers care more about e-mail than access to content. Several publications that summer picked up Odlyzko's comments as he reminded Edgar Jr. of his remarks in San Jose the previous month: "What would the Internet be without 'content'? It would be a valueless collection of silent machines with grey screens." Not so, said

Odlyzko. "The author of this claim is facing the possible collapse of his business model. Content has never been king, it is not king now, and is unlikely ever to be king . . . because people are not willing to pay very much for it."

A more immediate issue was finding a buyer for the spirits and wine division, which had been quietly placed on the auction block even before the merger was announced. During the joint news conference in June, Edgar Jr. had said, "There is real interest on the part of the family to continue its investment in the spirits and wine business." His reference was to Charles, who at the time was part of a management group that intended to make a bid. The other members of the group included all of the senior officers in the spirits and wine division: CEO Steve Kalagher, CFO Donard Gaynor, chief manufacturing officer Jérome Hyafil, head of human resources Florence Pramberger, chief communications officer Vicki Nobles, and operations analyst Stephen Smith. When the group first told Edgar Jr. of their interest, he was encouraging and suggested that they hire an investment banker, so they retained Lehman Brothers, led by Chris Harned, head of Lehman's global consumer products mergers and acquisition practice.

As the management group sought industry partners who could be financial backers, the meetings were held on familiar grounds. Some sessions were conducted in the Seagram Building, one floor away from Edgar Jr. Others were held at the house on Cadogan Square where for years the Bronfmans stayed when they visited London. The elegant space included a dining room and kitchen on the main floor, a study and sitting room on the second. The third floor had two bedrooms, one large and one much smaller, each with ensuite bath. On the fourth floor were two more bedrooms and a study that served as an office. In the basement was more office space and staff administrative areas. The fifth floor had traditionally been the sole purview of Edgar Sr., but as Edgar Jr. took command as CEO, he used it too, although towards the end of his reign he often stayed at the Metropolitan Hotel.

The management group were successful in finding two powerful allies to join them in their bid: Kirin, the Japanese brewer, and V&S Vin & Sprit AB, the Swedish government-controlled wine and spirits co-operative that was behind Absolut vodka. Under their plan, Kirin, Absolut, and Charles would each invest $1.3 billion. The individual members of the management group hoped they could put together as much as $200 million of their own money, for a total of $4.1 billion. That amount in equity would be matched by a similar amount of debt financing, for a bid of $8.2 billion.

When it began to look as if the management group might have some big-name backers and the necessary financial wherewithal to make a solid bid, the group sensed a growing concern coming from Edgar Jr. and Morgan Stanley, the investment bank running the auction. It was one thing for the spirits and wine division to be sold to a competitor; all the Seagram beverage alcohol products would then disappear into a larger entity. However, if the management group won the auction, the Seagram spirits and wine division would continue as a stand-alone company. If the "new" owners did well and the overall value grew, it might look as if Edgar Jr. had sold at too low a price or was not participating in the rising worth of the historic division. In the past, his detractors had enough reasons to mock the mistakes he made; he didn't want to give them more ammunition. In such a scenario, spirits and wine could end up joining DuPont on a list of companies Edgar Jr. sold that went on to do well without his involvement.

While no one ever told the management group why Edgar Jr.'s attitude cooled towards their bid, that worry about how well they might do as owner-managers was the only explanation they could come up with. If that concern about his image was accurate, it would be better from Edgar Jr.'s point of view to have an industry consortium, such as Diageo and Pernod Ricard—two firms that were showing a joint venture interest—buy Seagram's spirits and wine group and then divvy it up between them. That way, no one could ever make odious comparisons that reflected badly on him.

Charles's participation in the group, never a certainty, began to fade. As the summer passed and the Vivendi share price fell, Charles worried that his net worth was going down the drain. He might be better off to husband his resources rather than make an investment. Moreover, Charles was loyal to the family. In permitting the sale of Seagram to Vivendi, Charles had shown that he ceded full control of Seagram's future to Edgar Jr. As a result, he did not want to be seen as adversarial to Edgar Jr.'s views or put him in an awkward position. Since Edgar Jr. was getting out of spirits and wine, a management bid for beverage alcohol with financial support from Charles had the wrong optics. Charles withdrew from the bidding group without giving any reasons. He was replaced as an investor by the merchant banking arm of Lehman Brothers.

In September, events took another twist. During the Vivendi negotiations in the spring, Edgar Jr. had spoken to Allied Domecq, the British spirits and wine company. He fully expected that Allied would bid for and win Seagram's spirits and wine division, thereby creating the world's largest beverage alcohol company. But on the September day that Allied was scheduled to make its presentation at a New York hotel, the company didn't show up.

At about the same time, the management group learned that they were no longer in contention. The group were never officially told not to bother making an offer, but they began to wonder if they had ever stood a chance. They could only surmise why they got the cold shoulder from Edgar Jr. "His plan was for Allied to buy us and create the number one. I just think he got pissed off that his plan did not materialize. I've seen him do that on a whim," says one member of the group. "The way this company was run, you did not always hear everything. We couldn't get access to Edgar and that was pretty much the end of the conversation. He is who he is. Like the British royals say: never complain, never explain."

With both the management group and Allied gone from the scene, there still appeared to be two serious bidders: Diageo/Pernod Ricard as well as another industry consortium, Bacardi and Brown-Forman. In the end, however, the only bid came from Diageo/Pernod Ricard. When the winner, and the winning bid of $8.15 billion, was announced on December 20, 2000, the management group were shocked and angry. From a financial standpoint, they had been in the running all along but didn't know it.

There would have been no antitrust issues if the management group had won, but a merger of this magnitude, involving three companies, required close scrutiny. Necessary regulatory approvals in three jurisdictions dragged on for a year. The U.S. Federal Trade Commission, worried about a monopoly on rum, ordered Diageo to sell Malibu, allowing the company to keep Captain Morgan. To meet requirements of European Union authorities, Diageo sold Four Roses bourbon and was told to make certain that Captain Morgan distribution in Iceland was kept separate from the rest of the portfolio. In Canada, Diageo had to sell Gibson's Finest Canadian whisky. Distribution of

Absolut vodka reverted to its Swedish owners. Sam, who for twenty years had been the Bronfman family member most closely associated with wine, remained in California and was appointed chairman of Diageo Global Wines when the deal finally closed on December 21, 2001. Unlike Charles, Sam's continued role was apparently acceptable to Edgar Jr.

Diageo, formed in 1998 by the merger of Grand Metropolitan and Guinness, paid $5 billion for 61 percent of the spirits and wine group, and got such brands as Crown Royal, V.O., Captain Morgan, 7 Crown, and Seagram Chateau & Estate Wines. Pernod paid $3.15 billion for the other 39 percent of the assets, including Chivas, Glenlivet, and Martell.

The after-tax proceeds to Vivendi from the $8.15-billion sale were $7.7 billion, $1.3 billion more than the $6.4-billion debt that Seagram carried on the books when Edgar Jr. sold it. He had delivered more than he'd promised, not just a debt-free company but one with a surplus. Messier would make short work of that.

Within days of announcing the Seagram–Vivendi merger, Messier showed he would listen to no one. He even refused to heed the most basic advice on how to describe the merger when selling the deal to institutional investors and securities analysts. He was told to stay away from grand claims about Vizzavi and spend time describing Cegetel, thereby offering the kind of growth story that investors want to hear. Instead, as he and Edgar Jr. took to the road in July to sell the merger in the U.S., Canada, England, Scotland, Germany, France, Hong Kong, and Japan, he talked about how he didn't overpay for Universal and how Vizzavi was worth $15 billion to $20 billion. Edgar Jr. didn't help the cause when he told one group of investors that the best thing about owning an entertainment company was selling it.

By fall, Vivendi's share price was down 25 percent. Institutional investors were bailing out. Jarislowsky Fraser Ltd., a Montreal-based pension fund manager, had held Seagram shares in some of its investor accounts for forty years. The firm sold one-third of those shares in 1995 when DuPont was sold, and got rid of 60 percent of what was left at the time of the Vivendi merger. Says Stephen Jarislowsky: "The Bronfmans had never managed Seagram's well, but you didn't need to manage Seagram's well. When they owned DuPont, DuPont was managed well. The liquor business more or less managed itself. For a certain number of years the movie part of the business wasn't important enough in relation to the total thing to do too much harm, even though it was my opinion all the way through that Edgar Bronfman was a blowhard and bully and his son was basically uneducated and certainly was not the man to run a big corporation."

Jarislowsky did not see Messier as any improvement over Edgar Jr. He unloaded the remaining Seagram shares the firm held for its investors—about one-quarter of the original holding—in the twelve months after the merger. Messier's flaws were becoming more widely apparent. He won few fans when he spoke on July 10 to four thousand employees at the Universal Amphitheatre in Los Angeles. "I worked at Universal for twenty years and I never saw anything like it. He was prancing around the stage. I get real skeptical about people who haven't earned credibility," says Blair Westlake. "There are people in Hollywood who don't have as big an ego."

Messier's convergence strategy was equally unconvincing. "I never quite understood what Vizzavi was," says Ron Meyer. "I always questioned whether people were going to look at movies, videos, or listen to music on a cellphone. The technology hadn't really, especially in the United States, come to fruition. In Europe, at least cellphones worked on a regular basis. You weren't cut off every few minutes. Try and do that in the United States. Having music playing over your cellphone, or looking at a tape over your cellphone and having it cut out on a regular basis, would be very annoying."

Some analysts were puzzled about the supposed synergies between the merged companies. "I'm not sure I ever understood the logic of that, even at the time. It was not clear what Vivendi brought to the table, how were they going to grow the business in a way that Universal couldn't on their own," says Jessica Reif Cohen, top-ranked media analyst with Merrill Lynch. "Messier turned out to be a deal-junkie. He put the company in serious jeopardy. A lot of people thought he was brilliant. Edgar wasn't the only one."

Necessary regulatory approvals for the Seagram–Vivendi merger were granted by three jurisdictions, the U.S., the European Union, and Canada. Each ordered some changes, but nothing the company couldn't live with. U.S. rules forced Vivendi into modestly improved corporate governance by reporting financial results quarterly, not every six months as had previously been the case. In Canada, Vivendi was required to spend C$225 million over five years in local manufacturing, film production, and post-production, as well as finding and promoting Canadian talent. The EU ordered Vivendi to sell its BskyB holding and share Universal music and movies with other Internet portals. So much for Vizzavi's exclusive content.

Edgar Jr. made adjustments too. Since he was now commuting to Paris weekly from New York and had no Hollywood responsibilities, he sold his Malibu beach house for $10 million, twice what he'd paid.

∽

On December 5, 2000, Vivendi shareholders in Paris approved the merger, celebrated with champagne, and watched movie trailers. By contrast, when Seagram shareholders held their final meeting that same day in Montreal, there wasn't even a glass of V.O., Mr. Sam's favourite drink, to honour the past or toast the future. Said Edgar Jr., "My father and my uncle and other members of the family simply felt that a matter-of-fact meeting was called for—that it was not a good time to trumpet the history of the company or celebrate the future of Vivendi Universal." He did, however, haughtily remind shareholders that they should be grateful for what he'd accomplished despite everyone's disbelief in him. "The media and the stock market were skeptical of every deal I did. But as my friend Barry Diller once said to me, every new thing starts with a mess." Shareholders approved the takeover by a 90.4 percent vote. The meeting took all of eighteen minutes. As he headed for the door, Charles said to his driver, a former policeman, "Get me the hell out of here."

After telling employees in July that a chief executive could not be sentimental, Edgar Jr. now waxed nostalgic in his opening statement at the news conference that followed. "It's not easy letting go of so much of our past, and none of us—myself, my father Edgar, my uncle Charles, my brother Sam—have taken this decision lightly. I've often said to many people as we've gone through the merger process over the last six months: The heart is more stubborn than the mind," he said. "It's not been without a great deal of emotion—as a third-generation Bronfman and the third to lead this company—it's been particularly difficult to make dispassionate decisions about a company that has been so integral to my family's life."

The rest of Edgar Jr.'s session with the media was an embarrassment. A reporter from TVA, the Quebec-based French-language network, asked Edgar Jr. a question in French. Handlers jumped in to say the boss could not speak French, a fact well known to the Montreal media. "Oh, *pardonnez-moi*," said the reporter, who then switched to English. "I thought because you were making business with French companies that your French was improving." "It is improving," insisted Edgar Jr., who said he would answer the question in French, but did not.

By contrast, Messier was unstoppable in either language. In September he published his autobiography, *j6m.com: Who's Afraid of the New Economy?* Most CEOs don't bother writing an autobiography or do so only at the end of their career, when they might have something to say, but Messier saw himself as a breed apart. He was such a showboat that he used in the title the spoof name conferred on him by *Les Guignols,* the satirical show on Canal +. Messier signed his e-mails J2M; the show mocked him as J6M, which stood for Jean-Marie Messier, *moi-même, maître du monde* (Jean-Marie Messier, myself, master of the world).

In the six months since the deal was announced, the business world had been turned upside down. Internet-related stocks were in free fall and the panic was spreading to the broader market. Consumers had no interest in content-delivery business models. Most personal computer users were connected to the Internet by slow-speed modems; downloading anything very complicated took too long. People liked the interaction of playing games or participating in chat groups; they had no interest in sitting passively watching a movie on the computer screen. Most important, no one wanted to pay for anything.

Shareholders who sold their Seagram shares into the market when the takeover was announced did just fine. Shareholders who decided to remain owners along with the Bronfmans lost out. On December 8, 2000, the final day of trading for Seagram, the share price was $50.50. The value of the family's 106.5 million shares of Seagram had fallen from $8.2 billion in June to $5.4 billion a mere six months later. If the family had sold all of its shares in June, they would have been better off. At the deal price of $77.35 per share, the family's shares would have put $6.6 billion in their pockets even after paying the 20 percent capital gains tax. "I think I've seen more money lost by people trying to avoid taxes than any other single issue. It's funny, if you just pay the taxes you're ahead of the game for the most part," says investment banker Herbert Allen Jr.

Vivendi officials had originally proposed December 7 to sign the documents and close the deal. John Preston, who was handling matters for Seagram, pointed out that December 7 was the anniversary of the Japanese attack on Pearl Harbor. He suggested that the next day would be far more appropriate; December 8 was the Feast of the Immaculate Conception. The French got the message and the joke. The closing date was changed.

It was quickly evident that Messier's commitment to maintain Vivendi's debt-free condition meant nothing. He was a deal addict. Two weeks after receiving shareholder approval for the merger, Messier visited Morocco, met King Mohammed VI, and spent $2.2 billion for a 35 percent stake in the country's telephone system. "I was furious. It was done without my knowledge. In terms of the message we were trying to send to investors, it was disastrous. I'd just spent six months on the road selling the story," Edgar Jr. told Jo Johnson and Martine Orange, who wrote a book about Messier, *The Man Who Tried to Buy the World.* "In that context, the Maroc Telecom deal made no sense. Why did he do it? I have no idea. But then why did he do so many things?"

Edgar Jr. was a member of Vivendi Universal's newly formed executive committee, which also included two other former Seagram officers, John Borgia and Doug Morris. The other eight members were Messier, Vivendi chief operating officer Eric Licoys, Vivendi chief financial officer Guillaume Hannezo, Henri Proglio, chairman of Vivendi Environnement, Cegetel chairman and CEO Philippe Germond, CEO of Havas Agnès Touraine, and from Canal + CEO Pierre Lescure and COO Denis Olivennes. The group was supposed to debate prospective deals and discuss strategy, but Messier's practice was to present acquisitions that were almost finalized and ask for quick approval so he could take them to the board.

Messier's spree did not stop with Maroc Telecom. During the first ten months of 2001, Messier paid $2.2 billion for Boston-based publisher Houghton Mifflin, $372 million for music-sharing site MP3.com, and $1.2 billion for Elektrim, a Polish telecom company.

It's difficult to take seriously Edgar Jr.'s claim to have been "furious" about Maroc Telecom when he did not use any of the tools at his disposal to halt that deal or any of the others that followed. Edgar Jr. never lifted a finger to stop Messier at the executive committee, nor did he display his "furious" response or raise any of his concerns at meetings of the full Vivendi board. If he wanted to make the ultimate statement, he could have resigned from the board, he could have sold the family's shares, or he could have done both. In such circumstances one of Edgar Jr.'s basic character flaws got in the way: he was congenitally unable to have a confrontation, state a strongly held view, and try to change a situation. The best he could muster were mild rebukes that Messier did not take seriously. "He tells me on numerous occasions that he and Messier had a real good talk," says John Borgia. "And Messier would agree, 'We've got to have more restraint. You're right. We're not going to do any more of these. We've got to get cash, we've got to concentrate on operating the business.' He's very agreeable when Edgar had conversations with him. I think Edgar was hopeful in the first part of the year that by helping Messier we were going to get straightened out. Edgar realized, I don't know exactly when, but before too long, that 'Oh my God, this is not going to work. This guy can't pull this off.' It unravelled extremely quickly."

As the lead representative of the largest shareholder, Edgar Jr. could have and should have made more noise. He stood the best chance of stopping Messier, but he did not have the courage to do so. As a result, Messier did exactly as he wished. As time passed, he became even less likely to listen; he saw himself as impervious to errors. Anyone who disputed his judgment was rewarded with an outpouring of his volcanic temper. His behaviour became dictatorial. He'd summon executives who would fly to wherever he was then wait outside his office door only to be told at day's end that he would not be receiving them after all.

Agenda items at board meetings involving Edgar Jr.'s areas of responsibility were given short shrift. Messier took every opportunity to remind Edgar Jr. how little he mattered. The theme park in Osaka, Japan, was set to open in March 2001. Universal's involvement had been approved under Edgar Jr. Normal corporate niceties would include giving him some involvement in the opening ceremonies. Messier drew up a program that had no role for Edgar Jr. Rather than complain, Edgar Jr. simply stayed home.

The shareholding public had no way of knowing that Edgar Jr. was anything but pleased by Messier's performance. In March 2001, Vivendi reported profits for 2000 of $2.14 billion, a 60 percent increase over the previous year. Edgar Jr. was supportively at Messier's side during the news conference as Messier declared that Vivendi was on track to see revenues grow by 10 percent, earnings by 35 percent, in each of the next two years. Even when viewed from a vantage point within the company, Edgar Jr. gave no sign he was opposed to Messier's acquisitive strategy. He graciously included Messier in a celebratory dinner held in May at The Four Seasons. The event brought together Bronfman family members with some of the old Seagram hands, many of whom were retired, people such as Ed McDonnell, Phil Beekman, Mel Griffin, Jim McDonough, and Gabor Jellinek.

Even when the Bronfman family announced on May 29, 2001, that they had sold 16.9 million shares of Vivendi worth $1.1 billion, Edgar Jr. had nothing but praise. "I am personally gratified that Vivendi Universal is off to a very fast and successful start," Edgar Jr. said in an official statement. "I look forward to continuing to work closely with Jean-Marie and the rest of our very strong management team to realize the enormous potential of Vivendi Universal." Of the 16.9 million shares, 15.4 million were sold by entities related to the Edgar side of the family, including 1 million shares held by a charitable foundation. Charles's Claridge Foundation sold the other 1.5 million shares.

Of course, Edgar Jr. had a vested interest in making reassuring sounds. Messier and Vivendi were the buyers of those shares. If Edgar Jr. was worried about Vivendi taking on too much debt, it didn't stop him from adding to the load. In 2001, when Messier spent a total of $10 billion buying back Vivendi shares to support the share price, some of that money went to the Bronfmans to pay for shares they sold. In May Edgar Jr. also said that his side of the family, which still owned 33 million Vivendi shares, would not be selling any more that year. Charles made no promise about the disposition of his 34 million shares, but he too issued a complimentary statement.

In August 2001, Messier and his wife, Antoinette, moved from Paris to New York, bringing with them four of their five children. Edgar Jr. was part of the board approval process that provided Messier with a two-storey apartment on Park Avenue at East Sixtieth Street worth $17.5 million. Messier spent Labor Day weekend *en famille.* They walked across Brooklyn Bridge and took photographs of each other against the Manhattan skyline dominated by the twin towers of the World Trade Center.

Messier was in New York, Edgar Jr. in Los Angeles, on September 11, 2001, when terrorists destroyed the World Trade Center. News coverage of the attack and the aftermath curtailed Messier's plan to continue raising his profile, but his desire to get rid of Edgar Jr. continued. On October 11, Edgar Jr. was honoured at the City of Hope *Spirit of Life* award dinner on the Universal Studios back lot. The evening's entertainment, with a Motown theme, featured Smokey Robinson, the Temptations, Mary J. Blige, and Jon Bon Jovi. Money raised established a medical research fellowship in Edgar Jr.'s honour. It was his last major public event as a Vivendi executive.

On December 6, two days before the first anniversary of the closing of the deal, Edgar Jr. announced he would be stepping down as executive vice-chairman of Vivendi, effective the end of March 2002. In return for quitting, Edgar Jr. received severance pay of $17 million. Severance is usually paid when an executive is fired without cause or the company changes hands. In this case Edgar Jr. was able to collect by pulling the rip cord himself because a special provision had been written into the original merger for Edgar Jr. to take the money and run in the thirteenth month of their union. For Edgar Jr., the easy money proved to be irresistible. He stayed on the Vivendi board of directors; his family remained the largest individual shareholders.

Edgar Jr.'s colleagues understood how he had chafed under Messier and felt sorry for him. Of all the emotions a business leader might evoke, pity must be the least desirable. Says John Borgia: "Edgar saw, after being in charge [at Seagram], Messier was the sun, the moon, the stars, and the driving force in that company. Edgar was not. He wasn't just another employee, there was a lot of respectability shown between the two, [but] it wasn't his idea of how he wanted to live his life." Doug Morris, who, along with Borgia, was a member of the executive committee, agrees. "I think he resigned because he felt like he was being pushed into the background by Messier, who was a large figure, and it was embarrassing. I thought it was humiliating myself. I would have resigned too. Messier, for all his good points, did have the desire to be out front, and there can't be two of them. The stage wasn't big enough. Edgar took it well. It must have been painful after always being out in front himself, suddenly to be pushed into the background with all the penguins."

Edgar Jr. tried to sound philosophical. "Obviously, this was a very difficult decision, but I believe it is the right choice for me and the right time for the company. Given all that we have achieved, this is a good time for me to step back from my executive responsibilities and take some time to consider my next step," he said in his official statement. He talked about the smooth integration, the first year's financial performance, how well he and Jean-Marie Messier had got along, and how they'd become fast friends. "I share his vision and I believe that his energy and focus are the necessary ingredients to drive this company forward. As a representative of the company's largest shareholder, I believe under Jean-Marie's leadership Vivendi Universal will continue to grow and evolve and create exceptional value for all its stakeholders." Edgar Jr. extended the family pledge another year by saying that neither he nor his father planned to sell any of their Vivendi shares in 2002.

It was an odd statement, really, a little too full of heartfelt prose to be credible. Moreover, its purple prose went well beyond the usual explanations offered when an executive resigns, such as "leaving to pursue other interests" or "for personal reasons." Messier was likely closer to the truth when he said that he understood Edgar Jr. would find it difficult to work for someone else after being a CEO himself. "It's never easy to go from being No. 1 to not being No. 1 any more." But Edgar Jr. should have been aware of that when he signed the deal. His departure was in keeping with his decision to sell Seagram. He did not have the strength to fight for anything in which he believed, not even himself.

Edgar Sr. took his cue from his son. His executive duties at Vivendi were less onerous, but he resigned from them too. Both father and son remained on the Vivendi board, but Edgar Sr. also got a severance package, which consisted of a New York office and assistant, as well as a leased car and a driver for the next ten years, until December 2011, when Edgar Sr. will be eighty-two. Assuming two annual salaries at $50,000 each, vehicle costs of $25,000, and office rent of $25,000, that goodbye gesture was worth $1.5 million. For a man who claimed to be furious, Edgar Jr. remained fully prepared to let his so-called nemesis, Jean-Marie Messier, send a little lucre their way.

Eleven days after Edgar Jr.'s well-funded farewell, Messier announced that he'd paid Barry Diller $10.3 billion to buy back the cable and TV production assets that Edgar Jr. had sold to Diller in 1998 for $4.1 billion. Praise was heaped upon Edgar Jr., who sat in the front row at the news conference in the Versailles

Room of New York's St. Regis Hotel. "I am pleased to see Edgar Bronfman Jr.'s vision come into reality," said Messier. Diller called any criticism of Edgar Jr. "hogwash" and showered more praise. "What Mr. Bronfman did was sell his television assets . . . for what was then a full and fair price with the hope, clearly stated at the time, that they would grow in value better than they could inside Seagram and with absolute certainty be repatriated back to the company," Diller said.

Messier had now spent a total of $60 billion in his two-year acquisition binge. Repatriating the television and cable assets made no sense at all. There was no need for Messier to buy them, and Edgar Jr. had pointed that out. The shares would have one day been his anyway. Even after stepping down as vice-chairman, Edgar Jr. continued to be the good soldier that Messier wanted him to be and kept quiet about any apprehensions he might have had.

Diller, who was widely seen to have outfoxed Edgar Jr. on the original USA Network deal, came out a winner again. He was appointed chairman and CEO of Vivendi Universal Entertainment while retaining ownership of USAi with its profitable holdings in Ticketmaster and Home Shopping Network. "You can say that the arrangement makes no friggin' sense. But it certainly makes sense to those of us who did the deal. It makes perfect sense to me," said the irrepressible Diller. As for his role at Vivendi, "It is not incumbent upon me to do anything." To him, the deal was "without precedent. And so, by the way, is my whole life."

Almost lost in Diller's dust was another Messier acquisition, announced the same day. Edgar Jr. had been asked by Messier two months earlier to look into EchoStar Communications, a satellite TV company. He did, and urged Messier not to invest. Messier went ahead anyway, paying $1.5 billion for a 10 percent interest.

How the mighty had fallen. Until 2001, *Entertainment Weekly* had ranked Edgar Jr. in the top ten on their annual list of the fifty most powerful. In April 2002, Yahoo! hosted a website fan club for "those who think Bronfman is the cutest man on this planet." Gushed the site: "Members are invited to post photos of our dream guy. Come on in and let's get horny over Edgar!" At its peak, the club listed three members.

THIRTEEN

THE OUSTER

EDGAR JR. HAD BEEN A RISING corporate star since 1982. Now, for the first time in twenty years, he had no management responsibilities, no meaningful duties to perform on a daily basis. Following his resignation as an officer of Vivendi, he must have felt like a deep-sea diver who came up too quickly and got a bad case of the bends. He remained a director on the board of Vivendi, of course, but that part-time position occupied him for only a few days each month.

As far as Jean-Marie Messier was concerned, he'd banished Edgar Jr. and was now free to strut the global stage alone. On January 31, 2002, Messier emceed an extravaganza the night before the opening of the World Economic Forum, held that year in New York rather than Davos, Switzerland, in support of the city's recovery after September 11. The show in the Grand Ballroom of the Waldorf-Astoria was produced by Quincy Jones and included two dozen icons of the music world, including singers Bono and Peter Gabriel, and jazzman Herbie Hancock. U2's Bono, who was born in Ireland, told the crowd how wonderful it was to have a European running a Hollywood studio.

Messier was featured that month in *Paris-Match,* the French photo review more often dazzled by movie stars or European royalty than business leaders. The publication called him "our mega-CEO," and ran photos of Messier flying on his corporate jet, skating in Central Park, and posing with a Mark Rothko painting. Seeing Messier with the Rothko must have been particularly galling for Edgar Jr. Messier had wanted Rothko's *Brown and Blacks in Reds* moved from the Seagram Building to his Park Avenue apartment. When Edgar Jr. and his father asked him not to do so, Messier commandeered the canvas for his office, thereby controlling access to one of the masterworks from the former Seagram collection. European publications were not alone in praising Messier. *Fortune* called him France's "first rockstar CEO." *Vanity Fair* published an obsequious profile in its April 2002 edition, saying, "He is Donald Trump and Lee Iacocca and Jack Welch rolled into one."

On February 24, Edgar Jr. sent Messier an e-mail urging him to stop worrying about his personal profile and pay more attention to the company. Edgar Jr. sought Messier's assurance that cash flow would continue to be available for shareholder dividends. "If the dividend is cut, while the perception persists that your very expensive personal productions have not come to an end, you are potentially placing yourself in a very dangerous position. If, added to that, the reality of the downturn in the market is confirmed, and the employees' resentment increases even more, your margin to manoeuvre will become increasingly tenuous," Edgar Jr. wrote. At eighty-nine cents per share, the annual dividend on the 33 million shares held by the Edgar side of the family was $29 million. His complaint was a little self-serving, but at least it was a plainly stated point of view, a first for Edgar Jr.

He was unaware that Messier had previously been warned about something far more serious than dividends. On

December 13, 2001, four days before Messier announced the Diller buyback and EchoStar investment, Vivendi's chief financial officer, Guillaume Hannezo—who had known Messier for twenty years—sent him a handwritten note that said, "I've got the unpleasant feeling of being in a car whose driver is accelerating in the turns and that I'm in the death seat. All I ask is that all of this not end in shame."

Hannezo, who never shared his concerns with the board of directors of Vivendi Universal (VU), continued to prod Messier, urging him to sell assets. "Our jobs, our reputations are at stake," he said in a March 4 e-mail to Messier. Investors, he said, want to know, "Is VU a total fraud like Enron? Is VU threatened by its debt? Has JMM completely lost it?" The problem isn't the business, Hannezo concluded, "It's you."

During that same period a third, more vituperative assault was launched against Messier by Sam Minzberg, president and CEO of Charles's investment company, Claridge Inc. In March 2001, Minzberg, a tough and outspoken lawyer, had replaced Charles, who attended one Vivendi board meeting after the merger then resigned as a director. Minzberg spent his first few meetings getting to know his fellow board members and gaining a fuller understanding of the newly merged company. By early in 2002 he'd decided Messier had to go.

For Minzberg, two incidents tipped the balance. Messier had said he would not sell any Vivendi shares but changed his mind and in January 2002 sold $3 billion worth of shares to Goldman Sachs and Deutsche Bank in order to raise cash. Minzberg believed that Messier's turnabout had impaired his credibility with U.S. financial markets. The second event occurred during a meeting between Minzberg and Messier at Minzberg's New York office on February 26. Messier accused Minzberg and Edgar Jr. of leaking damaging information about him to the *Financial Times,* claiming he had been told by a *Financial Times* reporter that they were the newspaper's source. Minzberg denied Messier's allegation and said it was unlikely that any journalist would reveal a source, whoever that source might be. Minzberg concluded that if Messier would lie to him about that, he would lie about anything. He told Messier he wanted him to submit to a performance review and a vote of confidence by the board of directors. According to Minzberg, Messier said, "I have to keep on running this company." Replied Minzberg: "You sound like Bill Clinton saying 'I have to keep on running this country and I did not have sex with that woman.' The problem with you is that you're a very passionate liar but you're not a very good liar."

In the weeks that followed, Minzberg mounted a personal campaign against Messier. He telephoned, wrote letters to, and e-mailed all the Vivendi directors to denounce Messier's integrity, demand a performance review, and hold a vote. However, Minzberg was a lonely voice. At first even the other four North American directors nominated by Seagram—Edgar Jr., Edgar Sr., Marie-Josée Kravis and Richard Brown—paid little attention. Minzberg's tactics won no converts among the rest of the board. Simon Murray was British and Esther Koplowitz was Spanish; all the other directors were French. "It's clubby. They protect each other. He'd been the golden boy of French entrepreneurship. He came out of Lazard and the Ministry of Finance. The style in France is that they sit around and have a smoke and a beer and decide who should run what company. The idea that North Americans were telling them to kick this guy off was not very appealing to them," says Minzberg.

Messier was able to keep the European directors in line by claiming that Edgar Jr. wanted to get rid of him so he could have the job for himself, a position no self-respecting French company could allow an American to hold. But Messier's convergence strategy was imploding. On March 5, Messier announced Vivendi had lost $11.8 billion in 2001, the largest loss in French corporate history. Dividends to shareholders would continue, but Vivendi was operating so close to the bone that Messier had to borrow the $1 billion required to pay that year's dividends. AOL Time Warner's year-end numbers, announced a month later, were even worse. The company took a $54-billion charge against earnings, the biggest write-off in U.S. corporate history. AOL Time Warner shut down CNNSI, the electronic marriage between CNN and *Sports Illustrated,* for lack of consumer interest.

Convergence was suddenly out of vogue, but Messier blamed underlings for his problems. He publicly reprimanded his two top executives at Canal +, Pierre Lescure and Denis Olivennes, for losing money at Canal + for the last three years. Messier chose to deliver his message to them via an interview with *La Tribune,* a French business daily. Olivennes and Lescure sent a reassuring e-mail to their four thousand employees saying there would be no layoffs. Messier considered the message to be a slap in the face. He railed against Olivennes and Lescure in front of fellow executives during a company retreat in Deauville. Within days, Olivennes resigned. Messier fired Lescure on April 16.

Lescure's departure became a *cause célèbre.* Staff at Canal + interrupted programming for a live broadcast of a tearful Lescure pleading for support and complaining that Messier's actions threatened editorial independence. Unhappy Canal + employees took to the streets in support of the departed executives, particularly Lescure, who was a popular former TV anchor and had run Canal + since 1994. For Edgar Jr., the French inclination for street action was a surprise. Whenever he had fired anyone at Seagram, a hefty severance payment was all it took to keep matters quiet.

Messier's problems were not limited to rebellions about management. Almost two years after being launched, Vizzavi was not the pre-eminent portal that Messier had imagined. In fact, it was nothing more than an e-mail service. Vizzavi had lost $343 million the previous year. The CEO resigned and one hundred employees were laid off.

Even the language spoken in the Vivendi boardroom was proving to be a barrier. Prior to the merger, Vivendi board meetings were conducted in French. After the merger, directors could use either English or French. Simultaneous translation was provided through headphones, but the translation was sometimes slow and not always accurate. When directors met prior to the April annual meeting, Messier spent thirty minutes explaining Vivendi's cash flow using a complicated chart. At the end of the presentation, no one was any the wiser in either language. "As the Vivendi stock price fell, Messier probably felt more pressure from the board," says Laura Martin, who had been a media analyst with Credit Suisse First Boston before joining Vivendi in November 2001 as executive vice-president for investor relations. "In the face of Enron, Global Crossing, and Arthur Andersen, the credit markets closed and started hating debt. He changed less rapidly than the context changed. They insisted on cash flow, and we didn't change fast enough. It went from 'buy anything' to 'capital availability and cash flow is king, queen, and jack' within six months."

Messier's attempt to rally support from the seven thousand shareholders who attended the annual meeting on April 24 was marred by raucous interruptions. Electronic voting was plagued with malfunctions, but shareholders were able to demonstrate their unhappiness by rejecting a management proposal to set aside more shares for stock options. In spite of the previous year's disastrous results, the Vivendi board of directors had approved a $3-million performance bonus for Messier. As a sop to shareholder complaints, Messier pledged to invest his bonus in Vivendi shares at market prices. By the first week of May, Vivendi's share price had fallen to $29, down 50 percent since the beginning of the year.

Since February, Edgar Jr. had listened to Sam Minzberg promote his anti-Messier views at board meetings but had not joined him in agitating for action. "Edgar Jr. is a total gentleman. He's got a very European manner. He doesn't easily get into yelling matches or confrontations with people," says Minzberg. "I don't think he was ever taken in by Messier. Edgar knew when he was lying or stretching the truth. He's not a fool, believe me. I just think he was, as I say, more of a gentleman than I am."

During the question-and-answer portion of the April annual meeting, Edgar Jr. finally concluded that Messier could no longer continue as CEO. A shareholder asked Messier a broad question about operating expenses. Messier answered by pointing out that Vivendi had sold two Gulfstream IVs to reduce costs. He then went on to deny rumours that Vivendi owned an Airbus. Edgar Jr. knew Vivendi owned a company that in turn leased an Airbus and couldn't understand why Messier had strayed into a topic that hadn't even been raised and then lied about it. He leaned over to Minzberg and said, "This is what he does. He just lies."

Edgar Jr. had been talking to some of his friends about Messier since January. "He said on numerous occasions that he felt he had been betrayed and the guy had run amok," recalls John Bernbach. "For a long time he didn't say anything, even to people who were close to him, because he was the good soldier.

He tried to do whatever he could from the inside. By the time he began to recognize the enormity of the problem, he got very upset. He galvanized himself and his forces and moved in to try to make a change."

Minzberg, who had been badgering directors for two months, should have softened up the European directors and made them more open to challenging Messier, but they had stopped listening to Minzberg's harangues. "Everything was conspiratorial from Sam. I only knew half the agenda. If he made it clear where he was coming from and what the attack was all about, that would have really maybe saved us an awful lot of trouble," says Simon Murray, a Vivendi director who was British but spoke French fluently and served on other French boards.

Members of Vivendi Universal management were aware of Edgar Jr.'s discontent, but they remained loyal to Messier. "Monsieur Bronfman thought that Monsieur Messier was not capable of guaranteeing the company's revenues. He believed that M. Messier had become a menace for the Bronfman family; he believed that M. Messier was a menace for Vivendi," says Xavier Couture, who in April replaced Pierre Lescure at Canal +. "I do not think he persuaded anyone in the management. Management was behind M. Messier. M. Bronfman was committed to persuading French politicians, or the French establishment, or financiers who had considerable influence at the stock exchange, that M. Messier had become dangerous for French capitalism."

A powerful French businessman had come to similar conclusions on his own. Claude Bébéar, the chairman of the AXA insurance group, did not hold any Vivendi shares, but when Messier fired Lescure, Bébéar decided that Messier no longer deserved membership among France's commercial elite. He feared Vivendi would go bankrupt and bring shame to all of

France. In April, Bébéar spoke to some of Vivendi's French directors, urging them to sell assets, pay down debt, and restore profitability. When Bébéar made no progress, he took his views public during a radio interview in May, saying that the board should devise a strategy with management's agreement or, if necessary, get rid of management.

Much of the nine-hour board meeting held in the Seagram Building on May 29 was taken up by Minzberg hammering at Messier. With the support of the human resources committee of the board, chaired by Edgar Sr., Minzberg renewed his demand for a performance review of Messier. When the matter came to a vote, Minzberg's motion was defeated ten to five, with the European directors supporting Messier against the North American directors. Messier later found a handwritten note that had been passed to Minzberg by Edgar Sr. telling Minzberg to back off, that he was just uniting the French directors against their cause.

The Minzberg campaign and the general unhappiness of the North American directors did finally have an impact in one area. Edgar Jr. won consent for a new corporate governance committee with himself and Marc Viénot, chairman of Vivendi's audit committee, as co-chairs. Edgar Jr. also received board approval for a comprehensive audit of Vivendi's cash condition by Goldman Sachs.

On June 13, a somewhat contrite Jean-Marie Messier appeared with Stephen Shepard, editor-in-chief of *Business Week,* as part of a series of executive interviews held at the Ninety-second Street Y in New York. "We did make errors and we have to correct them," said Messier. He admitted that Vivendi had "shot too high, too quick," but then hinted that he might like to challenge MTV by starting a new music video channel. As for his own future, he said he had the support of his board and expected to be in charge for another fifteen years.

Minzberg's constant and cantankerous performances reached their nadir during the June 17 board meeting, when directors were linked via video conference facilities in Paris, New York, Dallas, and London. Directors had previously agreed to sell off 15 percent of Vivendi's 63 percent holding in Veolia Environnement, Vivendi's renamed water division. The June 17 meeting had been called to consider an opinion from J.P. Morgan, the investment bank, about the valuation given to the transaction.

Minzberg, who was in New York, complained that he had not read the report because he'd just received the document minutes before the board meeting began. He asked that the meeting be delayed for an hour. "Only an idiot would vote against it, but, nevertheless, I'm not going to vote until I've read this fairness opinion," said Minzberg. Simon Murray, in London, had another idea. "Given that the rest have all read it, and we're happy to vote, may I suggest that those who are prepared to vote, vote. Those who are prepared to wait for an hour or two while Sam reads may vote later, when Sam has finished reading his documents. And, since Sam said only an idiot would vote against it, I would be very interested to hear how he votes."

Minzberg, who was plainly visible and audible on every director's monitor, stood and shouted: "Fuck you, fuck you, fuck you." Recalls Murray: "Fifty percent of me was in hysterics. The other 50 percent of me is saying, here we are, one of the largest, at the time, media companies in the world, and we've got this going on. There was pandemonium." Directors voted to accept the report and the meeting ended. Minzberg later apologized to Murray.

Meanwhile, the board was shrinking in size. Three directors had resigned from the Vivendi board since January: René Thomas, honorary chairman of the Banque Nationale de Paris, retired because of his age; Jean-Louis Beffa, chairman and CEO of Saint-Gobain, resigned after his company sold its Vivendi holdings; and Philippe Foriel-Destezet, chairman of Adecco, a temporary employment firm, resigned prior to the May 29 meeting, without stating his reasons. A fourth resignation, the day before the June 25 board meeting, was the most significant. Bernard Arnault, the chairman and CEO of Moët Hennessy Louis Vuitton, the luxury goods company, had just been appointed to a four-year term in April. He was a friend of Messier, so his departure amid rumours about a cash flow crisis added to the forces that were dragging down Vivendi's share price.

The same day as Arnault resigned, Edgar Jr. met with Messier. The Goldman Sachs report, which was by then available to directors, concluded that Vivendi would escape a financial crisis only if the company retained the continued support of all of its banks and there were no external shocks to the financial system. Emboldened by what he saw as the report's damning conclusion, Edgar Jr. told Messier he had to resign. Messier refused. Edgar Jr. met with him the next morning, before the board meeting. Again Messier dismissed Edgar Jr.'s demand.

The first agenda item at the June 25 meeting showed that Messier was fighting back with powerful allies. Messier presented as a candidate for director Dominique Hoenn, chief operating officer of BNP Paribas. The fact that Hoenn was prepared to join the board seemed to indicate that Messier and Vivendi had the backing of at least one French bank. Hoenn was present and ready to take his seat, but there was a procedural flurry. His candidacy had not been reviewed by the board's human resources committee. The committee meeting, scheduled for the day before the board meeting, had been cancelled because committee chairman Edgar Sr. was ill. Messier suspected Edgar Sr. had come down with a case of diplomatic flu. The vote went ahead anyway. Hoenn's appointment was approved.

Citing the Goldman Sachs report, Edgar Jr. referred to "the Messier discount," a term he used to explain why share price was falling. Investors and rating agencies eyed Vivendi warily because Messier remained in charge, he said. Edgar Jr. then called for a vote of non-confidence in Messier, mistakenly assuming the Goldman Sachs report was sufficient to bring him down. Edgar Jr. had the support of the other four North American directors, but all of the other directors backed Messier again.

In the parlance of the boardroom, Edgar Jr. had not lined up his ducks. According to Simon Murray, who might have supported the motion from Edgar Jr., there was no advance warning of the vote. "Edgar was always studiously correct, very polite, appropriate in his manner and the way he conducted himself at the board meeting. As a person, I liked him. He was a good guy, you could get on with him. But he was mysteriously silent on so many of the issues that were clearly bubbling underneath. A lot of this would have been much more healthy if it had been on the boardroom table."

Edgar Jr.'s performance was reminiscent of his management style at Universal, where there were two groups of managers. There were those whom Edgar Jr. respected, like Ron Meyer, but there were also those, such as Ron Bension and Frank Biondi, with whom Edgar Jr. was not as close. The latter group didn't always know what was happening and couldn't always figure out what Edgar Jr. wanted. Simon Murray and the French directors of Vivendi were relegated by Edgar Jr. to the same in-the-dark status. He didn't communicate to them clearly, then was upset when they didn't support his plan.

Sam Minzberg couldn't comprehend how Murray and the others could possibly have been unaware that Edgar Jr.'s demand for a vote was coming. As far as the North American directors were concerned, Edgar Jr. had been clear about his goals and had previously told the corporate governance committee that Messier should resign. In fact, there were some French directors who agreed that Messier had to go, but they had not yet lined up a replacement CEO. As a result, they did not want to support Edgar Jr. because that would have left a vacancy if Messier was dumped. They voted to back Messier rather than risk making the company look even more troubled by creating a vacuum at the top.

Edgar Jr. had met earlier in the month with Claude Bébéar, and they sought the same outcome, but there was no united approach. "Bébéar's concern was mostly to work on the French directors and bring them to the decision that they should oust Messier," says Pierre Briançon, Dow Jones Paris bureau chief, who wrote a book, *The Messier Story,* published in French in October 2002. "The pressure that Bronfman brought on the board, on some directors, to try to oust Messier probably ended up having the opposite effect inasmuch as Messier could then try to rally some people and say, 'See, there's kind of an offensive by the Americans to try to oust me.' The case can be made that maybe Bronfman's actions delayed, if anything, by a few days or a few weeks, Messier's ouster."

External events that had nothing to do with Edgar Jr.'s efforts brought about Messier's demise. Later that same day, a few hours after the board had confirmed its support for Messier, revelations of an accounting fraud at WorldCom sent markets into a tailspin. Messier had hoped to raise cash for ongoing operations through a bond issue, but that plan was scuttled as global financiers worried there might be other companies like WorldCom on the edge of insolvency. German lender Bayerische Landesbank decided not to proceed with a line of credit promised to Vivendi. Barclays, the British bank, did not renew its loan. Deutsche Bank and two French institutions, Société Générale and BNP Paribas, refused to provide new funding. "It was a perfect storm. You've got WorldCom, you've got all the Enron crap still going on, you've got the credit markets tightening up. Goldman said if everything went well, nothing was going to happen, but the world doesn't always proceed the way you want it," says Minzberg.

At last, the French directors admitted they had a problem. "When the French banks pulled the plug, the French directors couldn't ignore that. Edgar never could have predicted what day the French establishment was going to rise up and take out Messier. There's no reason he should have been able to predict that, because it was political," says Laura Martin, head of investor relations at Vivendi.

The French directors had their own, made-in-France solution, one that did not depend on Edgar Jr.'s support or knowledge. On Friday, June 28, two emissaries from the board, Henri Lachmann, chairman and chief executive of Schneider Electric, and Jacques Friedmann, a director of BNP Paribas, called on Messier and told him he had to resign. In the three days since the board meeting, with the help of Bébéar, they had lined up a replacement for Messier. He was Jean-René Fourtou, vice-chairman of Aventis, the French pharmaceutical company.

But Messier had one last card to play. Since a board meeting had just been held, ninety days had to pass before the next meeting could be called. Only Messier, in his capacity as chairman, could convene another session before September. Without a board meeting, directors could not fire Messier. He said that he would step down only if he was given a severance package as bountiful as the one Edgar Jr. had received the previous December. "His attitude was 'unless I get my money, I'm not going to call a board meeting,'" said Edgar Jr. "But we couldn't wait until September. The company would have been gone by then. My view was that, however repugnant it may be to give that cocksucker anything, it was more important to save the company. It was blackmail and any agreement negotiated under duress would of course not be valid. But it was my duty to agree [to] it. It was €20 million or so to save a company with €13-billion equity value. I take that deal any day."

Cocksucker. Not a word often uttered publicly by a senior executive. Yet there it was, in an interview Edgar Jr. gave for *The Man Who Tried to Buy the World*, the book about Messier. *Cocksucker* has a particular resonance in the Bronfman family. It was Mr. Sam's favourite swear word. Leo Kolber tells the story about being summoned to Mr. Sam's house at seven one Sunday morning. When Kolber offered an opinion on a matter, Mr. Sam called him a "no good cocksucker." Kolber later spoke to Charles about the incident; Charles told him not to worry. According to Charles, if Mr. Sam had said "no good cocksucking son of a cocksucking cocksucker, then he's really mad. If he just says cocksucker, no problem, forget it." On that basis, Edgar Jr.'s description of Messier was at the inconsequential end of the family profanity scale.

Chief operating officer Eric Licoys officially approved Messier's severance deal. Messier resigned as chairman and CEO on July 2. Edgar Jr. had helped to precipitate the ouster, but he had not acquitted himself well. His plan was poorly executed, his communication efforts non-existent. "Somehow he could have played his cards better and I think got the board with him in a rational manner to examine some of these issues and investments," says Simon Murray. "Messier is no more. So Edgar achieved what he wanted to achieve, but it didn't save the company. He succeeded but in a way that brought about the collapse of the whole shebang at the same time. Everybody died with Messier."

❧

Edgar Jr. chaired the Vivendi board meeting on July 3 when the French directors chose Jean-René Fourtou, one of their own, to replace Messier as chairman and CEO. Fourtou, sixty-three, had privatized Rhône-Poulenc, the state-owned chemical giant, then created Aventis in 1999 by merging with Hoechst, the German pharmaceutical company. Fourtou had already agreed to the job after having his arm twisted over dinner with Bébéar and former president of France Valéry Giscard d'Estaing. Edgar Jr. pitched in and helped the new management secure a line of credit until a longer-term strategy could be devised to create more stability.

In an interview conducted by the weekly newspaper *Le Point* on June 5 but not published until July 4, Messier blamed the "bootlegger methods" of the Bronfmans for his downfall. "His dream is to replace me by an American and regain control of the group," said Messier. "And all that without spending a single dollar." With Vivendi's business and accounting practices under investigation by French authorities, most of those involved have not commented in detail about what happened. "Everyone is still lying about events at the end. They're covering their asses, probably because things got so ridiculous," says Pierre Briançon.

The Bronfman family fortune was ravaged as the Vivendi share price, a healthy $84 at the time of the merger, fell below $10 in the weeks after Messier was deposed. Here, in the simplest terms possible, is a reconstruction of the Bronfman holdings in Vivendi— what they owned, what they sold, and when. The two sides of the family started in December 2000 with about 88 million shares of Vivendi, 48 million held by the Edgar side and 40 million by Charles and his family, for a total of 8.6 percent of all Vivendi shares. Over the next two years the Bronfmans sold about 45 million shares at various prices, for pre-tax proceeds of $1.9 billion, or about $1.6 billion after tax, assuming a 15 percent capital gains tax. By December 31, 2002, they owned 43.2 million shares. Of those, 26.4 million were held by the Edgar side, 16.8 million by Charles.

Those 43.2 million shares represented about 4 percent of the total number of Vivendi shares. Because the Bronfman family's combined ownership had fallen below 5 percent, they were no longer required to make their transactions public, so it is impossible to know their current holdings. If they still held all 43.2 million shares in mid-June, 2004, four years after the merger was announced when the share price had climbed back to $27, those shares were worth $1.2 billion. Add that to the $1.6 billion in proceeds from divestitures and their Vivendi holdings were worth the equivalent of $2.8 billion, up from $2.2 billion eighteen months earlier but still a two-thirds drop from the peak in 2000. "The lesson is, when you have run a business for a long, long time as a family and then you subordinate your position to somebody else, don't stay, just get out, take your money, and leave," says Sam Minzberg. "We should have done that."

Better yet, Edgar Jr. could have simply held on to those boring DuPont shares. In 1995, Seagram owned 164 million shares of DuPont, which in 1997 split two-for-one, meaning Seagram would now have 328 million shares of DuPont, worth $14.3 billion in mid-June 2004, almost twice what Edgar Jr. collected when he sold DuPont in 1995. That stand-pat strategy would have kept the family abreast of their fellow billionaires. The Bronfmans have other investments in addition to their shares in Seagram that were converted to Vivendi shares. On the definitive annual list of the world's richest people, in 2004 *Forbes* put the combined net worth of Edgar Sr. and Charles at $5.2 billion—about the same as in 1996, when the total was $5.3 billion. During that eight-year period, however, their place in the standings fell. *Forbes* ranks the two brothers separately but their combined net worth in 1996 was good enough for twenty-sixth position. In 2004, their combined net worth would have put them at number eighty. By contrast, Ken Thomson, Canada's wealthiest individual, saw his net worth more than double from $7.4 billion in 1996 to $17.2 billion in 2004, a hefty increase that meant his ranking stayed about the same, four-teenth in 1996 and fifteenth in 2004.

Instead, Edgar Jr. and the other Vivendi shareholders saw about $75 billion in value wiped out in the two years following the merger. A similar collapse in the share price of AOL Time Warner also savaged those shareholders, including Ted Turner. At their peak, Turner's shares in Time Warner were worth $10 billion. In July 2002, he was worth about $2 billion. Nor was Messier the only convergence leader to fall into disrepute. In 2002 and early 2003 Gerald Levin, Steve Case, and Bob Pittman all left AOL Time Warner and Thomas Middelhof departed Bertelsmann.

Charles was devastated by the debacle. He and his wife, Andy, spend four months of the year in Israel. From there he regularly sends e-mails to a small circle of friends, describing current events in the region. Tom Axworthy, executive director of Historica, an education foundation that Charles established in 1999, told Charles in the summer of 2003, "That last one was really good. If you keep it up, I'll ask you to be a researcher and writer on my next book." Charles's response was both witty and winsome. "If the business keeps going the way it is," he replied, "I'm going to take up your offer."

Charles has not commented publicly about his misfortune, remaining tight-lipped even with old friends and former col-leagues. While golfing in Florida with Phil Beekman, Charles would say only, "I'm not a happy camper." Long-time employees of Seagram's spirits and wine division have not been as reticent.

"I don't know what ever possessed them to do what they did, but it's very difficult for me to accept, to see a great company built up and now it's no more," says Alan Sharp, who joined Seagram in 1944, was secretary to the board until he retired in 1980, then served as honorary secretary until the sale to Vivendi. Sharp wrote to Charles detailing his disappointment about selling off spirits and wine. Charles wrote back, saying, "You know I was against it." Explains Sharp: "He didn't want to rip up the family, brother against brother."

The relationship between Charles and Edgar Sr. has never been worse, but Charles holds his deepest disregard for Edgar Jr. After years of biting his tongue and doing his brother's bidding, Charles was almost more wounded by Edgar Jr.'s public comments than by the actual monetary loss. "One of the things that appears to be difficult for the Charles side of the family generally to do is take responsibility for its own decisions. They could have sold all of their position for $65 or $70 a share," said Edgar Jr. in an interview in *Fortune* in 2002.

In the past, such a snide comment about a family member would have been made in private, if at all. But Charles's actions *were* hard to explain. When the family sold 16.9 million shares in May 2001 at $64 a share, only 1.5 million of those belonged to Charles. In the period from August to October 2002, when Vivendi's share price was languishing near its all-time low, Charles sold about four million shares for proceeds of $60 million, a relative pittance in the former scheme of things. But Charles had also sold about 10 million shares in the last half of 2001, for about $500 million. Still, there is no obvious explanation why Charles did not fully cash out when he could have at $64.

Edgar Jr. had agonized about presiding over this kind of dynastic tragedy ever since Mr. Sam's 1966 prediction. Patsy Puttnam had listened to his expressions of concern when he was a fifteen-year-old working on *Melody.* "He used to laugh [and say], 'Oh well, it's always the third generation that loses everybody's money.' You know a lot about people when they joke about something that's that serious. It's obviously in their mind that that is the last thing they must do. I felt particularly sad when the thing didn't work just because he would have taken that as such a huge knock to his self-esteem. What had come to him was what he'd prophesied as a young kid."

Only Barry Diller managed to find sunshine amid the gloom. "One of the heroes—the unreported heroes—of this process is Edgar Bronfman Jr., who potentially has not slept for a month while he has worked to stabilize them financially," Diller told analysts on July 23, 2002, while commenting on earnings of his company, USA Interactive. "He has done a great service for all Vivendi Universal shareholders." Of course, Diller had every reason to be cheerful after Messier's ouster. Diller had come through the carnage unscathed. The $10.3-billion sale of USA Interactive to Vivendi had successfully closed in May. Diller had received $1.6 billion in cash and the return of 360 million shares of his company that had been given to Edgar Jr. as part of their deal in 1997. Messier had made Diller chairman of a new entity, Vivendi Universal Entertainment. Now he was also designated co-CEO with Fourtou. Not only did Diller's company, USA Interactive, own 5.4 percent of Vivendi, not only did Diller himself own 1.5 percent worth a guaranteed $275 million, Diller also stood to have tax liabilities of $620 million paid for by Vivendi if the U.S. entertainment assets were sold. Diller referred to his Vivendi duties as his "night job."

By then, Edgar Jr. and Diller had got over their falling-out as former joint venture partners. Each had been on the other's board. Even though there was no longer any ownership connection between the two men and there was no Seagram board for

Diller to serve on, Diller asked Edgar Jr. to remain on his USA Interactive board. Edgar Jr. agreed to stay. "I truly respect him. I think he's really smart, and I'm fond of him. We have a long life relationship with each other, and so I hope he stays on our board and we are associated in some way forever," says Diller.

As Edgar Jr.'s personal net worth was falling, Diller's was rising. According to *Forbes,* Diller's personal fortune is $1.4 billion. Edgar Jr.'s personal fortune is more difficult to assess. Like most things in his life, much of his wealth is controlled by his father. The EMB Trust, set up by Mr. Sam in 1942, provides for Edgar Sr.'s seven children and twenty-two grandchildren. Edgar Jr.'s share of the capital in the EMB Trust could be as much as $250 million. Edgar Jr.'s own $20-million trust fund, also set up by Mr. Sam, should now be worth $50 million. Add another $100 million for the value of his houses, their contents, and his art collection. During the six years he was president and CEO of Seagram, his salary and bonus totalled $24 million. At Vivendi, Edgar Jr. earned another $5 million as vice-chairman and a consultant. When he left in December 2001, his severance pay was $17 million. In January 2002 he exercised Vivendi stock options worth $33 million. Assuming at least part of that $79 million total income has been set aside for investment, add another $50 million for a personal fortune of about $450 million—nowhere near enough to make the *Forbes* billionaires' list.

Edgar Jr. did not live the American Dream. He was not an immigrant who started with nothing and made a fortune, he was never the brazen entrepreneur with a brilliant new concept, like Ted Turner dreaming up CNN. Turner may have had many a professional failing, and much of the value of his empire collapsed around his ears just as it did with Edgar Jr., but there was a difference. At twenty-four, Turner inherited his father's billboard company and went on to create a global media empire.

Despite his substantially reduced wealth, Turner was able to retain his self-esteem because he knew that whatever he achieved, and for whatever time he rode a high horse, it was his doing and his alone. By contrast, the arc of Edgar Jr.'s life was set at birth. Edgar Jr. simply appeared onstage in the starring role that his father had designated for him.

Still, one last chance remained to confound his critics, confirm his father's faith in him, and, more importantly, make it on his own.

FOURTEEN
ROAD TO REDEMPTION

IN JANUARY 2003, Edgar Bronfman Jr. watched what appeared to be a film shoot in the lobby of the Seagram Building. About one hundred people were packed tightly together, bathed in bright lights, preparing for a scene. His reverie was interrupted by a colleague who saw the activity and said, "Maybe it's the life of Jean-Marie." Edgar Jr. let a small smile play on his lips, and said, "No, it's too small a crowd."

The surroundings from which he viewed the cinematic proceedings were nothing like his previous life. In his new role at his venture capital company Lexa Partners, there were no global brands to command, no movie openings or record launches to attend, few fawning supplicants on bended knee. In December 2001, when Edgar Jr. resigned as vice-chairman of Vivendi, he had bravely said, "I am excited at the prospect of building another business. I am proud of my record so far. Now begins what's next." More than a year later, "what's next" had not amounted to much. Edgar Jr. had joined two boards: Equitant, an outsourcing firm, and Fandango, an on-line movie ticket service. In an effort to reclaim a few shards of his former self, in

October 2002 Edgar Jr. paid $4.3 million to reacquire the 51 percent interest in The Four Seasons restaurant that had gone to Vivendi in the sale of Seagram. The family fortune had been eviscerated, but redemption could be more enjoyably contemplated over cracked crab and mineral water while Julian Niccolini, the maître d' and a minority owner, hovered nearby.

Throughout his adult life, The Four Seasons had offered him continuity along with the comestibles. Edgar Jr. was a mere stripling when he first dined in what was long regarded as the Seagram Building cafeteria. Because he wore jeans in those days, he was assigned Table No. 45 in the far left reaches of the narrow mezzanine overlooking the Grill Room. After Edgar Jr. joined Seagram in 1982 and began wearing more appropriate attire, he was offered a better table, but declined. And so he sat ensconced in that same aerie for twenty-five years, aloof and aloft, gazing down upon the rest of the power lunch crowd.

Edgar Jr.'s only other acquisition during that first year after leaving Vivendi was the purchase in June 2002 of a 40 percent stake in Asprey and Garrard, the British luxury goods retailer. A new Asprey flagship store was under construction on New York's Fifth Avenue; London's Bond Street location was being renovated. There were plans, with his partners and fellow co-chairs Laurence Stroll and Silas Chou, to open ten to fifteen stores by 2007, fifty by 2012.

Edgar Jr.'s baby steps back into business seemed geared more to his personal comfort and social standing than any commercial possibilities. Along with his interest in high-end retail and fine dining, he returned to a former love. In March 2002 he joined a group backing a new play called *Never Gonna Dance,* based on the movie *Swing Time* with Fred Astaire and Ginger Rogers. While no merry musical could ever match his former mogul status, at least it was a fresh start on familiar ground.

The cast, the crew, the financing, the songs, everything was set. But after months of searching, they still had not found a venue in New York. Theatres in other cities were willing to book the show for the two-month tryouts, but the backers needed a Broadway destination to establish the pre-opening schedule. "The problem is that plays are staying too long," said Edgar Jr. on that January day. "It started with *Chorus Line,* then *Cats,* and *Les Misérables.* Four hundred years ago, when I first started in this business, a play might stay eighteen months. Now they play for seven, eight, nine years. We're getting to the point where we're going to have to let it go. I mean, everybody involved is doing something else, but if we can't get a venue, we're lost." Edgar Bronfman Jr. had never been lost before.

If Edgar Jr. had been able to pick the era in which he lived, it would probably look a lot like *Swing Time,* made in 1936. Prohibition had ended and Seagram was legitimate again, growing by leaps and bounds. In this fantasy world Edgar Jr. would see himself as Fred Astaire, all silk scarf and ceaseless smile. His detractors would become Ginger Rogers, following his lead, a twosome so inseparable as to be seemingly of one mind. For Edgar Jr., those salad days had never happened. All that remained was the hope of what might yet be.

Even on that smaller theatrical stage, far from global conglomerates, Edgar Jr. could not avoid business blunders. The show eventually found a New York venue, but when *Never Gonna Dance* opened at the Broadhurst Theatre on December 4, 2003, the reviews were scathing. "A spiceless production," said *The New York Times;* "whenever the show stops dancing it falls down" (*The New York Sun*); "corniness that's kind of sweet when it works" (*Newsday*); "dawdles too much of the time" (Associated Press); IT'S NEVER GONNA LAST, blared the headline on the Clive Barnes review in the *New York Post.* By the end of

January, the theatre was often half empty. After forty-four pre-
views and eighty-four regular performances, *Never Gonna
Dance* closed on February 15, 2004. (A revival is scheduled for
Japan in 2005.) Peter Gerety, who played an unemployed Wall
Street broker, uttered one of the show's more memorable lines
when he said: "I've put all your money into a Broadway show!
You're ruined!"

Edgar Jr. spent the rest of his time trying to explain his own
near-ruination. In September 2002 he was the keynote speaker
at an investors conference in Quebec City sponsored by CIBC
World Markets. "I thought it odd, as did some others, why
Edgar Bronfman Jr. had to come to a group like this to explain
how he didn't screw up," says Ira Gluskin, a Toronto-based
investment manager. "My impression is that Edgar Bronfman Jr.
will tell anybody, cab drivers, bus drivers, he didn't screw up.
The reason he did it with this group was that he was practising
it, he was refining it. And also because he wasn't dead and he
thought there was some possibility that he may emerge as a
CEO." Edgar Jr. made a similar confession that same month to
Forbes. "I went in with my eyes wide open, but it turned out to
be a disaster. Putting a wireless distribution platform together
with entertainment assets was ill-conceived."

By October, Edgar Jr. could summon moral outrage. "I
think anybody that either worked for the company, invested in
the company, should feel betrayed," he told CNBC's Maria
Bartiromo. "I do feel betrayed, because this was a situation
where Jean-Marie, remember, had a real record of achievement.
He lost his head and because he did, people got hurt." Edgar Jr.
blamed poor corporate governance in France for allowing
Messier more power than was possible for a CEO in the U.S.

"Within eighteen months we basically put on debt at a rate of about a billion dollars a month, much of that without the board even knowing about it."

But if French business practices were the problem, why would they come as a surprise to such an able American director on that board as Edgar Bronfman Jr.? Wasn't this company run by the French, the same bunch who were beaten so easily by Nelson?

Moreover, Edgar Jr. should have known the foibles of French commerce better than most. The Bronfmans had owned French companies since 1952, when Mr. Sam acquired Mumm and Perrier-Jouët. Edgar Jr. had continued those commercial ties when he bought Martell in 1988. The following year, on the occasion of the two-hundredth anniversary of the French Revolution, a laser image of the Eiffel Tower was projected onto the Seagram Building. That day, Edgar Jr. phoned his best wishes to Jacques Chirac, then mayor of Paris. For his part, Edgar Sr. had been appointed a Chevalier of the Legion of Honour by the government of France. To the Bronfmans, France was not exactly uncharted waters.

Even if corporate governance in France was as lax as Edgar Jr. claimed, how different was that from the easy ride he'd enjoyed during his own career? Corporate governance at Canadian companies tends to lag behind that facing American firms. His directors were a docile bunch. Institutional and individual shareholders rarely complained. Annual meetings moved along like clockwork. DuPont executives who were on the Seagram board used to marvel at how the Bronfmans got away with annual meetings that were so brief and uneventful.

Shareholders were sanguine no more. Class action lawsuits had been launched in Los Angeles, New York, and Paris. As part of the civil fraud settlement with the Securities and Exchange

Commission, in December 2003, Jean-Marie Messier paid a $1-million fine and relinquished his claim for the €21-million severance, by then worth about $25 million given the stronger euro. Messier, who had started Messier Partners, an investment banking firm with offices in New York and Paris, was also prohibited from serving as an officer or director of a U.S. public company for ten years. Vivendi paid a $50-million fine; former CFO Guillaume Hannezo was fined $120,000 and cannot serve as a U.S. director or officer for five years.

Prosecutors in Paris and New York continued to investigate Vivendi, but no one anticipated that Edgar Jr.'s name would appear on any indictments. He lost a fortune and damaged his own business reputation—but unlike some chief executives, who only looked out for themselves, he was honest. In the aftermath of the Internet bubble, when stock markets suffered their worst three years since the Second World War, Edgar Jr. was one of those rare CEOs who lost money along with everyone else. As captain of the SS *Seagram,* he went down with the ship. Usually, after such tragedies, the captain is revered as a man of honour. Instead, Edgar Jr. was reviled. To Edgar Jr.'s numerous detractors, that humiliating outcome merely proved that they had been right about him all along. *New York* magazine columnist Michael Wolff called Edgar Jr. "possibly the stupidest person in the media business."

Other observers concurred, saying Edgar Jr. had managed to give nepotism a worse name than it already had. "Edgar is the largest reason why they ought to have a 100 per cent estate tax. I rarely have seen anyone screw up something as royally as he has," says Howard Anderson, founder of the Yankee Group, a Boston-based firm that analyzed cable, media, computer, and communications companies. "You talk about shirtsleeves to shirtsleeves in three generations. This is actually one of the great reasons that you hire professional money managers, not to make you money, but to keep what you have. You only have to get rich once in this world. Hang on to it. Hell, you did it. You don't have to do a trifecta out here, and this is what he was trying to do. What a shame."

Even close colleagues could not fully comprehend what had happened. "Edgar made a mistake with Messier. As I worked with Edgar all through the years, I had not seen a mistake like that," says Bruce Hack, who joined Seagram in 1982 and held senior positions at Tropicana and Universal Studios. "It was catastrophic and wrongly substantiated years of misconceptions about Edgar."

At root, Edgar Jr.'s philosophy of life, as taught to him by his father, was a major cause of his failure. When Edgar Jr. was thirteen, in 1968, his father had told him, "Always remember, son, you never have any power if you have to use it. That means if you walk into a room and you have to tell people who you are, you are not powerful." The lesson was so well learned that Edgar Jr. had repeated that philosophy in the speech he gave in 1996 when he won the Steven J. Ross Humanitarian Award. Yet such thinking yields an unlikely leadership style in business, depending as it does upon power that has been bestowed rather than earned. Power is earned through a combination of vision, communication skills with colleagues, and the ability to execute that vision. By contrast, the Bronfman view of power is more aristocratic in nature; it flows from their celebrity status and their capacity to control employees. Followers are enlisted to the cause and then are somehow supposed to be enlightened about their duties and responsibilities by osmosis. In such a situation, whatever the actions of a crown prince or his father the former king, the family is always right. If things turn out badly and mistakes are made, well, it must have been the fault of underlings as was the case at Tropicana, stubborn opponents like Gerald Levin of Time Warner, ink-stained wretches in the fourth estate who ask rude questions, or a Judas in their midst like Jean-Marie Messier.

In September 2002, Jean-René Fourtou declared that if Messier had not been forced out, Vivendi would have gone bankrupt within ten days. Fourtou's plan to restore health required selling assets to reduce debt. Sold were Houghton Mifflin, Telepiù, EchoStar, the European publishing assets, and Veolia Environnement. Among the smaller divestitures was Vivendi's 50 percent stake in Vizzavi. At $140 million, the proceeds were a long way below Messier's valuation, which ran into the billions. Also put up for sale were corporate jets, a palazzo in Venice, a soccer team, Messier's New York apartment, and the 600-year-old Château de Méry-sur-Oise outside Paris, which had recently been restored by Vivendi for use as a concert venue. By the end of 2003, Vivendi had sold about $12 billion worth of assets but acquired control of Cegetel and made other investments, so debt remained high at $14 billion. The company's stated aim was to reduce debt to $6 billion by the end of 2004 and begin paying dividends again in 2005.

Of all the steps taken by Vivendi's new management, the most controversial was the decision to sell the Seagram art collection. Phyllis, the unofficial Bronfman family curator, had assembled most of the 2,500 items. "This is part of a whole Greek tragedy," she said. "I'm heartbroken. These collections are really part of the heritage of New York." Auctioned were Rodin sculptures as well as paintings by Roberto Matta and Pablo Picasso. *Brown and Blacks in Reds,* the Rothko that Messier wanted to hang in his apartment, went for $6.7 million. Seven hundred black-and-white photographs of American urban life taken by Alfred Stieglitz, Lee Friedlander, and Walker Evans, among others, fetched $2.9 million.

The Four Seasons was stripped. Sold were the tapestries in the lobby based on designs by Joan Miró; gone too was a painting by Larry Rivers that hung in a private dining room. Christie's unsuccessfully tried to sell the 22-foot-high theatre curtain painted by Picasso in 1919 for *Le Tricorne,* a ballet by Diaghilev staged the following year. In the end Vivendi donated the curtain to the city of New York so it could remain where it had hung since 1960, on the wall between the Grill Room and the Pool Room.

Vivendi also donated Seagram's former headquarters on Peel Street in Montreal to McGill University for use by the development and alumni relations department. The bequest, made in 2002, stipulated that the castellated façade could not be altered and Mr. Sam's office had to be preserved just as it was during his lifetime, complete with wood panelling, oak furniture, and his ashtray on the sill of the stained-glass window.

Vivendi's asset disposal did more than kick-start the possibility of corporate rebirth; it also created an opportunity for Edgar Jr.'s redemption. When the U.S. entertainment assets were put up for sale, he assembled a bidding group to buy the movie studios, television, and theme parks, but not music, which Vivendi decided to keep until filesharing abated and the division's value improved. His partners included Cablevision Systems, Wachovia Securities, Merrill Lynch, Blackstone Group, and Thomas H. Lee Partners. In order to avoid any conflict of interest, Edgar Jr. and Edgar Sr. suspended their participation as Vivendi directors.

Edgar Jr.'s competitors in the bidding included the NBC division of General Electric, Liberty Media, MGM, and Viacom. At the end of August, as rumours spread that NBC looked like the winning candidate to buy Vivendi Universal (VU), Edgar Jr. went on the attack. "The transaction with NBC is exactly the wrong outcome for shareholders. It's not VU selling entertainment, it's VU buying an interest in NBC. What they're doing is turning over the keys to the car, hoping someone else will drive it faster and that someone will pay more for the car ten miles down the road. NBC are very good at what they do, which is buying programming and selling advertising, but they have never run a studio, an entertainment cable network, or a theme park." The auction wasn't over and already Edgar Jr. sounded like a sore loser.

Just as he feared, a week later Vivendi chose NBC's offer over his bid. The deal closed in May 2004, finally putting NBC together with USA and Sci-Fi (as well as CNBC, Bravo, and twenty-nine television stations), just as Barry Diller had envisioned in 1998. Ron Meyer, who remained in charge of Universal Studios, said it was the best thing to happen to Universal in a decade, a time period that obviously included Edgar Jr.'s Hollywood sojourn. "We've been rescued," said Meyer. "I can't even describe the difference. We're finally around a company that's in our business."

Edgar Jr.'s next chance for redemption came when Time Warner put Warner Music Group up for sale in the fall of 2003. Because of his failed Vivendi Universal bid, he already had a close relationship with moneyed partners. Edgar Jr. bid $2.6 billion in conjunction with Thomas H. Lee Partners, Bain Capital, and Providence Equity Partners. The four partners contributed a total of $800 million in equity and arranged $1.8 billion in debt. Unlike his losing duel with NBC, this time Edgar Jr. had an advantage. The other bidder for Warner Music was EMI. If a major record company like EMI acquired Warner Music, antitrust approvals would be required. With the

proposed merger of Sony and Bertelsmann already under official scrutiny, Time Warner worried that a sale to EMI might
not go through because it would further reduce the number of
major record companies. Since Edgar Jr. did not intend to
merge Warner Music with any other company, his bid had no
such impediment.

This time, he won. Edgar Jr. and his father resigned from the
Vivendi board permanently. The family kept their Vivendi shares,
but the boardroom relationship had to be abandoned because
Edgar Jr. was in direct competition with Universal Music. The only
original Seagram appointee remaining was Marie-Josée Kravis.

Founded in the 1950s, Warner Music had famous labels such
as Warner Bros., Atlantic, and Elektra. With 18 percent of the
market, Warner ranked third after Universal and Sony-BMG.
Among Edgar Jr.'s new stable of recording artists, the most aptly
named was Junior Senior, a Danish duo with the equally fitting
debut album *D-D-Don't Don't Stop the Beat*.

Edgar Jr.'s role as chairman and CEO of Warner Music
Group will be far different from his former job at Seagram.
Because Warner Music is a private company, he will not have to
put up with the same analysis by Wall Street or try to please
shareholders as he did when he headed a public company. In
another sense, however, he will be under more pressure to perform than he ever was in the past. After all, Warner Music is no
family business run with the blessing of a father blinded by
affection. Said Scott M. Sperling, a partner in Thomas H. Lee,
"The deal with Edgar is, he does a good job or someone else
comes in to do a good job." In all his life, no one had ever before
spoken so bluntly about Edgar Jr. or his role.

The first priority was cost reduction. Edgar Jr. retained
Boston Consulting Group, the same firm he'd hired for the
Universal–PolyGram integration, to find $250 million in

savings. Although Warner Music had reduced its workforce by 30 percent over the previous three years, Edgar Jr. cut a further 1,000 jobs. Some members of management took pay cuts, artists with poor sales were dropped, and prices on older CDs were slashed by half.

With that acquisition, Edgar Jr. demonstrated he was done with licking his wounds and lying low. He'd spent almost three years since stepping down from Vivendi looking for his next venture, the one that would prove he had talent, that his previous problem was caused by Jean-Marie Messier, not by his own failings. Warner Music could be his road to redemption. "From a Wall Street perspective, it depends on how well Warner Music turns out. He may have the last laugh on this one. If the music industry continues to go down, then he won't," says Jessica Reif Cohen, the Merrill Lynch analyst.

The timing of Edgar Jr.'s return to power might be perfect; maybe his luck has changed. Legal action against filesharing launched in 2003 by the Recording Industry Association of America has had an impact. Downloaders appear to be in retreat. Before the subpoenas and fines, 29 percent of Internet users admitted they had downloaded music. By year-end, that proportion had dropped to 14 percent. In Canada, however, court rulings have gone the other way; downloading has been declared acceptable. But the slump in global sales that began in 1999 seems to have stopped. Album sales began growing again in the last half of 2003, and that strength continued into 2004. In February a new album by Norah Jones, *Feels Like Home,* sold more than one million copies in a single week, the best launch in almost three years. Legal downloading sites, such as Apple Computer's iTunes, are becoming more popular.

Just as important as the improved business environment is the fact that in his new role Edgar Jr. is no longer an inheritor

CEO with the stigma that comes with being a scion. Families rarely get to run Fortune 500 companies. Third-generation leaders are even scarcer; only 10 percent of family businesses survive that long. In 2001, when William Clay Ford Jr., great-grandson of Henry Ford, was named CEO of Ford Motor Co., he was the first family member to run the firm in twenty years. Success remained so elusive that Bill Ford refused a salary during the first few years. When August Busch III stepped down as CEO of Anheuser-Busch in 2002, professional management took over while August Busch IV waited in the wings. Christopher Galvin, grandson of Motorola's founder, was named CEO in 1997 but left six years later amid investor unhappiness with his efforts.

Willingness to work hard is not the problem; talent is usually the issue for family leaders. Everyone agreed Edgar Jr. worked hard when his vast wealth would have allowed him to do otherwise. "He puts himself through an awful lot when he doesn't really have to. I have said to him on numerous occasions, 'What do you have to prove? You've got nothing else to prove.' For those of us who really know exactly what he has accomplished, his accomplishments are legion," says John Bernbach. According to Ron Meyer, "The sad part is that in hind, hind, hindsight, had it not been Vivendi at that particular time, I believe Edgar would have proven them wrong. I never found Edgar to be a dilettante. Edgar worked very hard, he was focused, he cared about his businesses, he cared about the people in his businesses."

As always, in the other camp, his critics were unimpressed by his motives. "It was commendable that he didn't want to spend his entire life being a playboy, he wanted to do something. It was just a shame that what he wanted to do was stupid," says Michael Palmer of First Associates. "His record in the liquor business wasn't bad. Maybe he deserves some credit for that."

But Edgar Jr. cared only about entertainment, and not just for business reasons. Linked to his third-generation sense of duty and responsibility was a desire not only to do right by his father but also to do better than him. Only by investing in entertainment could Edgar Jr. both vindicate the family name after his father's embarrassing foray at MGM *and* beat him at his own game, the ultimate victory for any son who grew up in the long shadow of a powerful father.

Jean de Grandpré, a Seagram director from 1979 to 1992, sees a parallel between Edgar Jr. and Paul Martin Jr., who in 2003 became prime minister of Canada. In 1968 his father, Paul Martin Sr., ran against Pierre Trudeau and lost out in his last opportunity to lead the Liberal Party and the country. Paul Jr. followed Paul Sr. into politics and accomplished what his own father could not. Says de Grandpré, "Maybe [Edgar Sr.] said, 'Are you going to redeem my name in the entertainment business because I didn't do well? Maybe you will do better.' Neither of them did very well. Very often you see the father who has not succeeded helping his son to try. The son wants to succeed where his father did not."

While Edgar Jr. has been made the scapegoat, everyone played their assigned role. Edgar Sr. encouraged his son, as always, to do just whatever he wanted with Jean-Marie Messier. Charles, who never said no to any acquisition or sale that his brother or nephew proposed, didn't deny them the Vivendi deal either. Members of the board of directors posed a few questions, but none among them pushed, prodded, or asked: "Is this the right move? Do you really know what you're doing?"

There was nothing inherently wrong with Edgar Jr.'s diversification strategy to move away from DuPont into the more risky area of global entertainment content and distribution. Edgar Jr. firmly believed that he was a trends-spotter, but maybe all he ever saw was already in plain view. "He was young, he was impressionable, and he was likely to listen to—not to his own voice—but the voice of the popular press," says analyst Harold Vogel. "He wasn't listening to that inner gut feeling like a Barry Diller does, a Michael Eisner, Fred Silverman, Sumner Redstone, Rupert Murdoch. They have the intellect, they have the knowledge, but they have their own way. The fundamental flaw is that he was not driven by his own gut, he was driven by whatever was popular that day."

A successful CEO must have intuition, that internal compass that provides an unerring view of the marketplace. Right from his early days when he discussed possible films with Andrew Birkin or Broadway plays with Bruce Stark, Edgar Jr. had no sense what the audience wanted and did not seem to care. Perhaps that was because the face he presented to the world was not the real Edgar Jr. The middle child, the one who never felt totally accepted, had to fabricate a persona. For Edgar Jr., that false front was well dressed and handsome, gracious and caring. He would carefully gauge the temperature in the room then try to blend in and be accepted—all the while fearing deep within that he would be rejected by the very people he most sought to please because they would see him for the fraud he was.

As for leadership, he could be inconsistent with underlings and uncertain of himself. Sometimes he left people alone, on other occasions he was a micro-manager. His followers never knew which Edgar Jr. would show up. "In some respects he wasn't tough enough. He didn't push his own people hard enough to move more quickly, and I think he probably regrets that," says Hilary Rosen, CEO of the Recording Industry Association of America.

Nor did Edgar Jr. ever properly come to grips with another of life's great questions: Whom do you trust? Edgar Jr.'s problem wasn't so much that he was naive, as many have supposed. His biggest failing was *misplaced* trust. He'd trust someone who lied to him, he'd trust a big name in the business, he'd trust his money to solve his problems. He never knew if people liked him as a person or simply because he had a fountain of funds.

For a long time, the poor little rich boy could always satisfy his every desire. Want to be in a band? Get your dad to buy one of the members a set of drums. Want a Hollywood deal? Agree to whatever terms it takes. Don't like the job I've assigned you to do? Swallow your pride, here's more money to wash away the sour taste. On any given day Edgar Jr. could put on the market a house he'd recently renovated, lose faith in an executive he had just hired, or give up on an entire business that had fascinated him only last week. Edgar Jr. got used to doing whatever he wanted because for most of his life there were never any consequences for his actions. Mere mortals who make a mistake might fear job loss, but Edgar Jr. had been able to walk away from a string of failures: Oddbins, Soho Beverages, Golden Wine Coolers, Hervé Léger, and Time Warner. If people fell from favour, he could magically make them disappear: Pietersen, Bension, Biondi, McGurk, Peck, Nichols.

Edgar Jr. had every reason to succeed. He fought against all the predictions that he would fail, but no matter how hard he tried, he had been unable to alter his destiny. Edgar Sr., who supervised and supported Edgar Jr.'s every move, saw the error of his ways too late. When Leo Kolber sent Edgar Sr. a copy of his memoirs, published in 2003, Edgar Sr. wrote a thank-you note to Kolber in which he admitted that maybe he had given his CEO son a little too much leeway. "Not to pooh-pooh the money, but that's not the real disaster," said Edgar Sr. "The real

disaster is bad judgment. [We] took something my father had
built and my son had converted into something which was really
dynamic, and put it in with these guys to get the kind of size we
needed. And suddenly it blew up in our faces."

Edgar Sr. had grown up receiving lots of direction from Mr.
Sam but too little love. In vowing not to make that mistake with
his own son, Edgar Sr. did the opposite, which was equally misguided. He gave Edgar Jr. affection but no direction. "I think he
tried hard. He didn't have an awful lot of training at anything. I
think it was probably a pretty tough life for him in its own luxurious way," says Herbert Allen Jr., the investment banker who
advised Edgar Jr. on media deals. "He had a combination of
things that were missing. It would be similar to being a beautiful young girl who turns into a model and spends her adolescent
years being adored or ignored but never corrected. There was no
learning curve, there weren't steps along the way. By the time he
got into business, he had spent the years from eighteen to thirty-
two—which are important formative years for young people—
being a movie producer, and in Hollywood, going to the events
and all that stuff. It sort of hollows people out. Instead of building something, he had to operate with almost no background."

Successful entrepreneurs such as Sam Bronfman believe the
businesses they create will live on beyond their death as a mon-
ument to their mastery. Although some of Mr. Sam's brands still
exist, ownership has gone forever from family hands. His legacy
will be not in booze but in a few buildings that bear the family
name. In Montreal, the memorials include the Saidye Bronfman
Centre for the Arts, the Samuel Bronfman Building at McGill,
a library at the Université de Montréal, and the home for the
Jewish Studies program at Concordia University.

Edgar Sr.'s greatest accomplishment was not in business but in his role as president of the World Jewish Congress. As a citizen diplomat, Edgar Sr. secured an agreement from the Swiss banks to establish a $1.25-billion restitution fund for the families of Holocaust victims. He also exposed the Nazi past of Kurt Waldheim, president of Austria. Charles's most lasting contribution was not hinged on his execution skills at Seagram either. He will be remembered instead as the man whose financial backing brought professional baseball to Montreal and as the philanthropist whose Birthright Israel program has paid for tens of thousands of young Jews to visit Israel for the first time.

As for Edgar Jr., he has done nothing yet that will last, either in business or anywhere else. It will take a lot of hard slogging by him just to improve his beleaguered public image, let alone leave any legacy. Toronto investment manager Ira Gluskin sees an analogy between Edgar Jr. and major league pitcher Sandy Koufax. Even people who know little about baseball were aware that Koufax, a Jew, refused to pitch on Yom Kippur, the most holy of days. Says Gluskin: "I find the same thing with Seagram. If we had an elevator operator and you said to him 'Seagram' he'd say, 'Why did Edgar sell DuPont?' People who don't ordinarily know nothing about nothing have got it in their heads that these guys screwed up. I'm dumbfounded. You could say that about a lot of people: 'If they'd just held on to their Microsoft, or a piece of downtown property, they'd be worth a billion dollars today.' But everybody picks on this guy."

Edgar Jr.'s only hope for the future lies in the public's willingness to forgive someone who fell from grace and then worked hard for redemption. Individuals as diverse as Jimmy Carter and Jimmy Swaggart have come back from political defeat or public dishonour to more than regain their former following. "I think he wants it. I hope he gets it. If I could be any help with it, I would be fighting for him in the forefront. Now, that's after being with someone for eight years," says Doug Morris. "That's an interesting comment—after eight years to say I would do anything you would like me to do. How's that? And I mean it. He was a very good guy. And everything wasn't easy. We had times when we weren't successful. He was just as supportive when it was tough as when it was good."

If being a good guy were enough, Edgar Jr. would have succeeded long ago. In the past he was smart and worked hard. Now he needs to be hard and work smart. "All I want to do is go off and run my own little company and have nothing to do with family," Edgar Jr. once told Donard Gaynor. "He tried to get away, but in that family there are certain *requirements*," says Gaynor. In his fiftieth year, Edgar Jr. is at last being tested on his own. As second chances go, Warner Music is already risky enough without the guiding hand of his doting father. The sector may take years to recover from piracy, if recover it ever does. His venture partners could lose patience. Catcalls from journalists will again cause trouble.

Edgar Jr. rose to the top only because his name was Bronfman. That was his strength and his weakness. It was his strength because without the name he never would have had the opportunity to do what he did. It was his weakness because Seagram's entertainment strategy was not just about creating shareholder value and increasing family wealth but also about seeking vindication for the old man. As Edgar Bronfman Jr. sets out to swim against the current of his own past, this time without the burden of his father's failures, he has his best chance yet to make it to the safety of the other shore.

NOTES

There were numerous journalists who covered Seagram and the Bronfman family who shared their recollections with me or provided material. They include: Pierre Briançon of the Dow Jones Paris Bureau; James Harding of the *Financial Times;* James Ferrabee and L. Ian MacDonald of the *Montreal Gazette*; Richard Siklos and Anthony Bianco of *Business Week*; and Patrick Martin of *The Globe and Mail.* Librarians Pat Duggan of the Montreal *Gazette* and Scott Maniquet of the *National Post* helped with my research.

There were others whose published work was also valuable. They include Ken Auletta and Connie Bruck in *The New Yorker;* Johnnie L. Roberts of *Newsweek;* Geraldine Fabrikant and Bernard Weinraub of *The New York Times;* John Carreyou, Laura Landro, Martin Peers and Eben Shapiro of *The Wall Street Journal*; James Bates, Claudia Eller and Richard Verrier of *The Los Angeles Times;* and Brian Milner of *The Globe and Mail.*

What follows are notes on the secondary sources used in the book as well as specific information about those quotes from interviews personally conducted by the author. Once Edgar Jr. changed his mind about co-operating, other family members also declined to be interviewed. Charles had initially agreed then he, too, withdrew. Edgar Sr., however, has written three books so many of the quotes attributed to him were drawn from his own words.

INTRODUCTION

P. 1   "You know what they say . . . future of the generations to follow." *Los Angeles Times,* August 4, 2002.

P. 2   "Bronfman, one of Hollywood's favorite punching bags, may finally get some respect." *U.S. News & World Report,* June 26, 2000.

P. 2   "If ever they erect . . . and non-family shareholders." *Globe and Mail,* June 21, 2000.

P. 2   "It's the end of an era . . . run the company." *The Gazette* (Montreal), June 21, 2000.

P. 3   "There's something in life . . . The Great Equalizer at work." Culver interview, October 24, 2002.

P. 3   "Members of a family don't want . . . come and gone." *Fortune,* December 1966, 208.

P. 3   "Even to this day Senior thinks . . . of the Seagram Co. I knew." Griffin interviews, April 22 and 25, 2003.

CHAPTER ONE: BITTEN BY THE BUG

P. 15   "We loaded a carload of goods . . . the empty Seagrams bottles." *Fortune,* November 1966, 198.

P. 15   "Sam and his brothers kept . . . coast to coast." Michael R. Marrus, *Mr. Sam: The Life and Times of Samuel Bronfman* (Toronto: Viking, 1991), 11–12.

P. 15   " . . . the largest supply of aged whiskey." The word *whisky* comes from the Gaelic *ulsge-beatha* or *usquebaugh* meaning "water of life." The more vulgar *booze* has its roots in a Dutch word, *bulzer,* which means "drinking to excess." As for how the word is spelled, it's Canadian or Scotch *whisky,* American or Irish *whiskey.*

P. 17   "Now I know . . . a poor relation." Stephen Birmingham, *Our Crowd: The Great Jewish Families of New York* (New York: Harper & Row, 1967), 378.

P. 17   "But those Bronfmans . . . out of the trees." Marrus, *Mr. Sam,* 385.

P. 18   "It was like going . . . was quite amazing." Schulson interview, March 19, 2003.

P. 18   "They both were very impactful . . . our lives." Edgar Bronfman Jr. interview, March 3, 2003.

P. 19   "I would settle fights . . . take care of you." Edgar Bronfman Jr. interview.

P. 20 "We want to go bowling . . . my little jewels." *Financial Times of Canada,* May 21, 1990.

P. 20 "The father was a very standoffish person . . . same type of environment." Reif interview, April 20, 2003.

P. 21 "More than anything . . . deal with them." Edgar Bronfman Jr. interview.

P. 21 "I don't think . . . working for his father." Edgar Bronfman Jr. interview.

P. 22 "In those days . . . and so did we." Edgar M. Bronfman, *Good Spirits: The Making of a Businessman* (New York: G.P. Putnam's Sons, 1998), 66.

P. 22 "As he was growing up . . . for his siblings." Ibid., 186–7.

P. 22 "I remember being bored . . . bored to death." Edgar Bronfman Jr. interview.

P. 23 "It was very established . . . whatever he wanted." Bernstein interview, March 25, 2003.

P. 23 "I don't remember . . . you are not powerful." *The Daily Telegraph* (London), June 30, 2002.

P. 24 "He wanted to be in the group . . . at their homes." Reif interview.

P. 24 "I liked the camaraderie . . . it was over." Edgar Bronfman Jr. interview.

P. 25 "It had so much wrong . . . started at Collegiate." Reed interview, March 13, 2003.

P. 25 "We had real awareness . . . separate environment." Edgar Bronfman Jr. interview.

P. 25 "Nearly everybody in the school . . . they were doing." Reed interview.

P. 26 "You need to have a market . . . in the middle sixties." Edgar Bronfman Jr. interview.

P. 26 "He didn't seem to be . . . rest of us kids." Moore interview, March 18, 2003.

P. 26 "Edgar was much more a phantom . . . social class apart." Major interview, April 22, 2003.

P. 26 "We cribbed answers . . . it was hysterical." Wolfson interview, April 24, 2003.

P. 27 "That always absolutely . . . interesting person." Reed interview.

P. 28 "Tell me Edgar . . . get laid." Peter C. Newman, *Bronfman Dynasty: The Rothschilds of the New World* (Toronto: McClelland and Stewart, 1978), 187.

P. 29 "Hey look . . . five whole minutes!" *The Gazette* (Montreal), July 23, 1971.

P. 29 "We all became jolly buddies . . . Edgar had a villa." Joan Collins, *Past Imperfect: An Autobiography* (New York: Simon and Schuster, 1984), 282.

P. 30 "He didn't seem . . . he got to us." Patsy Puttnam interview, June 30, 2003.

P. 31 "He wasn't one of those . . . learn about film-making." Lieberson interview, August 29, 2003.

P. 31 "He was a quick learner . . . to be his world." David Puttnam interview, June 25, 2003.

P. 31 "He had cameras and gadgets . . . things like that." Lester interview, May 18, 2003.

P. 32 "a pure delight." *Newsweek,* April 12, 1971, 113.

P. 32 " . . . Tracy Hyde actress of the year." For detailed information on *Melody* including photos, movie clips, and reviews, go to the Tracy Hyde website www.tracyhyde.net.

P. 33 "It was very Efer . . . streak of irresponsibility." Birkin interview, July 23, 2003.

CHAPTER TWO: COMING HOME

P. 35   " . . . would be the last time." It was only after Mr. Sam's death in 1971 that the family learned he'd been born in 1889, so he was actually eighty-two. He'd taken two years off his age.

P. 36   "I made a toast back . . . 'You're the one.'" *Whisky Man: Inside the Dynasty of Samuel Bronfman,* David Paperny Films, 1996.

P. 36   "Well, at least it . . . I love you." Bronfman, *Good Spirits,* 138.

P. 37   "I made the mistake . . . not a good idea." Bibb interview, January 22, 2003.

P. 38   "I hadn't had a hit show . . . beyond his years." Stark interview, May 13, 2003.

P. 38   "Edgar got a little . . . bunch of sharks." Stark interview.

P. 39   "I can't," replied Edgar Jr. . . . And I did." Commencement Address, Pine Manor College, Chestnut Hills, Mass., May 21, 1989.

P. 39   "Edgar engineered himself . . . write you a cheque." Isaacs interview, May 17, 2003.

P. 40   "He had very little . . . making of the film." Rees interview, May 20, 2003.

P. 40   "The film was going . . . a lot more generous." David Puttnam interview.

P. 41   "It has been my very good fortune . . . were self-imposed." Commencement Address, Pine Manor College.

P. 43   "It was difficult . . . it was a hard time." Edgar Bronfman Jr. interview.

P. 43   "She has five kids . . . here we go." *Detroit Free Press,* September 20, 1985.

P. 44   "What do you think . . . a start." Source.

P. 45   "If you're given . . . then he wasn't." Edgar Bronfman Jr. interview.

P. 47   "Kass was a pussycat . . . Fuck you." Keys interview, April 15, 2003.

P. 48   "She was absolutely radiant . . . fell in love." Faison interview, April 23, 2003.

P. 48   "Rich men's sons . . . the fast life." Collins, *Past Imperfect,* 112–13.

P. 49   "I learned about theatre . . . Mr. Know Nothing." *The New York Times,* May 5, 1978.

P. 49   "Because of the lower salary . . . lost $75,000 in Philadelphia." *The New York Times,* July 6, 1978.

P. 50   "Edgar was a theatre idealist . . . wanted something else." Stark interview.

P. 50   "The content needed to change . . . It was a little terrifying." Mount interview, October 13, 2003.

P. 51   "I didn't think twice . . . kill his parents." Stark interview.

P. 52   "I very much wanted . . . not the point." Bronfman, *Good Spirits,* 187.

P. 52   "It was a very thoughtful . . . prepared for it." Beekman interview, April 17, 2003.

P. 52   "Being a closet liberal . . . with the other." Bronfman, *Good Spirits,* 187.

P. 52   "Don't be an . . . cocktail party." *Fortune,* March 17, 1986, 30.

P. 53   "I thought he was smart . . . the possibilities were." Diller interview, May 5, 2004.

P. 53   "He didn't hesitate . . . impressed by that." Freeman interview, October 7, 2003.

P. 54   "Even though he was . . . star-struck." Green interview, October 21, 2003.

P. 54   "What's pertinent is . . . hands dirty, and he did." Freeman interview.

P. 55   "I joked with him . . . picture to picture." Freeman interview.

P. 56   "I want to see . . . and that child's mother." Mount interview.

P. 57   "He slouched and muttered his way back and forth across *The Border*." David Thomson, *Biographical Dictionary of Film* (New York: Knopf, 2002), 635.

P. 57   "It was the wrong movie . . . it was my fault." Tanen interview, October 24, 2003.

P. 57   "Though the movie was . . . fed up.'" Bronfman, *Good Spirits*, 188–91.

P. 57   "Will you join . . . bestowed on you." *The New Yorker*, June 6, 1994, 60.

P. 58   "I knew that's what . . . yes over the telephone." *Fortune*, March 17, 1986, 30.

P. 58   "He was being the peacemaker . . . personality at all." Patsy Puttnam interview.

P. 59   "The day I joined . . . was uncanny, *uncanny*." *Vanity Fair*, November 1987, 176.

CHAPTER THREE: UP THROUGH THE RANKS

P. 61   "This letter starts . . . projection of him." Speech by Phyllis Lambert at the Royal Ontario Museum, Toronto, February 7, 2003.

P. 61   "The day we moved in . . . memos bore its image." Bronfman, *Good Spirits*, 81.

P. 63   "He worked very hard . . . his West Coast contacts." Beekman interview.

P. 64   "You're in real trouble . . . jinx it for you." *Vanity Fair*, November 1987, 176.

P. 64   "He was very aloof . . . a lot of people." McDonough interview, May 1, 2003.

P. 65   "I'd kill for that job." Beekman interview.

P. 65   "Didn't anyone tell you . . . pretty tough to beat." McDonnell interview, July 1, 2003.

P. 66   "I was dumbfounded . . . I was impressed." Bibb interview.

P. 66   "He chose a very nice . . . beneath her feet." Patsy Puttnam interview.

P. 67   "Is he the best . . . the top person." Bernbach interview, August 7, 2003.

P. 67   "It didn't amount to . . . from the subject." Beekman interview.

P. 67   "The acquisition of Matheus . . . they didn't bite." Preston interview, March 4, 2003.

P. 68   "expensive introduction." *Fortune*, March 17, 1986, 30.

P. 70   "That works in a growing . . . with greater intensity." *The New York Times*, January 17, 1985.

P. 70   "I suppose you can always . . . not fundamental." *Fortune*, March 17, 1986, 31.

P. 71   "I find them not . . . have them tell you." Beekman interview.

P. 71   "It was clear even . . . the nicest man I know." Bronfman, *Good Spirits*, 185.

P. 71   "The man had a slight . . . center of the court." Bronfman, *Good Spirits*, 191.

P. 72   "Sam had a bad temper . . . than play sports." Edgar Bronfman Jr. interview.

P. 73   "There were a few raised . . . pro or con." Griffin interview.

P. 73   "When Edgar Jr. was appointed . . . the decision of the family." Jean de Grandpré interview, October 24, 2002.

P. 74   "I don't want to say . . . the board what to do." *The Gazette* (Montreal), April 12, 1986.

P. 75   "He seems like a nice . . . in your life." Leo Kolber, with L. Ian MacDonald, *Leo: A Life* (Montreal and Kingston: McGill–Queen's University Press, 2003), 48.

P. 75   "He's a guy that would rather run than fight." Beekman interview.

P. 75   "I agree with him." *The Wall Street Journal*, May 22, 1986.

P. 76 — "I could call him father . . . Edgar U.S.A." *Wall Street Journal,* December 3, 1987.

P. 77 — "He resents the senior . . . he is not senior." Chancery Court, State of Delaware, *MCA v. Viacom,* testimony of Edgar Bronfman Jr., Vol. 6, October 28, 1996, 1286.

CHAPTER FOUR: AT THE TOP

P. 81 — "That would be foolish . . . do the right thing." Bronfman, *Good Spirits,* 176–77.

P. 82 — "Edgar was very involved . . . the Martell line totally." Millet interview, April 24, 2003.

P. 83 — "Edgar had been very self-assured . . . won't make that mistake again." Gaynor interview, April 14, 2003.

P. 84 — "Edgar relished deals . . . too much stock in a company." Pietersen interview, March 4, 2003.

P. 85 — "He was not too interested . . . like fire people." Hauswald interview, April 24, 2003.

P. 85 — "I don't think Edgar . . . knowing if they were bright." Marram interview, April 25, 2003.

P. 85 — "Tropicana reminded me of Sicily . . . no consequences." Swain interview, November 25, 2003.

P. 86 — "It sounds like a funny thing . . . our retailers to buy it." Marram interview.

P. 87 — "Running a brand . . . these special brands." Collier interview, August 26, 2003.

P. 88 — "I will always . . . admit it had happened." Patsy Puttnam interview.

P. 89 — "I don't mean to be flippant . . . you can't stop them." *Financial Times of Canada,* May 21, 1990.

P. 90 — "He'd be pretty short . . . touch of arrogance later on." Beekman interview.

P. 90 — "Let me put it . . . of us is right." *The Wall Street Journal,* December 3, 1987.

P. 90 — "To this day this guy . . . knew how to use that." Marram interview.

P. 91 — "He was actually flirting . . . money during Prohibition, too." Hendy interview, January 29, 2003.

P. 91 — "He is actually more comfortable . . . almost be gentle." Hauswald interview.

P. 91 — "You know, Richard . . . the right question." Source.

P. 91 — "You never knew whether . . . father right next to him." De Grandpré interview.

P. 93 — "He's brilliant at that . . . lounging out in Southampton." McDonnell interview, April 8, 2003.

P. 94 — "He was a gentle, sensitive . . . I think not." Hendy interview.

P. 94 — "There was just a touch . . . possibly more fun–activity." Collier interview.

P. 94 — "Having Steve on his team . . . making the final mistake." Hauswald interview.

P. 96 — "In an earlier interview . . . job through nepotism." *The Wall Street Journal,* December 17, 1993.

P. 96 — "While 2 percentage points . . . a family company is for, isn't it?" *Newsday,* June 13, 1993.

P. 98   "Would you rather he . . . worked against you." Semel interview, November 17, 2003.

P. 99   "I tried to talk . . . he wants to move." Gaynor interview.

P. 99   "You have to remember . . . right company to go after." Vogel interview, January 30, 2003.

P. 99   "When he bought it . . . it wasn't easy for him." Allen interview, June 5, 2003.

P. 100   "Edgar was mesmerized . . . he wouldn't have been." Kolber, *Leo: A Life,* 72.

P. 100   "My relationship with my . . . meaningful to retire *to.*" Edgar M. Bronfman, with Catherine Whitney, *The Third Act: Reinventing Yourself After Retirement* (New York: G.P. Putnam's Sons, 2002), 4–5.

P. 101   "Psychotherapy alone was not . . . Edgar and I have grown." *Vanity Fair,* July 1995, 80.

P. 102   "Is it true you just wanted . . . pissed away the family fortune." *Business Week,* January 16, 1995, 78.

CHAPTER FIVE: GOING HOLLYWOOD

P. 104   "We have our limits." Source.

P. 104   "If there's anyone . . . love to meet her." *The New Yorker,* June 6, 1994, 62.

P. 104   "She's very strong-willed . . . great about her." Bernbach interview.

P. 105   "There are a few things . . . he's got three children.'" *Vanity Fair,* July 1995, 81.

P. 105   "Once again . . . hope over experience." Bronfman, *Good Spirits,* 187.

P. 106   "I told Peter two things . . . my Latin upbringing." *The New York Times,* September 23, 1999.

P. 107   "Being happy is better . . . in that regard." *Canadian Business,* October 1994, 26.

P. 107   "It didn't fit . . . we lost money every year." Millet interview.

P. 108   "It's the one that . . . generations ain't happening here." *Whisky Man,* David Paperny Films.

P. 108   "It was clear that . . . large part of that." Bernbach interview.

P. 110   "DuPont was the deal . . . liquor business any more." De Grandpré interview.

P. 111   "The whiskey business . . . run that business?" *The New Yorker,* May 11, 1998, 68–69.

P. 111   "It's something he obviously has always wanted to be a part of." *USA Today,* April 7, 1995.

P. 112   "We had gone from . . . than the film business." Westlake interview, October 6, 2003.

P. 113   "Junior said that the sale . . . it was breathtaking." Kolber, *Leo: A Life,* 198.

P. 114   "I always thought . . . didn't have much experience." Falkenberg interview, April 15, 2003.

P. 115   "The one problem . . . is *no* business." Source.

P. 116   "I'm sixty-four years old . . . the same profile." History Channel, *Big Deals: The Good, The Bad, and the Ugly,* September 18, 2002.

P. 117   "You don't always win . . . but not a serious one." *The Jerusalem Post,* June 29, 1999.

P. 117   "Woolard accepted the offer . . . heart was elsewhere." Adrian Kinnane, *DuPont: From the Banks of the Brandywine to Miracles of Science* (Wilmington: E.I. du Pont de Nemours and Co., 2002), 238.

P. 118   "We can take this company . . . get screwed by Hollywood." History Channel, *Big Deals.*

P. 118   "I just can't figure . . . what he should do." McDonnell interview.

P. 119   "You're joining a family . . . upset about that." Gaynor interview.

P. 120   "Edgar Sr., and . . . at board meetings." Griffin interview.

P. 120   "When you agree to . . . look like an ass." Source.

P. 121   "It was absolutely unbelievable . . . mutual admiration society." McDonnell interview.

P. 121   "My recollections at the board . . . was being presented." Bill Davis interview, December 22, 2003.

P. 122   "He really went and . . . done, with great stealth." Diller interview, May 5, 2004.

P. 122   "Obviously, the inflamed issue . . . accomplished his objectives." Allen interview.

P. 122   "This will dog Edgar . . . people in the business." Vogel interview.

P. 123   "Do me a favour . . . through the deal again." Source.

P. 123   "Now the rules are . . . let's get on with it." Bronfman, *Good Spirits,* 214–15.

CHAPTER SIX: MOVING IN

P. 125   "Guess where I am . . . the next time." Mount interview.

P. 126   "I hope you'll take courage . . . Citizen Kane." Birkin interview.

P. 127   "There's a guy . . . very supportive," Boberg interview, October 9, 2003.

P. 127   "He remembered my name . . . work for him." Bension interview, October 15, 2003.

P. 127   "So it's all solved . . . winked at me." Source.

P. 128   "The asshole only had . . . should paint it." Tanen interview.

P. 129   "*The Border* was a good picture . . . a great success." *Los Angeles Times Magazine,* July 30, 1995, 32.

P. 129   "According to a *Forbes* calculation . . . worth more than $13 billion." *Forbes,* July 3, 1995, 46.

P. 129   "As far as I know [he] has . . . write a big check." Newsmakers of the Year, *Newsweek,* November 1995, 53.

P. 130   "When you were told . . . drinking Crown Royal." Bill Davis interview.

P. 131   "I don't want this to be . . . I'm going to say yes." Tom King, *The Operator: David Geffen Builds, Buys, and Sells the New Hollywood* (New York: Random House, 2000), 548.

P. 132   "Are you here with . . . with my pilot." *Esquire,* June 1997, 58.

P. 132   "He is trying to be . . . world that shafts you." Patsy Puttnam interview

P. 133   "According to Bernard Dick's . . . a total of at least $360 million." Bernard F. Dick, *City of Dreams: The Making and Remaking of Universal Pictures* (Lexington: The University Press of Kentucky, 1997), 211–12.

P. 133   "Can't we just enjoy the moment?" Source.

P. 133   "Part of the negotiation . . . would be a difficult dynamic." Page 22, Report by Deborah DeMott, a Duke University law professor and corporate governance expert retained by the plaintiffs in a suit against Disney Chairman and CEO Michael Eisner. The twenty-nine-page report was among thousands of pages unsealed by Delaware Chancery Court in February 2004.

P. 134   "There is no plan B." Source.

P. 134   "He saw [MCA] as a sleeping . . . talent to do that." Meyer interview, October 13, 2003.

P. 135   "Efer, what are all these people doing in *our* room?" *Fortune,* April 15, 1996, 102.

P. 136   "There were certain people . . . required changing people." Meyer interview.

P. 137   "I've seen the movie . . . it's a passion." Morris interview, March 6, 2003.

P. 138   "That really changed . . . force to be reckoned with." Morris interview.

P. 138   "The fact that he had personal . . . made a big difference." Rosen interview, July 22, 2003.

P. 139   "As the owner . . . e-mail response we had." Hack interview, December 2, 2003.

P. 139   "Edgar wanted a fresh . . . grown up in the industry." Olson interview, November 11, 2003.

P. 139   "I think Doug Morris . . . use of that capital." Martin interview, December 16, 2003.

P. 140   "What Edgar set out to do . . . 375 Park Avenue." Westlake interview.

P. 140   "He was out here . . . of the company." Meyer interview.

P. 140   "There were a lot of . . . face-to-face with him." Bension interview.

P. 141   "The team that he put . . . a big movie company." Crawford interview, October 8, 2003.

P. 141   "On the street it became . . . a huge change." Palmer interview, May 29, 2003.

CHAPTER SEVEN: RE-ENGINEERING THE CORPORATION

P. 145   "This was as broad . . . so people hid problems." Gunby interview, May 22, 2003.

P. 146   "Entertainment companies occupy . . . conquistadors of modern business." Michael J. Wolf, *The Entertainment Economy: How Mega-Media Forces Are Transforming Our Lives* (New York: Time Books, Random House, 1999), 28–29.

P. 146   "Re-engineering was very costly . . . have lost my job." Westlake interview.

P. 147   "A lot of kids in their . . . money-minded manager to Wall Street." Pollock interview, October 13, 2003.

P. 147   "You could read him . . . committed to something." Falkenberg interview.

P. 148   "They were like royalty . . . disagree with you." Marram interview.

P. 148   "I thought it was . . . circus come to town." Meyer interview.

P. 149   "Tropicana went from a . . . excited and motivated." Gunby interview.

P. 150   "People had to fly in . . . by profligate spending." Source.

P. 151   "Should the kings eat less caviar?" Source.

P. 151   "Rob Cohen had every . . . he's had success." Meyer interview.

P. 152   "There's nothing like being . . . against the best?" Patsy Puttnam interview.

P. 152   "He's very private . . . did for himself." Rosen interview.

P. 153   "We shared a unique connection . . . way to blissfully coexist." My thanks to Gerry Schwartz for his help in obtaining Michael Douglas's handwritten speech notes.

P. 154   "Edgar came into the business . . . sharks out there." Cohen interview, December 1, 2003.

P. 154   "In Hollywood there never . . . CEOs who ran companies." David Davis interview, October 10, 2003.

P. 154   "Nobody wants to believe . . . actually, he's stupid." Source.

P. 155   "Have you noticed a whirring . . . turn in the barrel." *Variety*, April 13, 1998.

P. 156   "In the film business . . . tough conditions." Diller interview.

P. 156   "I have a plan . . . happen often enough." Peter Bart, *The Gross: The Hits, the Flops—the Summer That Ate Hollywood* (New York: St. Martin's Press, 1999), 56.

P. 157   "Rosemary wouldn't let him . . . rude questions?" Hendy interview.

P. 157   "It was tough . . . win over the naysayers." Tofalli interview, January 27, 2003.

P. 157   "It was one of the most . . . a killer instinct." Reguly interview, March 16, 2004.

P. 157   "Some people, and its no . . . not a sympathetic character." Diller interview.

P. 158   "The way he explained . . . imperious at all." Marram interview.

P. 158   "Knowing him personally . . . gloss over something." Boyce interview, November 24, 2003.

P. 159   "I always found him . . . never should have been CEO." Siklos interview, January 22, 2003.

P. 159   "His baggage was checked . . . he was given." Meyer interview.

P. 159   "I find a lot of . . . always impressed me." Valenti interview, November 24, 2003.

P. 160   "This is my least favourite . . . tough to conduct business." *Barron's*, April 27, 1998, 36.

P. 160   "Hit him and money comes out." *The New Yorker*, May 11, 1998, 77.

P. 161   "Hollywood thinks it was dumb . . . a dumb town." Ibid., 68.

P. 161   "Today is a very important . . . in *The New York Times*." Source.

P. 161   "Edgar's always above . . . any good professionally." Mount interview.

P. 162   "I heard him tell . . . no longer with us." Hullin interview, January 21, 2003.

P. 162   "At least he was . . . the right change." Bill Davis interview.

P. 163   "Watch us and judge us . . . the Sound of Silence." Testimony by Bill Bennett before the Senate Committee on Commerce, May 4, 1999.

P. 163   "I have more to lose . . . my answer to you." *Maclean's*, November 16, 1998, 44.

P. 164   "The magnitude of the hemorrhage . . . management move." *Los Angeles Times*, February 22, 2000.

P. 165   "I was always concerned . . . much better results." Matschullat interview, April 16, 2003.

P. 165   "Edgar was impressed . . . screws up in the beginning." Mount interview.

P. 166   "There were a lot of comings . . . took three years." Meyer interview.

CHAPTER EIGHT: SHARK ATTACKS

P. 168   "The partnership agreement . . . not going to screw." Chancery Court, *MCA v. Viacom,* 1117.

P. 170   "So, we have an agreement . . . in thirty days." Transcript, 1163.

P. 170   "This is ridiculous . . . kind of behavior." Transcript, 1170.

P. 171   "No, I didn't understand that meant everything." Transcript, 1470.

P. 171   "Edgar, I don't like . . . you asked me for." Transcript, 1183.

P. 171   "I haven't lost my marbles . . . what your view is." Transcript, 1476, 1483.

P. 171   "Well, Edgar, that's the only language Sumner understands." Transcript, 1203.

P. 172   "I know how to wage war . . . you're my partner." Transcript, 1793.

P. 172   "I have been trying . . . pretty intractable." Transcript, 1216–7.

P. 172   "You propose things . . . your own proposals." Transcript, 2530.

P. 173   "The job was a natural . . . execute the plan." Biondi interview, November 2, 2003.

P. 173   "He made the bold . . . to bat like that." Olson interview.

P. 174   "To Bronfman and Redstone, USA . . . would be crowned victor." Bernard F. Dick, *Engulfed: The Death of Paramount Pictures and the Birth of Corporate Hollywood* (Lexington: University Press of Kentucky, 2001), 232.

P. 174   "MCA's sole opportunity . . . be it film or television." Chancery Court, *MCA v. Viacom,* 1251–52.

P. 175   "I certainly now wish . . . more than that." Ibid., 1272.

P. 175   "This is not like you . . . actually ran Seagram's." Ibid., 1771–72.

P. 175   "There has been a consistent . . . meeting of the minds." Ibid., 1242–43.

P. 175   "Q: Are you an expert . . . I continued to work." Ibid., 1161.

P. 176   "it is simply unreasonable . . . multi-billion-dollar agreement." *Variety,* May 15, 1997.

P. 178   "You're competing against . . . we couldn't do both." Matschullat interview.

P. 179   "We came up with the . . . a really clever idea." Diller interview.

P. 180   "for all the world like . . . thrill of their new partnership." Kay Koplovitz, with Peter Israel, *Bold Women, Big Ideas* (New York: PublicAffairs, 2002), 29.

P. 180   "In men who lost prowess . . . on his own terms." Gail Sheehy, *Understanding Men's Passages: Discovering the New Map of Men's Lives* (New York: Random House, 1998), 116.

P. 181   "To the Hollywood establishment . . . strip him of his constituency." Bart, *The Gross,* 52.

P. 181   "I didn't like the deal . . . of intellectual property." Vogel interview.

P. 182   "You're selling the best asset . . . increased his borrowing power." Biondi interview.

P. 182   "I guess you don't . . . play tennis today." Source.

P. 182   "He had commissioned an agency . . . not one of his strengths." Biondi interview.

P. 183   "Doug and Edgar can talk music . . . It never really connected." Borgia interview, April 15, 2003

P. 183   "I guess what I learned . . . overlook that possibility." Biondi interview.

P. 184   "The competition were people . . . to do on their own." Semel interview.
P. 185   "The highest performing assets . . . Diller got him." Pollock interview.
P. 185   "Diller on the movie side . . . than those two." Valenti interview.
P. 186   "Edgar was not a popular . . . to do the work." Diller interview.
P. 187   "Barry is always going . . . Edgar's best interest." Bibb interview.
P. 188   "I had worked for a company . . . everlastingly good business." Diller interview.
P. 189   "He'd gone through some . . . full speed ahead." Bernbach interview.

CHAPTER NINE: THE MUSIC MAN

P. 192   "Music is where his heart . . . information to him." Olson interview.
P. 192   "That's how you get deals . . . that was important." Matschullat interview.
P. 193   "drastic measures." Matsushita suffered similar dilution. Because the Japanese put in no additional money, its 20 percent share in Universal fell to 16 percent after the 1997 deal with Barry Diller. The PolyGram purchase further cut Matsushita's stake to 8 percent.
P. 194   "The thing that intrigued me . . . had the same passion." Bibb interview.
P. 196   "We could have bought Allied . . . much as we did before." Millet interview.
P. 197   "This wasn't a job . . . Can I get a piece of that?" Borgia interview.
P. 197   "The spirits division was . . . better for the shareholders." Jellinek interview, April 24, 2003.
P. 199   "He had a certain cachet . . . that goes so far." Boberg interview.
P. 200   "We look around and . . . so much fun." Morris interview.
P. 201   "I always counted Edgar . . . things in that context." Rosen interview.
P. 203   "He understands the importance . . . message and when not." Gerson interview, May 1, 2003.
P. 204   "Viacom, NewsCorp, Disney . . . increasing programming ownership." Westlake interview.
P. 206   "I think I am uniquely qualified . . . have filled this job." Nichols interview, October 20, 2003.
P. 207   "I won't bonus on 12.5 . . . make it more exciting?" Nichols interview.
P. 208   "I was never totally happy . . . he inserted himself." Biondi interview.
P. 208   "I can't recall . . . just to be different." Bension interview.
P. 209   "The fear was that . . . he wasn't there." Nichols interview.
P. 210   "I'm beginning to hear . . . at that moment in time." Nichols interview.
P. 211   "He'd go through the right . . . coming the other way." Biondi interview.
P. 211   "This is a person who . . . know that they do." Nichols interview.
P. 213   "I want my pound of flesh." Sources.
P. 213   "Edgar's an encouraging boss . . . [and] got whacked." Borgia interview.
P. 214   "You have no power . . . don't follow. Care." Video of proceedings, UJA-Federation of New York, Steven J. Ross Humanitarian Award, 1996.
P. 215   "He's so nice . . . with his eyes." Award video.

CHAPTER TEN: WHISKY INTO WATER

P. 216 "It was one of the few . . . would call expectations." Westlake interview.

P. 218 "With all apologies . . . fight the French." Sources.

P. 222 "It's better to pick . . . What's the hurry?" *Variety,* November 20–26, 2000, 6.

P. 222 "I'm sure I'm exaggerating . . . in no man's land.'" Borgia interview.

P. 224 "It was meant to . . . his whole life." Marram interview.

P. 228 "I'd prefer to merge . . . in the water business." Berger interview, February 3, 2004.

P. 231 "The company is not . . . especially to lie." *Los Angeles Times,* June 23, 2000.

P. 231 "Jean-Marie, if you were . . . run for president." Jo Johnson and Martine Orange, *The Man Who Tried to Buy the World: Jean-Marie Messier and Vivendi Universal* (London: Viking, 2003), 11.

P. 231 "You were extremely impressive . . . have the green light." Ibid., 13.

P. 231 "I stopped before a magnum . . . good year for Bordeaux wines." Jean-Marie Messier, *j6m.com: faut-il avoir peur de la nouvelle économie?* (Paris: Hachette Littératures, 2000), Chap. 2, 4. (All citations from an English translation supplied by Vivendi.)

CHAPTER ELEVEN: DOING THE DEAL

P. 234 "We declare a dividend and have a drink." Bronfman, *Good Spirits,* 152.

P. 235 "We want the board . . . our Seagram shares." Source.

P. 235 "Presentations were always . . . they're talking about." Preston interview.

P. 239 "sole vice-chairman . . . senior to Mr. Bronfman." Proxy circular, November 2, 2000, 97.

P. 239 "Give me some more . . . give you my congratulations." Messier, *j6m.com,* Chap. 2, 9, 1.

P. 242 "I thought they were . . . friend of the court." Diller interview.

P. 243 "The wealth, the power . . . up in thin air." *Venture,* CBC-TV, May 25, 2003.

P. 244 "His father was always . . . no one could meet." Bianco interview, January 22, 2003.

CHAPTER TWELVE: COMING UNDONE

P. 246 "You know the way . . . grow these businesses." Berger interview.

P. 247 "Content certainly has all . . . very much for it." An expanded version appeared in *First Monday,* a peer-reviewed academic on-line journal, vol. 6, no. 2, February 2001.

P. 248 "There is real interest . . . spirits and wine business." *The Wall Street Journal,* July 13, 2000.

P. 251 "His plan was for . . . never complain, never explain." Source.

P. 253 "The Bronfmans had never . . . a big corporation." Jarislowsky interview, November 4, 2002.

P. 253 "I worked at Universal . . . big an ego." Westlake interview.

P. 253 "I never quite understood . . . be very annoying." Meyer interview.

P. 254   "I'm not sure I ever . . . wasn't the only one." Cohen interview.

P. 255   "My father and my uncle . . . future of Vivendi Universal." *Variety,* December 11, 2000.

P. 255   "The media and the stock . . . starts with a mess." *National Post,* December 6, 2000.

P. 255   "Get me the hell out of here." Source.

P. 255   "It's not easy letting go . . . my family's life." *Business Wire,* speech text, December 5, 2000.

P. 256   "Oh, *pardonnez-moi* . . . it is improving." *Variety,* December 6, 2000.

P. 257   "I think I've seen . . . for the most part." Allen interview.

P. 257   "I was furious . . . so many things." Johnson and Orange, *Man Who Tried,* 112–13.

P. 258   "He tells me on . . . unravelled extremely quickly." Borgia interview.

P. 262   "Edgar saw, after . . . live his life." Borgia interview.

P. 262   "I think he resigned . . . all the penguins." Morris interview.

P. 263   "It's never easy . . . No. 1 anymore." *The Wall Street Journal,* December 7, 2001.

P. 264   "I am pleased . . . back to the company." *Business Week Online,* December 27, 2001.

P. 264   "You can say that . . . my whole life." *Los Angeles Times Magazine,* March 24, 2002, 12.

CHAPTER THIRTEEN: THE OUSTER

P. 267   "He is Donald Trump and Lee Iacocca and Jack Welch rolled into one." *Vanity Fair,* April 2002, 248.

P. 267   "If the dividend is cut . . . become increasingly tenuous." *Le Monde,* December 13, 2002. My thanks to Dr. Alison McQueen for this translation and her other help *en français.*

P. 268   "I've got the unpleasant feeling . . . It's you." *The Wall Street Journal,* October 31, 2002.

P. 269   "I have to keep on running . . . very appealing to them." Minzberg interview, March 5, 2004.

P. 271   "As the Vivendi stock . . . within six months." Martin interview.

P. 272   "Edgar Jr. is a total gentleman . . . He just lies." Minzberg interview.

P. 272   "He said on numerous occasions . . . try to make a change." Bernbach interview.

P. 273   "Everything was conspiratorial . . . lot of trouble." Murray interview, February 16, 2004.

P. 273   "Monsieur Bronfman thought that . . . dangerous for French capitalism." Couture interview, February 5, 2004.

P. 274   "We did make errors . . . fifteen years." CBS Marketwatch.com, June 13, 2002.

P. 275   "Only an idiot would . . . There was pandemonium." Murray interview.

P. 277   "Edgar was always studiously . . . on the boardroom table." Murray interview.

P. 278 "Bébéar's concern was mostly . . . a few weeks, Messier's ouster." Briançon interview, March 8, 2004.

P. 279 "It was a perfect storm . . . way you want it." Minzberg interview.

P. 279 "When the French banks . . . it was political." Martin interview.

P. 279 "His attitude was 'unless . . . that deal any day." Johnson and Orange, *Man Who Tried*, 238.

P. 280 "no good cocksucker . . . no problem, forget it." Kolber, *Leo: A Life*, 32.

P. 280 "Somehow he could have . . . died with Messier." Murray interview.

P. 281 "Everyone is still lying . . . things got so ridiculous." Briançon interview.

P. 282 "their current holdings." As of December 31, 2003 the largest single share-holder in Vivendi was Capital Group International, of Los Angeles, with 72 million shares, or 6.7 percent.

P. 282 "The lesson is . . . done that." Minzberg interview.

P. 283 "That last one was . . . take up your offer." Axworthy interview, December 3, 2002.

P. 283 "I'm not a happy camper." Beekman interview.

P. 284 "I don't know what ever . . . brother against brother." Sharp interview, December 17, 2002.

P. 284 "One of the things that . . . $65 or $70 a share." *Fortune*, November 25, 2002, 118.

P. 285 "He used to laugh . . . as a young kid." Patsy Puttnam interview.

P. 286 "I truly respect him . . . in some way forever." Diller interview.

P. 286 ". . . options worth $33 million." Vivendi Universal has assumed the U.S. pension plan obligations applicable to former Seagram executives. In 2003, Edgar Jr.'s retirement pension was $1.9 million.

CHAPTER FOURTEEN: ROAD TO REDEMPTION

P. 290 "The problem is . . . we're lost." Edgar Bronfman Jr. interview, January 24, 2003.

P. 291 "I thought it was odd . . . emerge as a CEO." Gluskin interview, December 10, 2002.

P. 291 "I went in with . . . was ill-conceived." *Forbes*, September 30, 2002.

P. 291 "I think anybody that . . . even knowing about it." Transcript, *After Hours with Maria Bartiromo*, CNBC, October 21, 2002.

P. 293 "possibly the stupidest person in the media business." *New York*, September 30, 2002.

P. 293 "Edgar is the largest reason . . . what a shame." Anderson interview, July 24, 2003.

P. 294 "Edgar made a mistake . . . misconceptions about Edgar." Hack interview.

P. 295 "This is part of a whole . . . heritage of New York." *The New York Times*, December 12, 2002.

P. 297 "The transaction with NBC . . . or a theme park." *Financial Times*, August 27, 2003.

P. 297 "We've been rescued . . . that's in our business." *The New York Times*, May 13, 2004.

P. 298   "The deal with Edgar . . . do a good job." *The New York Times*, November 30, 2003.

P. 299   "From a Wall Street perspective . . . then he won't." Cohen interview.

P. 300   "He puts himself through . . . accomplishments are legion." Bernbach interview.

P. 300   "The sad part is . . . people in his businesses." Meyer interview.

P. 300   "It was commendable . . . credit for that." Palmer interview.

P. 301   "Maybe [Edgar Sr.] said . . . his father did not." de Grandpré interview.

P. 302   "He was young . . . popular that day." Vogel interview.

P. 302   "In some respects . . . regrets that." Rosen interview.

P. 303   "Not to pooh-pooh the money . . . blew up in our faces." Brian Milner, *Report on Business Magazine*, September 2002, 29.

P. 304   "I think he tried hard . . . almost no background." Allen interview.

P. 305   "I find the same thing . . . picks on this guy." Gluskin interview.

P. 306   "I think he wants it . . . when it was good." Morris interview.

P. 306   "All I want to do . . . there are certain *requirements*." Gaynor interview.

BIBLIOGRAPHY

Auletta, Ken. *The Highwaymen.* New York: Harcourt Brace, 1998.

Baime, A.J. *Big Shots: The Men Behind the Booze.* New York: New American Library, 2003.

Bart, Peter. *Fade Out: The Calamitous Final Days of MGM.* New York: William Morrow, 1990.

———. *The Gross: The Hits, the Flops—the Summer That Ate Hollywood.* New York: St. Martin's Press, 1999.

———. *Who Killed Hollywood? . . . and Put the Tarnish on Tinseltown.* Los Angeles: Renaissance Books, 1999.

——— and Peter Gruber. *Shoot Out: Surviving Fame and (Mis)Fortune in Hollywood.* New York: G.P. Putnam's Sons, 2002.

Bellow, Adam. *In Praise of Nepotism: A Natural History.* New York: Doubleday, 2003.

Bibb, Porter. *Ted Turner: It Ain't As Easy As It Looks.* Boulder: Johnson Books, 1997.

Birmingham, Stephen. *Our Crowd: The Great Jewish Families of New York.* New York: Harper & Row, 1967.

Bronfman, Edgar M. *The Making of a Jew.* New York: G.P. Putnam's Sons, 1996.

———. *Good Spirits: The Making of a Businessman.* New York: G.P. Putnam's Sons, 1998.

———, with Catherine Whitney. *The Third Act: Reinventing Yourself After Retirement.* New York: G.P. Putnam's Sons, 2002.

Bruck, Connie. *Master of the Game: How Steve Ross Rode the Light Fantastic from Undertaker to Creator of the Largest Media Conglomerate in the World.* New York: Simon & Schuster, 1994.

———. *When Hollywood Had a King: The Reign of Lew Wasserman, Who Leveraged Talent into Power and Influence.* New York: Random House, 2003.

Collins, Joan. *Past Imperfect: An Autobiography.* New York: Simon and Schuster, 1984.

Davis, L.J. *The Billionaire Shell Game: How Cable Baron John Malone and Assorted Company Titans Invented a Future Nobody Wanted.* New York: Doubleday, 1998.

Dekom, Peter, and Peter Sealey. *Not on My Watch: Hollywood vs. the Future.* Beverly Hills: New Millennium Press, 2003.

Dick, Bernard F. *City of Dreams: The Making and Remaking of Universal Pictures.* Lexington: The University Press of Kentucky, 1997.

———. *Engulfed: The Death of Paramount Pictures and the Birth of Corporate Hollywood.* Lexington: The University Press of Kentucky, 2001.

Drabinsky, Garth. *Closer to the Sun.* Toronto: McClelland & Stewart, 1995.

Eisner, Michael, with Tony Schwartz. *Work in Progress.* New York: Random House, 1998.

Evans, Philip, and Thomas S. Wurster. *Blown to Bits: How the New Economics of Information Transforms Strategy.* Boston: Harvard Business School Press, 2000.

Finkelstein, Sydney. *Why Smart Executives Fail and What You Can Learn from Their Mistakes.* New York: Portfolio, 2003.

Foster, Peter. *Family Spirits: The Bacardi Saga.* Toronto: Macfarlane Walter & Ross, 1990.

Fuller, Robert W. *Somebodies and Nobodies: Overcoming the Abuse of Rank.* Gabriola Island: New Society, 2003.

Gabler, Neal. *An Empire of Their Own: How the Jews Invented Hollywood.* New York: Anchor Books, 1988.

Goldman, Victoria, and Catherine Hausman. *The Manhattan Family Guide to Private Schools.* New York: Soho Press, 2001.

Gotti, Victoria. *Superstar.* New York: Crown, 2000.

Gray, James H. *Booze: When Whisky Ruled the West.* Saskatoon: Fifth House, 1995.

Johnson, Jo, and Martine Orange. *The Man Who Tried to Buy the World: Jean-Marie Messier and Vivendi Universal.* London: Viking, 2003.

Kent, Nicolas. *Naked Hollywood: Money, Power and the Movies.* London: BBC Books, 1991.

King, Tom. *The Operator: David Geffen Builds, Buys and Sells the New Hollywood.* New York: Random House, 2000.

Kinnane, Adrian. *DuPont: From the Banks of the Brandywine to the Miracles of Science.* Wilmington: E.I. DuPont de Nemours and Co., 2002.

Kipps, Charles. *Out of Focus: Power, Pride, and Prejudice—David Puttnam in Hollywood.* New York: William Morrow, 1989.

Klein, Alec. *Stealing Time: Steve Case, Jerry Levin, and the Collapse of AOL Time Warner.* New York: Simon & Schuster, 2003.

Kolber, Leo, with L. Ian MacDonald. *Leo: A Life.* Montreal and Kingston: McGill-Queen's University Press, 2003.

Koplovitz, Kay, with Peter Israel. *Bold Women, Big Ideas.* New York: Public Affairs, 2002.

Leacock, Stephen. *Canada: The Foundation of Its Future.* Montreal: privately printed, 1941.

Mair, George. *The Barry Diller Story: An Inside Look at Hollywood's Power Player.* New York: John Wiley & Sons, 1997.

Mariani, John, with Alex von Bidder. *The Four Seasons: A History of America's Premier Restaurant.* New York: Smithmark, 1999.

Marrus, Michael R. *Mr. Sam: The Life and Times of Samuel Bronfman.* Toronto: Viking, 1991.

McDougal, Dennis. *The Last Mogul: Lew Wasserman, MCA, and the Hidden History of Hollywood.* New York: Crown, 1998.

Menn, Joseph. *All the Rave: The Rise and Fall of Shawn Fanning's Napster.* New York: Crown Business, 2003.

Messier, Jean-Marie. *j6m.com: faut-il avoir peur de la nouvelle économie?* Paris: Hachette, 2000.

———, with Yves Messarovitch. *Mon Vrai Journal.* Paris: Balland, 2002. (Translated by E.J. Katz.)

Munk, Nina. *Fools Rush In: Steve Case, Jerry Levin, and the Unmaking of AOL Time Warner.* New York: HarperBusiness, 2004.

Newman, Peter C. *Bronfman Dynasty: The Rothschilds of the New World.* Toronto: McClelland and Stewart, 1978.

———. *Flame of Power.* Toronto: Longmans, Green, 1959.

———. *Titans: How the New Canadian Establishment Seized Power.* Toronto: Penguin Books, 1998.

Ostrow, Stuart. *A Producer's Broadway Journey.* Westport: Praeger, 1999.

Pitts, Gordon. *Kings of Convergence: The Fight for Control of Canada's Media.* Toronto: Doubleday Canada, 2002.

Powers, Tom. *Steven Spielberg: Master Story Teller.* Minneapolis: Lerner, 1997.

Puttnam, David, with Neil Watson. *Movies and Money.* New York: Random House, 1999.

Redstone, Sumner, with Peter Knobler. *A Passion to Win.* New York: Simon & Schuster, 2001.

Rensin, David, *The Mailroom: Hollywood History from the Bottom Up.* New York: Ballantine Books, 2003.

Sharp, Kathleen. *Mr. and Mrs. Hollywood: Edie and Lew Wasserman and Their Entertainment Empire.* New York: Carroll & Graf, 2003.

Sheehy, Gail. *Understanding Men's Passages: Discovering the New Map of Men's Lives.* New York: Random House, 1998.

Singular, Stephen. *The Rise and Rise of David Geffen.* Secaucas: Carol Publishing, 1997.

Slater, Robert. *Ovitz: The Inside Story of Hollywood's Most Controversial Power Broker.* New York: McGraw-Hill, 1997.

Swisher, Kara, with Lisa Dickey. *There Must Be a Pony in Here Somewhere: The AOL Time Warner Debacle.* New York: Crown Business, 2003.

Thomson, David. *Biographical Dictionary of Film.* New York: Knopf, 2002.

Vogel, Harold L. *Entertainment Industry Economics: A Guide for Financial Analysis.* Cambridge: Cambridge University Press, 1998.

Walker, Alexander. *Peter Sellers: The Authorized Biography.* New York: Macmillan, 1981.

Wolf, Michael J. *The Entertainment Economy: How Mega-Media Forces Are Transforming Our Lives.* New York: Times Books, Random House, 1999.

Wolff, Michael. *Autumn of the Moguls: My Misadventures with the Titans, Poseurs, and Money Guys Who Mastered and Messed Up Big Media.* New York: HarperBusiness, 2003.

Yule, Andrew. *Fast Fade: David Puttnam, Columbia Pictures and the Battle for Hollywood.* New York: Delacorte Press, 1989.

VIDEOS, CATALOGUES, AND OTHER PUBLICATIONS

Melody. Hemdale Productions/Goodtimes Enterprises. © Catullus Productions, 1970.
Seagram Co. Annual Reports, 1970–1999.
Shaft. MGM Home Video, Shaft Productions Ltd., 1971.
Stephen J. Ross Humanitarian Award. UJA-Federation of New York, 1996.
The Border. MCA Home Video, an Efer Production. © Universal City Studios, 1981.
The Seagram Collection of Photographs. Phillips de Pury & Luxemborg, sale catalogue,
April 25–26, 2003, New York.
Whisky Man: Inside the Dynasty of Samuel Bronfman. © David Paperny Films Inc.,
1996.

INDEX